RESOUNDING EVENTS

Resounding Events

ADVENTURES OF AN ACADEMIC FROM THE WORKING CLASS

William E. Connolly

FORDHAM UNIVERSITY PRESS   NEW YORK   2022

Fordham University Press also publishes its books in a variety of electronic formats. Some content that appears in print may not be available in electronic books.

Visit us online at www.fordhampress.com.

Library of Congress Cataloging-in-Publication Data available online at https://catalog.loc.gov.

Printed in the United States of America

24 23 22   5 4 3 2 1

First edition

In memory of Judy.
For David, Debbie, and Jane

Contents

"What? Hast thou not lived?" —MONTAIGNE

"For if the power of mind has been so changed
That all remembrance of the past has fled,
That is not far, methinks, from being dead."

—LUCRETIUS

"The simplest act or gesture remains immured as within a thousand
sealed vessels, each one of them filled with things of a color absolutely
different one from another, vessels, moreover, which covering the
whole range of our years, during which we have never ceased to
change if only in our dreams and our thoughts, are situated at the most
various moral altitudes and give us the sensation of extraordinarily
diverse atmospheres."

—MARCEL PROUST

"Out of damp and gloomy days, out of solitude, out of loveless words
directed at us, *conclusions* grow up in us like fungus: one morning
they are there, we know not how, and they gaze back upon us, morose
and grey. Woe to the thinker who is not the gardener but only the soil
of the plants that grow in him."

—FRIEDRICH NIETZSCHE

"This I is creative in that it alters and inflects what is taken in, taken
on, and taken up."

—JANE BENNETT

"Except in scale, the machinations for power are about the same in a
university as in the Roman Empire."

—JOHN WILLIAMS

"Let us Laugh together, on principle." —W. E. C.

Prologue

Event, Memory, Thinking...

I

He was walking glumly down the hall when he encountered the secretary. She was carrying a bundle of papers from the social science office to another office in the new Flint UM commuter college. "Aren't you going to meet the professor from Ann Arbor today?" she asked. They had said polite hellos to each other on occasion but had not before talked. "I've given up on the grad school thing," he said. "I didn't win a fellowship, so I need to go in a different direction." A desk job in the Cleveland branch of the Social Security Administration was the option that had surfaced, though he knew his composure could crack if he said that. "Look," she said with surprising severity. "Professor Laing is driving up to talk with potential graduate students and to offer *you* a staff position in the residence halls that covers room and board. Go home, change your clothes, and be back here by four." "Okay," he said. His graduate school career was thus launched at 1:30 P.M. on a spring day on a hallway during a chance encounter with a kind and direct woman who decided on the spot to take matters into her own hands. The contingency of timing was—and not for the last time—pressed upon him as he drove the old Chevy coupe home with more blue smoke than usual spewing from the tailpipe.

This report from the academy relates a few such contingencies and intellectual issues that arise in relation to them. It focuses on the bumpy relations between events, memories, and thinking in the life of an academic aspiring to be an intellectual. The Prologue highlights some textual strategies adopted to enact and dramatize those elusive relations.

1

II

Event, memory, thinking, action. They are entangled. Not in the stark way an efficient cause produces an effect, in which each entity is distinct from others it moves or is moved by. That latter relation may work okay for billiard balls with specific spins and velocities imparted to them by a player as they collide on a smooth, bounded, green table with bouncy edges. But not for much else. Even quantum processes of coherence and decoherence exceed that mode of causality. Neither are event, memory, thinking, and action related in exactly the way an organism is said to weave elements together to forge a unified whole. The variables do *infuse* each other to some degree in the constellations we explore; they also *impinge* upon one another; and many contain capacities for some degree of *creative self-variation* triggered by the impingements and infusions. They are entangled in *process*.

So, for example, a startling event may call up a sheet of memory composed of past events arrayed in nonchronological order, varying in degrees of consciousness, cloudiness, obduracy, and fecundity. As when, for me, a recent tornado warning amid black clouds called up several past events, including the shock of late-night pounding at the door when our parents were not home, another of a time I taught the "Theophany" in the book of Job to explore how the biblical story brings out the volatility of nature, and another yet of a tornado that rattled me and my friends in our teens. A sheet organized nonchronologically, with events weighted roughly according to relative affinity to this situation, sharpness of recollection, and visceral intensity. Dissonant conjunctions between an event and the sheet of past called up by it sometimes spawn a tipping point from which new thinking, action, or judgment springs. A novel conjunction of event, memory, and thought may shake something loose. It may enliven, or call up a cliché, or overwhelm.

Memory itself is essentially layered: one dimension takes the shape of *recollection images*; another of *unconscious dispositions* and habits without recollection consolidated from past shocks, joyous events, and routines; yet another of *residues, traces, or scars* in which, for example, an incompletely formed intention previously blocked from consolidation festers again in a new setting. So only one dimension of memory takes the form of recollection, and even recollections vary among themselves in the extent and ways to which they are affect-imbued. I call all three dimensions of memory because they may all be activated from the past—though in different ways—when a new event enlivens or disrupts life. Different layers on the same sheet of memory may then resonate together, making differences to what occurs later. Memory is thus many-splendored, often composed of shifting coalescences. Without memory, no thinking; with it, thinking can crawl along, freeze, or take flight. Thought itself can be an event, too.

To compose a political report that respects events and contingencies, then, is to place at least four elements into play—events, memory, thinking, and action. It is not, however, to *know* all the relays between the elements: How could you know a lively remnant or residue? How review rapid modes of preconscious coalescence between diverse dispositions or drives as they gather to face a novel situation? It is, rather, in some instances to recollect the past and in others to *tap* lively residues of it, doing so in the second instance to encourage remainder, event, and recollection to reverberate. It is, as the saying goes, to stew in your own juices periodically in ways that may foster new thinking—to carry thinking already underway to a distinctive point of crystallization.

A political report, so conceived, dwells in the past to activate experimentalism in the present. It suspends old settlements at some moments and ignites new possibilities at others. More awkwardly, this is an attempt to compose poliphilosophical reports, drawing upon personal events of consequence, experiences of dramatic public events, and more prosaic academic events.

This is not, then, a memoir, at least if that genre is understood to be one in which the author mostly confesses slights, achievements, and secrets of interest to others. It rather explores complex relays between event, memory, and thinking, particularly as they speak to one academic who entered graduate school after he had become a gathering place for preliminary assumptions, demands, and hopes in a white working-class atmosphere.

To compose or read a report of this sort is also to discern that there is more to thinking than either knowing or judging according to a settled format—though knowing and judging in some sense are also important. Thinking consists of several entwined processes: perfecting an agenda of thought, rattling old categories, dwelling in fecund hesitations, absorbing unfamiliar ingressions into thought, creative invention, and becoming worthy of a new event that disturbs previous expectations.

III

But why compose such a study? I will try to answer that question more closely in Chapter 5. Even then the answer will be incomplete. But preliminary reasons can be hazarded now. First, this report might help us to ponder how bifurcation points arise at key moments, so that it becomes more palpable how to take one fork invariably means to pass by others. "To do is to forgo," says Nietzsche. Not always or only through conscious deliberation, but thinking in a fecund sense is always involved. The fork taken is not simply determined by what precedes it, either, for a set of proclivities incited by resonances between a new event and a sheet of past may now open a new possibility for further reflection as it bubbles into awareness. The old, forsaken fork springs up not exactly as it was, of course, but as it can be when subjected to reflection in a specific linguistic regime. A mere past incipience on the way cut off in the past (as another was consolidated) may thus be tapped again in a new setting. A new thought sometimes emerges from reverberations between an incipience previously untaken and the new situation.

Reports of this sort thus provide one way to think about how creative interventions arise and how new interpretations become consolidated. Such a report also suggests how every consolidation *bristles* with incipiencies that exceed it because of how it arose. You are yourself, and you fester with more than yourself. Sometimes such a condition fosters anxiety, at other times joyous experimentation. It depends.

A second reason I am moved to issue these reports is more academic. Growing up as the son of a factory worker and labor activist in Flint, Michigan, I soon found myself breathing the professional/professorial air of the academy. I was inhabited by tendencies to thought and judgment that touched many colleagues, and yet my proclivities often diverged from them in this or that way. Our initial responses to the same events could readily swerve in different directions, doing so in ways that might eventually cast light on the overlapping problematics of explanation, ethics, politics, aesthetics, and/or metaphysics different people bring to everyday life, to capitalism, to the cosmos, to the state, and to the academy, let alone to the working class, Anthropocene, racism, pandemics, the shape of democracy, and the specter of fascism.

A third motive, explored in Chapter 5, concerns the death in 2019 of my younger, vibrant sister, who had lived just outside Flint. A short time after she was gone it hit me with a jolt—as now the only one remaining from our family of origin—how such an event renders a whole battery of memories at once more poignant and more precarious. There was no longer anyone with whom to share and test early recollections. Another connection was jangled, too: the tacit sharing of distinctive gestures, facial expressions, habits of intonation, ways of walking, routines of humor, and prompts to action. Several such routines and affinities between us had scarcely been noted when she was alive—though when we teased each other about this or that tendency some would pop to the fore. She teased me about the professorial mode of speaking I periodically adopted as an adult. I would sometimes declaim in an exaggerated professorial tone on a visit to Flint that it was time for her to stop pronouncing "creek" as "crick" and "roof" as "ruf," recalling to those in the room through that sentence how I too spoke while growing up in the same setting. And thus how

I had now become more precious. Preciousness can be either a sin or a laugh in Flint, depending on the situation. It can become a habit in the academy.

Intersecting layers of memory ignite the vitality and pathos of life. Writing with them, trying to amplify or dramatize a few, may honor the place of memory in thought and creative action without reducing such entanglements to any smooth model of determination, shaping, or expression. Here suggestion and intimation exceed report and delineation. Such a project may also illuminate how different dimensions of memory become insinuated into current feelings, actions, and collaborations. That is one reason this text is composed of scenes. A scene starts in one temporal moment and often bounces to a few others, enacting in this way, perhaps, some of the imbrications between memory, thinking, and event. Such a *political* report, then, both resists simple models of situational determination and encourages periodic bouts of experimentalism, for its composer and, it is hoped, for others.

IV

Another thing. Each of us becomes twosomes and threesomes over time, with several voices jostling around in the self at strategic moments, varying in degrees of cloudiness and insistence. These voices contend and coalesce to constitute proclivities and ambivalences of action. The "I" can become quite a crowd. It thus becomes helpful in this text to allow an Interlocutor to pose questions to the composer and, later in the text, to press sharper interrogations and objections. Is the Interlocutor, then, an interviewer? Well, it starts that way, and reverts to that mode on occasion. Sometimes it functions as a straight man, too. But it also becomes a Double or counter-voice haunting the I, posing from within doubts pressed against official patterns of insistence, as when, later on, it poses again the question of pessimism to an author who had resisted it before the perils of the Anthropocene and fascism became such obdurate objects of attention. Or, on other occasions, when it becomes a sparring partner who triggers a reflective turn. Sometimes, too, the Interlocutor relays a voice from the future. The interlocutor interrupts the flow of the text in something like the way thinking itself is marked by pauses, hesitancies, and interruptions.

If the self is a dynamic polyphony of voices poised in a precarious hierarchy, a new event can rattle or disturb the old balances. If and when thinking undergoes a sea change, the result is often inflected by underground struggles that had already been underway between affect imbued, proto-thoughts on the way, and your official self. Some simmering thoughts are larval; they are *incomplete incipiencies*, too unformed as they simmer to be articulate and too filled with pluri-potentiality to be implicit. Incipiencies exert strange efficacies

under the right circumstances. They are essential to moments of creative thinking, even as they can also promote blockages on occasion. They form ambiguous elements in thinking. For thinking is marked by a creative element, but
creativity itself is never the simple result of a preformed intention. It emerges
out of resonances back and forth between disparate elements.

The Doubles grow in number, complexity, and entanglement, then, as a
working-class boy grows up. Mother, father, sisters, teachers, coaches, friends,
teammates, children, partners, students, comrades in a social movement, college administrators, political leaders, media figures, colleagues in intellectual
dialogue: all shuffle in and out as internalized doubles on occasion, as events
accumulate and sheets of past proliferate. For the longer you live the thicker
and more convoluted becomes the past pressing upon you. Fortunately, brain
pruning also occurs as time passes (a process still not understood well by neuroscientists). We are strange, intentional beings whose brain pruning is not
subject to direct intentional control. There are also, fortunately, "tactics of
the self" that can help to rewire a few brain processes that exceed conscious
capture and remain beyond direct intentional control.

The Interlocutor may open a new line on one occasion, intensify a defensive line of thought on another, or provoke productive or unproductive stub-
bornness on yet another. The child, the adolescent, the athlete, the young
assistant professor, old scars and joys, the temptations of professionalism, and
the legacy of more recent actions do not entirely disappear as new problems
arise and fresh consolidations form. Some may take a back seat for a while
and then be reignited as larval subjects whose gestations and efficacies are
not themselves susceptible to full consciousness. They can only be suspected
through effects they engender on conscious thinking. Such an uneven layering of twosomes and threesomes is periodically invaluable to creative thinking and judgment; it also obstructs the smoothness of thought. The difference
between an Interlocutor and a Double is mostly that the latter functions as a
murky voice within while the former poses more articulated challenges and
issues. That means the two can shift places as time accumulates, as one ages.
It also means that nothing said here or elsewhere in this book denies the efficacy of conscious reflection; it merely situates it in cloudier processes that
subtend and provoke it.

I hope that the mosaic of scenes portrayed here occasionally taps larval subjects in other thinkers that carry strange efficacies of their own, even if they
remain too cloudy or unformed to be represented. To tap is to move and arouse
efficacious elements below representation. I do not know to what degree those
hopes will be fulfilled. I, me, he, she, we, you, they, them, us. A multiplicity
of intersecting voices and incipiencies on the way, with the self tending to settle

into a stable, hierarchical social structure for one period and to break into new confusions and adventures in another, even to sink into occasional bouts of nostalgia as life bumps along.

Finally, a few books "I" have written (at least the royalties go to my address) are reviewed at pivotal moments. Each book encases a settlement of thought. Specific events, academic issues, collective struggles, and sublime happenings have slipped into it, so it is set into a context. Each also assumes a texture of its own, related but not entirely reducible to the contexts of its production. No text is either simply determined by events or entirely autonomous. How to evoke such a zone of indeterminacy? If you fail to do so, intersections between events and texts may appear like modes of pure determination, with only a couple of additional details needed to render them complete. Or you may pretend that each text is an autonomous formation, reducible only to the logical arguments, explicit assumptions, and clean evidence it assembles. Those two contending cliches, however, dishonor thinking, artistry, politics, and life. They even simplify logic too much. One way to navigate the issue, perhaps, is to locate each text in its moment, to compress its summary into a style different from the rest of these reports, and to set that condensation in a distinctive font. The text under review now becomes a minor monument entangled with events that dig and tug at it—a crystallization, subject to new disruptions as events unfold. It is a consolidation that *bristles* with other possibilities. I will wait until after a few diverse types have accumulated to discuss closely what I mean by "event." Except to say that events find you before you find them.

One focus of this report is how discrepancies between my early experiences in the working class and the later ethos of the academy periodically face the jolt of a new event to ignite thought. Those discrepancies are notable when the boy enters graduate school, but they also arise again when he writes *The Politicized Economy* with a talented colleague also from the working class threatened with denial of tenure, and again when he sniffs out the dangers of aspirational fascism before and during the Trump era, and yet again when he finds himself compelled to work tactically on the visceral register of being to fold principled support for same-sex relations more securely into his own bodily dispositions.

The reported discrepancies between norms of the academy and my prior proclivities are mostly those that help to nurture productive thinking, not things about which to complain. It is the positive possibilities in frictions between a working-class past and the ethos of the academy, at least, that deserve emphasis, even if they are occasionally marked by negatives: jolts, losses, doubts, accusations, suffering. Thinking often profits from jolts that disrupt the train it is following.

V

Even if the *motives* behind this study have been at least introduced, what is its *purpose?* Well, one purpose is to probe anew the mechanisms by which new thoughts are prodded into being. It is to break up onto-epistemological strait-jackets of thinking in order to prime adventures of thought and to spur positive action as the world takes new turns. Another aspiration is to help a few young writers to see how and why initial misreadings of their work by others are sometimes unavoidable at first, something to address rather than merely to fume against. (Though a *bit* of fuming may ventilate things.) Another aim is to ponder more closely how the need for experimentalism surges up in the face of new events. Hopefully, and above all, such an inquiry may speak to a few young seekers negotiating rocky paths among accumulations of experience, the strictures of the academy, the volatility of the world, and the need to experiment.

1
Professionals and Intellectuals

Interlocutor: Memory, you might say, consists of at least three intersecting components: recollections called up in images, dispositions to action forged through intersections between past events and previous impulses, and remains that retain strange efficacy in relation to the first two but are too vague or fragmented to take the form of recollection. The latter, for instance, may add energy and vitality to conscious ideas or, to the contrary, they may incite ambi-valences that haunt conscious thinking. All three of these dimensions, I know, become pertinent to your later work, but you did not perhaps unsort or think about their relations during your graduate student days. For now, let's focus on recollections of norms, resistances, and events from graduate school and your first academic position, which may have come to serve as prompts and precursors to your later thinking.

I was very quiet in seminars during the first year of graduate school at the University of Michigan, finding rather stressful the vocabulary, assumptions, and references easily spilling from the lips of most graduate students. Things fell into place later, and eventually it became hard to shut me up.

My key mentors there became James Meisel and Arnold Kaufman. Meisel was an elderly, blond-haired, blue-eyed Jewish refugee from Germany who taught theory seminars in the Midwest well ahead of their time. He confided to me once—while advising me to introduce more caution into my dissertation—that he had waited almost too long before fleeing Germany at the onset of Nazism. He foolishly thought his eye color would protect him, he said. He introduced us to Hegel, Marcuse, Marx, Sorel, Mosca, Michels, and Pareto in seminars on modern theory, while other modern theory courses there focused on Hobbes, Locke, Burke, Mill, and Rousseau. They were mostly Anglo-centered.

Kaufman was a radical pragmatist in the philosophy department, working on democratic theory at the intersections of Rousseau, Marx, and Dewey. His course on "Human Nature and Participatory Democracy" in 1961 blew some students away, me most definitely included. More senior grad students in theory, who also migrated from political science to take this class in the Philosophy Department, found it to be unrealistic, even though Kaufman himself always noted both the element of unrealism in this agenda and the real need to pursue it nonetheless. Democracy could become unraveled unless that pursuit bore fruit. Tom Hayden—a senior taking the course too—loved it as much as I did. Kaufman's course soon found a presence in the *Port Huron Statement* of 1962, the early manifesto of the New Left in America.

The basic thesis of the seminar was that electoral democracy only flourishes if active citizen participation finds expression in families, localities, corporations, unions, schools, and social movements. Participation develops citizenship capacities. Kaufman worried a lot about the danger of authoritarianism in an electoral democracy that is only representational. If the authority structures of other institutions such as families, work life, localities, and corporations were autocratic, authoritarianism would be apt to creep into representational politics. Churches, as I recall, were not included on his list.

•••

In 1963, as we were strolling across campus one day, I asked friends whether anyone knew the professor standing rigidly in front of the campus flagpole next to the library. "That is Kenneth Boulding," one said, "an economist who thinks he can change the world by holding solitary vigils against the war in Vietnam." Some people found the event amusing, others illuminating. It prompted me to begin research into the origins of the Vietnam War and the "containment policy" widely held to vindicate it. I took a seminar with Inis Claude, who criticized the "realism" of Hans Morgenthau, a famous IR theorist who, surprisingly, also eventually turned against the war.

By the time Arnold Kaufman and other critical colleagues organized the first anti-war "teach-in" in the country—held all night in the spring of 1964 in university classrooms right after Lyndon Johnson had expanded the war—I was ready to participate in such events myself. I attended the huge teach-in and joined in its discussions, soon thereafter speaking against the war at a fraught meeting of the local Democratic Party in which dissidents sought successfully to censor Lyndon Johnson. These events launched a longer career of sporadic participation in anti-war, civil rights, university reform, and diversity movements. An early event was participation in fair housing protests, after an African American graduate student, Hadley Normandt, in the political science department called them to my attention. Otherwise I would have missed them, since the local newspaper barely noted these protests. I only gradually came to appreciate how such actions can work upon unconscious prompts to your thinking and change the world and how such work can also render future actions more strategic and timely. While Kaufman had primed those insights, it took involvement in these protests to develop them.

• • •

My oral qualifying exam was scheduled for November 22, 1963. As I hesitantly entered the department hallway that morning, five or six people were crouched silently in front of a radio in the staff office. John F. Kennedy had just been shot in Dallas, they announced, though there was no word yet whether the wound was serious.

The examiners, who included Kaufman, Meisel, Claude, and two others, arrived soon and huddled briefly. Since no one really knew yet what had happened, they decided to hold the oral—which served as a capstone after four written exams. Two events thereafter were conjoined for me: an assassination and an exam.

I do not remember the exam well, only that Kaufman asked me to tell them what was unique about humans. I knew I was supposed to say "language," but I opted to answer, "We have opposable thumbs." They smiled benevolently, knowing my hesitation about any philosophy anchored in mind/body dualism. I thought dualists were "dreaming with their eyes wide open," as Spinoza (whom I would only later read) said.

The discussion was engaging. No one posed a question about the perils of human exceptionalism; nor would I have known what to do had it arisen, despite my emphasis on the animality of human beings. The danger of "anthropomorphism"—the then unbreakable "fallacy" of attributing human capacities to animals—could have made an appearance in the discussion if the moment had not been so fraught and precarious. None of us wanted to commit that dreaded fallacy. The pressure to rethink its terms only arrived later in the American academy.

After the gentle oral was complete, the examiners told me to leave the room and ascertain what had transpired in Dallas. When I was invited back into the room, they told me I had passed. I told them that Kennedy was dead. We filed out in stunned silence.

•••

I had not been a highly enthusiastic John F. Kennedy supporter; he had seemed too hesitant to me, particularly with respect to race and labor. His assassination shattered my tacit sense of trust in the world, nonetheless, as it did to so many others. Something dark and dangerous was lurking in America. My parents and younger sister soon made a trip to Ann Arbor—their only visit during my five-year stint there—to spend a day with me and help pull me out of despair.

Each time the possibility of an assassination conspiracy was floated by this or that journalist, others replied generically by rejecting "a conspiracy model of the world." Jack Ruby's murder of Lee Harvey Oswald in the very center of the Dallas Police Department Building two days after the assassination, however, convinced me that there are *sometimes* conspiracies. Ruby was a low-level member of the Mafia, and evidence of an alliance between a section of the CIA and the Mafia troubled me along with millions of others. The assassination occurred two years after Kennedy had refused to expand the CIA-sponsored invasion of Cuba during the "Bay of Pigs," earning him the enmity of factions in the CIA and the Mafia gambling interests that had been driven out of Havana by the Cuban revolution. Besides, my youth in Flint had already taught me a thing or two about how powerful elites collude with organized crime when it is advantageous to do so, as we will see in Chapter 2. A powerful recent review of the evidence that came after the Warren Report about that assassination is provided in Mike Davis, *The JFK Assassination Evidence Handbook*.[1]

There was not enough proof at the time to convict in court, certainly, but there was sufficient evidence to make an informed political judgment. This event served as a dark prelude to the Nixon years and, later, the Trump years, with the latter oh-so-dangerous trio of Donald Trump, Mitch McConnell, and William Barr. Yes, Virginia, there are sometimes conspiracies. And, yes, a conspiratorial vision of the world is a paranoid delusion. The later assassinations of Martin Luther King and Robert Kennedy deepened this sense of foreboding; in each of these instances, too, the event was officially chalked up to the work of a lone assassin.

The event of Kennedy's death stuck, entering into my thinking each time a new event of its sort erupted.

• • •

Looking back, I see the late teens and early twenties as a period in which my experience bore a distant relation to what W. E. B. Du Bois calls "double consciousness." "I discern how you see me. I increasingly note distortions in your vision, even as I internalize stings and pains from it."[2] African Americans, says Du Bois in *The Souls of Black Folk*, are injured deeply by images of them advanced by those who both represent them in alien terms and otherwise oppress them; they must struggle to legitimate self-experiences profoundly at odds with those perceptions, disciplines, and judgments, generating a version of double consciousness that percolates into activism. Indeed, that is a key step to black pride, though a profoundly difficult one to take and sustain in a racist culture.

My condition was far more modest, since I was not marked by a skin color that attracts negative judgments in daily life, education, work, and promotion prospects, let alone by a history of forced Atlantic migrations, enslavement, lynching, Jim Crow, systemic job and education discrimination, police killings, mass incarceration, voter suppression, and redlining. So, even as a card-carrying member of the white working class, I was also a recipient of white privilege, since my skin color did not automatically trigger the aforementioned oppressions and dangers. This is a difficult lesson, however, to teach many white working-class men in particular—especially those whose parents were immigrants—though it is absolutely essential to do so.

Indeed, it may take whites and blacks together to teach it to working-class white males, since so many are bedeviled by their own experiences of subordination, insecurity, and grievance and identify white privilege as something only attributable to highly educated professionals. Many also know that their own grievances are widely ignored by others. Consider the assertion by a white worker who first supported Obama in 2008 and 2012 and then supported Trump in 2016, as a case in point. "You are white and so you have original sin and you can never do anything about it except publicly apologize to everyone."[3] Judy Beal, my sister in Flint, became effective in engaging male white workers on this score. She had a light touch, always starting by appreciating the class grievances and insecurities they felt. Then she would turn to the historic oppression of Blacks, trying to open lines of connection across a chasm. Her two daughters, Janelle and Tiffany, were and are effective in this regard, too; their lived experience with multifaceted diversities of race, gender, sexuality, and religion has expanded well beyond those Judy and I experienced as youngsters.

That trio has been effective in the micropolitics of white family life, class, neighborhood, town, and local election organization, though less so after the advent of Donald Trump.

• • •

With respect to graduate school, it is perhaps most accurate, then, to say that *embedded ambi-valences* marked my life during this period as I migrated from the white working class through grad school into an upper-middle-class, predominantly white male academy. I absorbed a series of cloudy discrepancies between academically accepted concepts and norms of scholarly judgment on one side and a lived history of events that challenged several of them. I was a bit of a stranger in a new world. My gait, pronunciations, memories, priorities, and engrained dispositions rubbed against several academic assumptions and norms, while attraction to intellectual life in the academy nonetheless cast an overwhelming lure. Embedded ambi-valence. Perhaps something positive could be extracted from it? For example, several seminars I took were governed by a positivist norm of explanation without evaluation, but a working-class kid could readily hear and feel how the dominant concepts and assumptions pervading those seminars propagated negative evaluations of workers and unions.

Karl Mannheim, in *Ideology and Utopia*[4]—a book I encountered as an undergraduate before reading Du Bois—explored the double experiences of those who imbibe a minority creed or inhabit a subordinate class position. He thought such ambivalences could spark creative thinking if the burdens were not too overwhelming. Such doublings also inhabit subordinate gender experiences and nonheteronormative sexualities, as Michel Foucault and Judith Butler later taught in such compelling ways. There are critical differences of scope and severity between the various dissonances with respect to class, race, gender, and sexuality; my attention for the moment is on loose affinities between them, affinities that could potentially be drawn upon to open avenues of collaboration across diverse minority constituencies in support of progressive social movements.

I refer to discrepancies of class experience to note how it soon became timely to synthesize some of them into positive themes. The intellectual task, it was beginning to dawn, was to give such experiences and orientations—including an appreciation of working-class struggles, the positive virtues of nontheistic gratitude as one existential faith among others, the pursuit of protean plurality, the aspiration to radical reductions in economic inequality, and the limits to academic professionalism—more room to roam; to transfigure a specific set of experiences into intellectual and political insights as you encounter new events; and to look for ways to transmit those insights to others in different social positions, as you also listen to what they can teach you. An expansive ethos of egalitarian pluralism.

The aim was becoming less cloudy; but the pathway remained uncertain. It took a while, for instance, to articulate more closely how received concepts of academic discourse often blur or distort working-class and minority experiences; how secular theories popular in American political thought of the postwar period are themselves inhabited by the remains of monotheistic theologies not addressed by secularists themselves; how the coldness of neoliberal capitalism, so congenial to the coddled investment class in America, could become entwined dangerously with the heat of white evangelicalism; how nontheists need to fold affirmative spiritualities into their own political practices to contest an evangelical/neoliberal constellation and promote a more encompassing creedal pluralism; how—after unions had been weakened and deindustrialization set in—white working-class evangelicals could become so susceptible to movements of aspirational fascism; or how stubborn traditions of "planetary gradualism," lodged in the humanities and social sciences, authorize deficient readings of manifold relays between climate change and imperial capital. None of these later findings was required by the specific dissonances in question; the dissonances merely opened a series of pathways to explore in the wake of new events. A deep pluralist will recognize that similar results can be attained through other pathways, too.

•••

Writing in 1936, Karl Mannheim, in his magnum opus *Ideology and Utopia*, had defined European intellectuals to be a "floating" stratum tied closely by background and occupation to neither the laboring nor the capital class. It could thus be experimental and exploratory; and it could, within limits, *choose* its affiliations. But in the early 1960s—at least in the United States—social science and humanities professors in the academy were predominantly white males speaking with upper-middle-class accents. Moreover, the professionalization of the social sciences—tethered to a disciplinary method held to be neutral between alternative theories—constricted the explorations a minority were tempted to pursue. The silent tyranny of method.

The Political Science Department at the University of Michigan became a case in point. It intensified the drive to professionalization during the last four years of my tenure there. Young, cutting-edge faculty members bought into a shiny new "behavioral revolution" that was consuming departments across the country. That movement was resisted by "traditionalists." The thinking of neither group appealed to me all that much—nor to Kaufman or Meisel, for that matter.

Behavioralists did not appeal because they were bent on studying political behavior through the lens of positivist categories too disconnected from the self-understandings of the "objects" of inquiry; they also searched for general cross-cultural probabilities to apply to every situation and culture. And they maintained a professional approach to academic life. They purported proudly, for instance, to keep their own "values" out of research, though an attentive person could detect them floating in the sentences they spoke, the histories they did not know, the timbre of their voices, and the data cards they coded. They aggregated data as if bits could be isolated and then recombined analytically to produce impressive explanatory power. To offer predictive explanations about future voting patterns, however, is to take one step toward presenting those predictions to elites who can afford to buy the information in order to shape an election and manipulate behavior. Behavioralists of that day were thus precursors to Big Data scraping processes through which the technocratic Right today seeks to manipulate people—doing so, say, through targeted disinformation campaigns of today that play upon the prejudices and anxieties of troubled constituencies.

This all rankled me, for concepts then advanced by behavioralists, such as "voter apathy," "social consensus," and the "value neutrality" of "investigators," demeaned working-class experience even before the data cards were filled out.

• • •

Traditionalists provided behavioralists with rather weak opposition, partly because they often shared much of the professionalism of their opponents while attacking their methods, certainties, and findings. By professionalism I mean, roughly, the judgment that researchers must adopt neutral methods as they maintain separation between their research and any public expression of values or political stance; nonetheless and somehow, the center of

American culture must provide the political measure through which to appraise the development of other regimes. So, for instance, "developing societies" were supposed to find their standard of aspiration in middle-class America of the early 1960s. To resist this mix of drives was to be labeled "unprofessional," or deficient in "methodological rigor," or both.

Professionals are often disciplined—by hiring practices, promotion criteria, reputational measures, dominant rhetorical recipes, and publication channels—to freeze thought at the current boundaries of their "discipline." Such a herd—or guild—mentality provides them with safety and with authority to discipline graduate students until the latter internalize the true method and substantive paradigms authorized. An ethos of disciplinary reproduction.

Professionals also tend to hew to the center of America as if it were a neutral place to lounge. It feels safe there, along several registers. Often, they unconsciously equate bureaucratic safety with value neutrality. They thus become rattled if the center itself slides to the right or comes under vicious attack from it. The trauma of McCarthyism, the student from Flint surmised, had left scars on both behavioralists and traditionalists in the academy, even though, in carefully designed polls of the day, most professors asserted firmly that their orientations had not been affected by that recent, rough history.

Certainly, once you insert *archival scholars* into that mix, the relations become more complex. A scholar will focus intently on a specific zone of research, often but not always resisting active participation in public intellectual life. To put it briefly, scholars are indispensable to intellectual life, though they may not always embrace its adventures themselves. If a cadre of intellectuals seeks, say, to identify and curtail the galloping Anthropocene that took so many geologists, humanists, and social science professionals by surprise, it becomes indispensable to absorb new scholarship in geology, climatology, neoliberalism, the imperial history of capitalism, decolonial theory, glaciology, racialized white working-class dreams, and other things besides. The cloudy line of division between scholars and intellectuals, then, is whether you seek—or appreciate others who do—to formulate political goals and support social movements appropriate to them. The intellectual, you might say, is somewhat more problem-centered while the scholar is more archival-centered, though the tasks of each cross into the priorities of the other. If you become governed by the dictates of a problem such as the Anthropocene, for instance, you may eventually find yourself even contesting the image of time—and related ontological assumptions—undergirding the methods and consensus of the day in the social sciences.

Intellectuals tend to move back and forth between ontology, ethics, cosmology, corporate-state practices, and the troubles people face, particularly when new events jostle a cultural synthesis already in place. They do so because an adjustment in any one of those domains cannot go far without jostling something in the others, too. For that reason, intellectuals also make themselves periodic objects of their own inquiry: how did I arrive at that assumption? How can I rethink it? What role definitions I have accepted now need to be challenged?

An intellectual thus moves to and fro, giving more weight to one task now and another later. It almost goes without saying that this or that intellectual may be more or less influential as an individual. A million drops of sweat, prose, and activism, however, sometimes accumulate from a variety of sources, with cumulative effects outweighing those of any individual— especially as they find expression in the classroom.

• • •

One might surmise that the danger of the professional is excess caution and conventionalism clothed in a dogmatic method that protects both from exposure. But the danger of the Intellectual? That might be narcissism, a periodic focus on the self that can grow into an exclusive concentration on one's own thoughts and priorities. Another danger is immobilization, as you become frozen by growing awareness of complexity and uncertainties. Foucault, you might say, worked upon those dangers as he struggled to expose "transcendental narcissism" in his work and to marshal political and intellectual resources against both it and immobilization. The saving grace of intellectuals, then, might be to cultivate attention and care for beleaguered constituencies outside their own circles of affiliation. But we are running ahead of ourselves. . . .

Perhaps we are. One example may dramatize how a minority of graduate students in the very early 1960s resisted the attractions and disciplinary pressures of the behavioral revolution, along with the other neopositivist revolutions that followed in rapid order. It speaks to physics as the model of aspiration for the behavioral revolution in the social sciences. Before the New Left had lifted far off the ground, a few students in theory in the early 1960s—including me—were inspired by a new book written by Thomas S. Kuhn called *The Structure of Scientific Revolutions.*[5] Each dominant paradigm in the natural sciences, the historian of science claimed, helps to shape the evidence scientists discern and sets presumptive parameters of explanation for the phenomena collected. Such paradigms are essential to science, according to Kuhn, but the dicey history of the authority systems through which they sustain themselves and the rocky historical transitions between paradigms should make positivist scientists (and philosophers of science) hesitant to claim that the latest paradigm corresponds to the way of the world itself. Or that these sciences are even on a steady road of progress.

"Fallibilism" does not suffice, either, since it typically seeks new evidence to falsify old claims while tacitly resting upon a settled ontology and episte-mology that themselves could become scrambled by emergence of a new paradigm, as the shift from Thomism to Newtonianism showed so dramati-cally during one era and the later shift from Newtonianism to quantum theory did later.

A science might be captured by a paradigm for a time and then crumble under the double pressure of accumulated "anomalies" and the bold introduc-tion of a new theory by maverick theorists. An accumulation of anomalies seldom suffices by itself; these anomalies are often cloudy and can usually be fitted into an old paradigm with the addition of new protective assump-tions. As, to take an instance arising well after Kuhn's book was written, how authoritative planetary gradualists and "uniformitarians" in geology and evolutionary theory instructed readers for two centuries that the strange gaps (or anomalies) appearing in the evolutionary record did not mean that periodic, deep "catastrophes" or mass extinctions had occurred (as their maligned competitors claimed); they pointed, rather, to future fossil evidence soon to be filled out of slow, steady, linear, progressive evolution. Those gaps in the record, Lyell (1830) and Darwin (1859) had said,[6] would eventually be confirmed by newly discovered fossils. Lyell, in particular, punctuated that promise with ridicule of theorists of "catastrophe" (such as the French geologist Cuvier) to protect the gradualist paradigm. The demean-ing rhetorical style Lyell adopted in discussing catastrophists placed them on the wrong side of the science/myth division he drew so confidently. What young geologist would want to be shuffled to the wrong side of *that* division? The authoritative gradualist paradigm began to explode only in the 1980s, and the new counter-paradigm was contested sharply for at least a decade longer before it gained hegemony. The new paradigm, for instance, now requires theorists of species evolution to draw periodically from other fields such as geology and climatology to do their own work, while the former allowed biology to be a more internally governed science in ways that comforted professionals. Paradigm protection thus draws upon evidence, rhetorical exclusions, theoretical authority, and methodological discipline to sustain itself.

Kuhn drew me in because I was facing, with the exception of the islands formed by Kaufman and Meisel, large discrepancies between the preliminary "paradigm" or baggage I carried into intellectual life and the themes presented by behavioral-professional-traditionalists of the day.

• • •

It is fascinating to pose the question: what kinds of assumptions about time and nature in Christian theology—with remainders also floating around in Euro-American secular theories—made it so difficult to break the old paradigm of planetary gradualism? How did those assumptions help to set the background of work in the humanities and social sciences during this period? What costs do we now pay for those delays, particularly with respect to the gathering clouds of climate change, the rapid decline of species diversity, and the periodic infusion of pandemics into cultural life?

Such issues were posed sharply several years after Kuhn's intervention in ways publicized by Stephen Gould in *Wonderful Life*.[7] What about those empiricists who so dramatically resisted thinking about metaphysical issues while unconsciously carrying the remains of a Christian theology of providential, progressive time into their secular inquiries? Remains of this sort encouraged many professional geologists to wait so long before coming to terms with the fraught relations between extractive, fossil capitalism and volatile planetary processes that recoil back upon it. More about that later. I was not alert to this condition myself during that period, though it was galloping along.

Note, too, how Kuhn introduces political language into the history of science—the terms "revolution" and "capture" are examples—in ways that suggest how power, observation, paradigm, models of explanation, rhetorical exclusions, the accumulation of anomalies, and revolutionary change mix together almost inextricably in scientific practices. The Kuhn book, it turns out, provided a modest preface to themes soon pushed more radically by Michel Foucault.

Most behavioralists found such a history of paradigm shifts in science to be anathema. Most philosophers of science in the analytic tradition and most natural scientists did, too. Such a history, they said, plays up too much the background role of culturally imbued, tacit judgments in sustaining a paradigm. It even runs the risk of eliding the fundamental lines of division between science and religious faith. For an authoritative element of faith would now be seen to inhabit both paradigms in science and religious theology, helping to hold each together. Such elisions may be okay to attribute to old, discredited theories in science but not to behavioral research being done *now* in a regime of study governed by new, rigorous methods. I think the risk of becoming once again entangled in religious wars played a background role in the vitriolic tone of the critiques Kuhn and Kuhnians faced.

The key, critics of the paradigm story typically contended, is to retain a sharp distinction between theory and data rather than to allow them to become intermixed. Along the latter route, only trouble reigns.

Behavioralists, indeed, claimed exclusive ownership over the word "rigor" rather than seeing it as a standard that varies to a degree across paradigms. They did so, however, more by showing how others outside their perspective did not live up to the standards of testability they set than by demonstrating how they themselves did so positively in their own work.

The behavioral movement soon collapsed into a new paradigm—rational choice theory—with the latter retaining many neopositivist assumptions of the approach it replaced. The replacement showed that it is often easier to maintain ideological primacy in the academy by replacing one worn-down theory with a shiny new one of pretty much the same sort than to rethink fundamentally the premises of both. Thomas Kuhn would not be startled.

● ● ●

Traditionalists, for the most part, feared paradigm talk would tempt students to stray too far from well-honed truths about the uniqueness of human nature, the wisdom of tradition, and, often enough, the authority of Christian theology. They often downplayed the practices of imperial exploitation lodged in those traditions and tended to ignore how contending traditions often clash in the same regime. A few professors in each camp thus refused to let students utter the word "paradigm" in seminars at UM. Most others, however, would smile benignly if we did so and then refuse to take the bait. Inis Claude, one of my favorites, was among the latter. He closed a long poem critical of new fads, including behavioralism, with the phrase, "Brother, can you paradigm?"

This array of professional dispositions foreshadowed the quick dismissals of other concepts later advanced by critics to challenge the behavioral tradition and other revolutions of that ilk. Arguments against a Kuhnian history of science were often enforced by disciplinary tactics designed to disarm and relegate to the sidelines those influenced by him. It was deemed commendable for a nontenured faculty member, for instance, to include Karl Hempel or Karl Popper in a philosophy of social science course, but the inclusion of

Thomas Kuhn, Paul Feyerabend, or Stephen Toulmin rankled. The latter
trio lacked rigor.

•••

I did not, however, face extreme trouble on this count in graduate school.
Kaufman, Meisel, and Claude exerted too much clout to allow that. Also, I
smiled a lot in class. And only a minority of professors were inclined to press
the issue too hard anyway. I note in passing that Kuhn focused on how
linguistic habits shape a paradigm in ways that encouraged later non-positivist
critics of him to emphasize how important nonlinguistic resistances encountered in experiments to a theory can be. A potential debate between Kuhn
and Michel Foucault was simmering in the wings.

Neither party to the behavioral/traditionalist debate ignored the importance of evidence to theory. They rather read its significance differently and
set available evidence in different paradigms. Do claims that perception is
memory-imbued and scientific data theory-imbued confound the scientific
enterprise so much that they must be rejected in favor of virginal images of
perception and data? Or do they suggest that science can be a problem-
centered enterprise in this world with no certainty that its temporal trajectory will be straight or linear?

*I trust you see how these ruminations do not connect closely to work in
political theory or even to the humanities more broadly. The risk, indeed, is
that they could carry you away from politics and political inquiry. They could
become a route to escapism. Do you see how you must either forge such connections or play into the hands of those who think that all this is an indulgence
going nowhere in particular?*
A good point, up to a point. The agenda was to find ways to loosen the
constraining terms of debate in the social sciences in which we were
expected to participate. I think the Kuhn detour helped me to do that, but
others have to make their own judgment on this point.

A substantive thesis advanced by many behavioralists of the day was that
America displays a distinctive political culture of "interest-group pluralism"
set in a deeper cultural consensus that allows competing interests to negotiate to achieve compromise solutions. The theory of interest-group pluralism
tended to place the array of interests on a horizontal axis rather than a
vertical hierarchy, when my experience suggested otherwise. Explicit
recollections of McCarthyism were fading fast in the academy, too, though
scars from it continued to find expression in entrenched academic disposi-

tions. The urgent quest for neutral explanation was one of those dispositions. The long, violent history of race in America was whitewashed in several paradigms, too. So was the history of corporate-sponsored and state-sanctioned violence against labor and the dangerous strikes labor had to foment to make advances.

The task, to purveyors of the old pluralist paradigm, was to show through rigorous tests how closely the United States fits this model of pluralism. Later social movements in the domains of race, gender, sexuality, antiwar sentiment, and creedal diversity had either not yet lifted off the ground or were hovering in postwar abeyance. Precursors to these movements simmered below the radar of the test procedures adopted.

My 1965 dissertation, examining that pluralist story, was entitled "Responsible Political Ideology"—with a long subtitle to make it appear sufficiently professional. It argued that the sharp separation between ideology and science now promoted by behavioralists and others throughout the social sciences had been oversold. The book growing out of it is called *Political Science and Ideology*. It was composed when many academics tried to avoid thinking too much about the Vietnam War and were wary of those who protested actively against it. To some, our protests were unprofessional, and we also showed disrespect for the outcomes of electoral democracy. You are supposed to elect leaders and let them govern until the next election, elite pluralists said. We increasingly insisted that such a story projects a one-dimensional image of democracy. It devalues activism outside the rubric of political parties; it thereby promotes conservatism within the party system. After a rather urgent quest to find a publisher, the book was accepted by Atherton Press.

The dominant themes of *Political Science and Ideology* (1967)[8] are, first, that the paradigm that behavioralists bring to the theory of interest-based pluralism in America disposes them unconsciously to test procedures supporting conclusions they already embrace; second, that the strategies by which they cast aside more radical interpretations dismiss the empiricism of their opponents on flimsier grounds than they acknowledge as they render their own test procedures too virginal in appearance; third, that implicit cultural assumptions governing those inquiries are tethered to norms of professionalism that tacitly bind political science and ideology more closely together than leading theorists of the day, such as Robert Dahl, Seymour Martin Lipset, Daniel Bell, Adolf Berle, Herbert McCloskey, David Easton, and Talcott Parsons, acknowledge; and, fourth, that an important task of critical intellectuals in the academy is to come to terms more reflectively with tacit ideologies that inhabit us as we also extend the narrow radius of social connections and acknowledged responsibilities within which we are confined, for to grow up in the world is to become instilled with preliminary dispositions to political interpretation.

The idea is to give critical intellectuality more room in the academy. G. H. Mead, Karl Mannheim, Herbert Marcuse, and C. Wright Mills inform positive themes advanced in the book. For while interest-group pluralists interpret "the implicit consensus" underlying political contests to be benign, critical theorists of elite governance discern a vague malaise permeating those silences undetected either by elites or the testing procedures they accept. For example, the "decision test," so beloved by theorists of interest-group pluralism, only speaks to issues after they have reached the governmental process; they thus miss vaguely defined constituency troubles floating beneath the reach of those tests.

Here is one quotation to capture some of the flavor of the book, for better or worse. It speaks to differences between those who advance a critical theory of a power elite and those who posit a pluralist image of actuality: "Both elitists and pluralists, then, recognize most of those facts that are presently subject to impersonal observation and test; they disagree on the placement and rating of those facts . . . in relation to crucial areas that cannot be readily brought to test. Is it a fact that broad segments of the population are experiencing latent discontents which are not fully articulated? This is one of the factual disputes that might, if brought to test, bring the two interpretations to a showdown. But a definitive test in this area is at present unlikely; and until there is such a test, each side is likely to accuse the other of making *ad hoc* assumptions which artificially bolster its case."[9]

The book closes with a call enunciated in the "we" voice I retained: "Is it futile to develop a profile of responsible ideology? Is the effort incompatible with existing moods and drifts in political inquiry? We think not. It is true that many social scientists have sought to expunge ideology from their research. [But] that dimension has been suppressed from research vocabularies and then reinserted into research results in ways that slide under conscious attention and thereby escape potential control."[10] Not everyone loved the book.

The book sounds like a critique of political science that is itself political sciency. . . . Did you note that at the time? Did the book itself embody ambivalence on this score in need of further excavation? If ambivalence is a term you are now ready to address, how would you define its expressions in

this book? What were the reactions to it, and where did it and they encourage you to turn next?
Yes, it was political sciency, and no, I was not highly alert to that fact at the time. Only later did that issue move front and center. A thinker encountered in the first study who entranced me, however, was the pragmatist G. H. Mead. He distinguishes the active role of the "I" as agent from the "me" as a largely unconscious repository of internalized social norms. He paid close attention to how these two are imbricated. The me is composed out of "generalized others" synthesized unconsciously as one absorbs a host of experiences from parents, friends, teachers, bosses, priests, political leaders, etc. Some of these experiences are dramatic, but many are highly repetitive. They may consolidate positive forms of thought or become filled with stubborn prejudices, or both at once. The me comprises social norms that slide unnoted into habits of perception and judgment—of both individuals and entire constituencies. These dispositions become coded into the background, say, of academic culture more than options tested by it.

The "I" unavoidably draws sustenance from some internalized others, but it is not entirely reducible to them. This is how, as I recall, the element of creativity in life is appreciated by Mead. I loved those formulations without drawing upon them sufficiently in my own book. I did not explore how pulses of real creativity bubble into life, an appreciation that encourages deeper critiques of the theories the text addressed. Nor did I know at the time how Mead's formulations were indebted to Alfred North Whitehead, a thinker I only much later engaged. Did residues from that early encounter with Mead help to steer me toward Whitehead later? I do not know, but it would not be too surprising.

Neither did I yet realize how no single genre suffices to register experiences of the world. Science, poetry, literature, philosophy, political theory, colonial studies, political economy, film, and liturgical practices lean on and into each other as we seek to become more sensitive beings and to incorporate those sensitivities into our work on politics, biology, oceanography, philosophy, colonialism, or theology. Without poetry, for instance, pulses of creativity may be stifled; without pulses of creativity politics becomes staid and arid, too rigid to respond to new events with suppleness. Without postcolonial theory, too many elide how profoundly the flourishing of Western capitalism and contained democracy in the luxurious regimes depend upon ruthless exploitation of other regions.

•••

Later, for instance, I would engage Anna Tsing as she explored ecological struggles that forge unexpected connections between, say, strategies adopted by ecologists in Southeast Asia and in the United States. Tree hugging took exactly that route. And Dipesh Chakrabarty, as he pressed us to bring studies of climate change and colonialism into close articulation. And Marcel Proust, as he *enacted* in long, undulating sentences how memory triggers without recollection slide into sentences we only partly orchestrate consciously. A preconscious thought-imbued trigger nudges a sentence this or that way, and resonances between it and an unexpected situation make a sentence become more than it was to be at its inception—the undulating sentence as a drop of time with its ending not settled at its start. Even to say that its end is *implicit* in its beginning is to iron out bumps in its formation.

When the narrator Marcel encounters poor old Charlus again—whom he knew previously as the overbearing, brilliant intellectual devoted to precise formulations—the old man now has aphasia. He has lost the precarious poise that allows unconscious triggers and trains of thought to balance and inform each other as a sentence proceeds.

Here is how Proust illuminates this ambiguity in a couple of sentences enacting it: "There were, however, two M. de Charluses, not to mention many others. Of the two, the one, the intellectual one, passed his time in complaining that he suffered from aphasia, that he constantly pronounced one word, one letter, by mistake, for another. But as soon as he actually made such a mistake, the other, M. de Charlus, the subconscious one, who was as desirous of admiration as the first was of pity and out of vanity did things that the first would have despised, immediately, like a conductor whose orchestra has blundered, checked the phrase which he had started and with infinite ingenuity made the end of his sentence follow coherently from the word which he had in fact uttered by mistake for another but which he thus appeared to have chosen."[11]

Marcel also learned how even a feeling of insane suspicion and jealousy could incite new adventures of thought. He saw how these adventures can teach you to prize encounters that shatter a few habits while they also teach you to transfer detective work from your own bouts of jealousy to other endeavors.

Unconscious memory triggers: without them, thinking becomes flat; with them, it is problematic, precarious, and wondrous. And such embodied cultural triggers play roles of prominence in politics, not only in theories about it.

•••

These were issues to be digested in the future. When *Political Science and Ideology* appeared, I assumed that mine would be a lonely voice. But between 1963, when the dissertation was launched, and 1967, events had moved fast. The burgeoning prominence of the New Left coincided with the book's publication. Also, two critical scholars—as the play of *Fortuna* or contingency would have it—were highly supportive. The first, David Kettler, then a professor at Ohio State University—not Ohio University in Athens, the smaller, older school where I worked—appreciated how the manuscript drew upon Karl Mannheim to explore the contours of ideology and the sociology of knowledge examining class and creedal relations in a society at large. Kettler was a deep scholar of Mannheim's work, and he persuaded the editor of Atherton Press to take a closer look at my manuscript. The second, Peter Bachrach, then a professor at Bryn Mawr, wrote a rave review of the book when it appeared. His book *The Theory of Elitist Democracy: A Critique*[12] had appeared six months earlier. It was richer in its critique of elitist democratic theory than mine and was perhaps complemented by how I brought Karl Mannheim, Arnold Kaufman, James Meisel, C. Wright Mills, and G. H. Mead to bear on the issues.

Those were two lucky breaks—breaks comparable, first, to growing up in a working-class setting that encouraged me to both prize university life and be skeptical of its professional pretensions; second, to those sweet professors at Flint UM who drove to Ann Arbor to secure me a position in the residence halls; third, to that secretary in the know who ordered me at a key moment to step up to the plate; and, fourth, to the tutelage of Kaufman and Meisel at the University of Michigan in graduate school. Debts were accumulating fast. Pay back by giving forward.

●●●

There are things, then, in that book I no longer accept. One is the too-sharp line it draws between what is possible for inquiry "in principle" and what is available "in practice." I accepted, at least officially, a predictive model of social inquiry then, while emphasizing how seldom it can be achieved in actuality. Today, as already indicated, I contend that periodic pulses of creativity fold both into social life and into dissonant conjunctions between social, biological, and planetary processes. Those ontological assumptions—assumptions that can be defended with evidence and argument, as we shall see—blow simple predictivism out of the water; they may also increase scholarly responsibility to make periodic participation in politics part of the intellectual vocation.

Another limit is how the book focuses on governmental rule without attending carefully enough to the bumpy intersections between governmental practices, the cultural organization of spiritualities, and economic life.

Most acutely—as you already suggest—when I now peruse the prose of an untenured assistant professor, I discern it to be suspended precariously between two agendas: first, to make more room for critical inquiry in a rather staid academy, and second, to find a niche for me in that very academy. The academy seemed the best place for me, and yet several of its norms were ill-suited to my aspirations.

Every place in life is replete with tensions, certainly. This specific set, however, worked upon me even more than they became objects of reflection by me. The exploration of "responsible ideology" in Chapter 5 displays the ambivalence previously noted.

I do not think, again, that such tensions can be eliminated. Nor should they be entirely smoothed out. One may, for instance, fold some norms of the professional into those of the intellectual, even though the institutional dangers of the latter project being overwhelmed are real. A critical intellectual, for instance, must draw sustenance from rich histories of political thought, decolonial thought, and, as we shall see, research in the earth sciences outside the ordinary purview of the humanities and social sciences. The latter connections help us to overcome what I later called "sociocentrism." *Political Science and Ideology* does not make those crossings.

•••

We write to others within a world that already insinuates itself through multiple modalities into the visceral register of affect-imbued thought, a register that carries subtle efficacy as it escapes full conscious awareness. Common norms and terms of discourse seep inadvertently into the dispositions of different cultural cohorts—we know not precisely how—setting collective proclivities to perception, aspiration, and judgment. They become insinuated into background norms and dispositions. It can be productive to thinking to become a bit of a stranger to the world you inhabit and even to aspects of the self you have become. That is why I later became so receptive to Nietzsche and Foucault on the importance of "techniques of the self" in intellectual work. These tactics work upon efficacious residues that exceed our capacities of articulation. Today I advise students to translate anxieties that plague them in their work into objects of inquiry, to the extent they can.

Thinking is inherently problematical. It can degenerate into mere calculation or, worse, collapse into writing blocks, or worse yet, lapse into a mere litany of accusations against others unless intellectuals include themselves among the objects of inquiry and unless they work tactically upon the very premonitions that exceed introspection. (More about that later.) And falling into a purely accusatory mode is almost as deep a trap to thinking as subscribing to a dogmatic model of objectivity.

• • •

Shortly after the first book was published, I encountered a fantastic article by Sheldon Wolin entitled "Political Theory as a Vocation."[13] Addressing the fetish of method in behavioralism, Wolin seeks to carve out space for critical intellectuality in an academy that too often squeezes it out in the name of professionalism and flat epistemologies One who practices theory as a *vocation* seeks to articulate large issues of the day and to participate periodically in their resolution.

The debate over the primacy of professionalism or intellectuality waxes and wanes. The problem is not merely one of strategy, either. For while the lines of division between behavioralists and intellectuals were often sharp during this period, archival scholars cut between them. Intellectuals need scholars, and scholars need them, too, though the institutional pressures toward mutual disavowal can become strong sometimes. The lines between them are cloudy. Negotiating relations between them can thus be difficult, particularly today when neoliberal university presidents are so prominent. Mead, Mannheim, Marcuse, Mills, and Wolin continue to be relevant to those who strive to contest the singular hegemony of professionalism, partly because they appreciated scholars and partly because they themselves were so active during a period when the hubris of professionalism was so high. I note Mills, *The Sociological Imagination* (1959),[14] as a valiant critic of academic professionalism during this period.

It is one thing to state such an agenda. It is another to practice it in ways that either convince others or show this to be one worthy path even if they do not follow it themselves. How did that go? Particularly when you were looking for a job?

I will answer the question, but I am not sure I entirely concur with your points. Even If a promising theory is developed—and I do not say the critics achieved that during this period—there are many reasons it could be resisted, ranging from the obdurate wish in a profession to protect a familiar paradigm, to desires to win grants, to unconscious identification with the perspective of specific constituencies, to layered desires not to displease higher university officials too much, to a lack of exposure to severe challenges to your own ontology or faith. Those were some of the issues Mannheim plumbed so carefully. But to your point, the first job interview I received while in graduate school did not work out well. So that does support your case.

A recent graduate of Dartmouth and a U of Michigan law student, Tom Dalglish, with whom I worked closely in the Michigan residence halls, commended me to Dartmouth. He must have carried some clout there. Amazingly, the politics department invited me to town for an interview even before my dissertation was far along. I traveled to Dartmouth in the dead of winter—aided this time by another former student there, Bill Hutton— whom I had come to know as a counselor at the Music Camp in Michigan. He drove me from Manhattan to Dartmouth after my connecting flight from New York had been cancelled by a severe snowstorm.

Roger Masters, a young Straussian in the political science department, worked me over as I tried to explain to the department the relation of Karl Mannheim's work to my dissertation. He announced that I was racing at breakneck speed toward solipsism, just as Mannheim had, a condition that would soon make it impossible to communicate with others. I could only wag my finger at them (as he was doing to me). I did not marshal a good reply. As I slowly walked away after that disastrous lunch, I heard from a distance the chair lightly remonstrate Masters for his lack of scholarly collegiality.

The chair's comments were kind, but I knew no job offer would be in the cards. I had not encountered previously either a Straussian or the charge of solipsism. I now realized that the thesis I was advancing faced intense opposition both from behavioralists and from more conservative forces.

• • •

Things proceeded differently at Ohio University, a sweet, mid-size public university at the foothills of Appalachia in southeastern Ohio. My dissertation was almost finished by then. I knew better what I was trying to do, the critiques to face, and the positive agenda underway. There were also no faculty members highly motivated to call everyone who disagreed with them relativists or solipsists. A job offer was tendered before I left town; it was not long before I accepted.

The teaching load was four courses a term at Ohio University; new teachers struggled to keep on top of the load. One of my newly appointed colleagues from Harvard decided that in principle he could not use "objective tests" on final exams, the kind of test in which students choose an answer from a fixed list of options. A month after the finals' period was over for the first term the poor bloke was still walking around with dark, sunken eyes and many papers to grade; he had to request a special dispensation from the dean to gain time needed to read the essay exams he had assigned for all four courses, two of which contained 150 students each.

I stuck with objective tests for my two large, introductory classes in American politics—drawing amply from predesigned questions distributed to faculty by publishers of Burns and Peltason, *Government by the People*,[15] the official departmental text for introductory American politics courses.

Once or twice during my first year at Ohio U I would suddenly decide that students of American politics needed to learn about the dialectical relation of Lordship and Bondage in Hegel's *Phenomenology*,[16] a dialectic I had studied carefully in grad school. Besides a panicky feeling about the prospect of otherwise walking into a large lecture class unprepared, I no longer recall the rationale for those decisions.

I also liked the school a lot. Many students were the first in their families to attend college, and I connected well with them. I, like them, also thought college secreted some amusing norms. I found that a fair number of students appreciated a pedagogy in which you move back and forth between key figures in the history of Western thought and reflection on contemporary issues. Those initial efforts later became transfigured into a philosophy of textual reading, one in which you place disparate thinkers from different places and periods into juxtaposition, seeing, for instance, how Sophocles unsettles Kantian themes and vice versa, or what happens if you place the work of Viveiros de Castro on the lived ontologies of Amazonians alongside the *Meditations* of René Descartes.[17] The idea is to open space for the possibility of new thinking through such dissonant juxtapositions

• • •

On a crisp fall day during my second year at Ohio University, my younger sister Judy, now in nursing school, called to inform me that our mother had suffered a severe stroke. I drove at a frantic pace for six hours to get to Flint Hurley Hospital from Athens, Ohio. By the time I arrived at the hospital, Pluma could no longer speak; she could only squeeze my hand in response as I talked quietly to her, reminding her again and again how much we and I loved her.

My sisters, Dad, and I soon had to make the agonizing decision to stop medical support for a fifty-year-old woman who became brain dead two days after her stroke. Only the machines kept her heart pumping. The family was shattered. The woman who held the fragilities together was now lost to life . . . and to us.

Things had to be reorganized; family assumptions had to be recomposed. There was no longer a central figure radiating care, stability, competence, and thoughtfulness throughout the family. We had assumed she would live into the deep, indefinite future. A hollowness slid into every aspect of life; it would not subside.

My father, whose short-term memory had been compromised in an auto accident fifteen years earlier, suffered immensely, quietly carrying around pictures of her in his shirt pocket to stare at whenever recollection of her image blurred. Judy, who still lived at home, suffered intensely, too. Her mother was her best friend. A short period after the funeral she suddenly flew to Oahu to marry her high school boyfriend, Bob Beal, who was now completing a tour in Vietnam. A few years later she began to fill the vacuum in the family left by this sudden departure. She became a wise counselor to others, one who could sink into their way of thinking for a time and then help them to negotiate a rough stretch. I suspect the greatest long-term toll, however, was felt by my two other sisters, Kathy and Sue, young adults then who seemed to lose considerable vitality for a long time after that event.

I had a nuclear family to fall back upon, as well as my teaching. As mourning began to slide through the months toward fond, vivid memories, I became acutely aware of how much those who lose a loved one appreciate contact and consolation from others. I had previously assumed—in my foolishness—that the grieving wish to be left alone. . . .

The anguished decision to end the life of our mother was repeated in spades a couple of decades later when our dad suffered from pancreatic cancer. Judy was still a nurse. She and I eventually had to convince two doctors to give our terminally ill father high doses of morphine to relieve the intense pain, even if that meant ending his life a few days sooner. It was all kept highly discreet. Those two agonizing events filtered into my thinking as I became a fervent supporter of doctor-assisted suicide for terminally ill patients who desire to end life. The horror of those instruments, uncertainties accompanying official definitions of death in a high-tech world, and a nontheistic faith encouraged consolidation of such a view. Judy and I supported movements to make such a decision legal, without suggesting that everyone should make that same choice for themselves. A few places have enacted such legislation.

•••

During three memorable years at Ohio University—despite the heavy teaching load—a series of events pressed me to punctuate teaching and research with bouts of activism. The first was the rapid expansion of the Vietnam War by Lyndon Johnson; second was the photogenic Ohio University president's strategy to consolidate control over the faculty; third was an illegal strike by nonacademic employees seeking more job security and higher pay; fourth was perhaps a desire to honor my mother through the actions I took.

I joined buses of students and faculty for two or three massive anti-war protests in D.C. and N.Y.C. The marches were energizing each time, and speeches on the mall inspired us to become even more active on the local scenes. Most liberals and the media, during this period, were either support-ive of the war or not highly concerned about it. The huge marches barely registered on the media, and when they appeared in ten-second blips, the focus was typically on isolated acts of violence.

I also worked with other young faculty members to organize a new faculty union at the school, as well as to mobilize a voting drive for the Faculty Senate that, among other things, soon catapulted three of us untenured "young hawks" to the senate. The senate had been entirely composed of tenured faculty before that. The fledgling faculty union acquired some clout, too.

When a strike of nonacademic employees began shortly after the faculty union had been formed—I was now treasurer of the union—the president of the school warned faculty that they could be fired if they refused to cross picket lines. I organized a Striker Relief Fund with a table manned every day at the very center of the campus by interested students and faculty. Like a vigil, perhaps. After a slow start, it began to collect enough funds to make a real difference; it also signified to a wider public in town that faculty and students increasingly identified with the strikers. The Faculty Senate also contested the university president's treatment of strikers. He had initially presented himself as a new kind of liberal to the faculty. But he was begin-ning to look more like something else: a squeaky-clean convert to the ethos and demands of neoliberalism even before it had reached a point of consoli-dation in the larger politics of the day. An early sign is usually projection of an aura of special entitlement joined to the demand that the university president of a university be treated like the CEO of a company. I had encoun-tered the type before in Flint, every time a General Motors CEO sent out a brochure to factory workers celebrating the virtues of a shared "community."

●●●

During a morning walk to campus one day, I saw posters advertising a student rally to ramp up support for the nonacademic employees. The strikers were under immense pressure from both the state and the university administration. When I took a closer look at one poster, I saw that I was scheduled to be one of the speakers. I had not agreed to this! Panic set in. The rally was scheduled for three hours later. I ran full speed to campus to prepare a talk. Then I reviewed its outlines rapidly with the chair of my department, Wid Elsbree. He was sympathetic to me and very much so with the strikers in Athens, Ohio, living on the edge of poverty; he was also savvy enough to rework sentences that might give an authoritarian, ambitious president an excuse for vindictive action against me as an untenured professor or against the department.

I informed the gathered students and locals what a "scab" was and why it was not wise for students to become strike breakers against employees struggling on the edge of poverty. I celebrated student government leaders for the initiative they had pursued on this issue. The speech by an untenured faculty member was replete with phrases such as "I am confident President Alden would not intend this, but this decision means. . . ." Wid inserted the first clauses, and I was grateful to him for doing so.

A year later, when the university president campaigned against tenure for an assistant professor in the philosophy department who had just become president of the faculty union, the gloves came off. I placed a guest editorial in the student newspaper, quoting a leading philosopher of science I had contacted who praised the quality of the young professor's work. The only lines I recall from the column are the last two. They said, "We must resist this President. He governs by giving a carrot to some, a stick to others, and a bland smile to everybody else."

I continue to embrace those lines. They apply to a large number of university presidents today as they buy eagerly into a corporate, CEO model of university governance, evince hostility to critical intellectuality within the liberal arts, practice servile deference to donors, and embrace the cruelties of a neoliberal economy. Many continue to undermine the critical mission of the university. They do not realize—or perhaps don't care—how their institutional commitments to a neoliberal model of CEO command in the academy intensifies an instrumental vision of education and undermines the value of critical intellectuality to a democratic culture. They are autocratic realists in relation to the faculty and innocent utopians in their failure to see how the cruelties of neoliberalism can even pave the way for fascist revolts. Back to those issues in a later chapter.

I now began to respect how an interplay among research, teaching, and role experimentation can enhance the quality of intellectual life. The latter activity involves experimental action upon roles you are assigned to play in consumption practices, church assemblies, teaching, family events, union meetings, corporation, and local life, experimenting with them to make little differences directly, to stretch prevailing norms, and to install more securely in the soft tissues of life new beliefs you have begun to articulate. Thus role experiments—say, working to organize a faculty union, or introducing a course that speaks to a new event, or joining protests—can not only exert small positive effects on the world, they can also help to entrench beliefs you have begun to espouse more firmly into the soft fibers of the self, rendering them more fulsome, thereby priming you to embrace more adventurous collective actions in the future. For a "belief" can have variable degrees of conviction embedded in it. New role experiments, indeed, can work to reverse the silent effects of unconscious immersion in role expectations that help to sustain injustices in an established order. A role experiment *enacting* this or that belief may thus help to consolidate it and to open the door to yet new thinking and teaching agendas. Pragmatists I had drawn upon, particularly Mead, Dewey, Mannheim, Kaufman, and Mills, already knew about inner connections among belief, disposition, and action. Their writings now became more vivid to me as I explored imbrications among teaching, writing, role experiments, and action in my new position.

Before we depart Ohio University, it might be wise to say a bit more about teaching there. This was, after all, your first real bout of teaching. And it is one of the sites at which those role experiments you extoll can be enacted.

It turns out that five years working in the residence halls at the University of Michigan prepared me for teaching more than I had realized. I started off at UM as a hallway counselor who also punched meal tickets, advanced to head of a house in South Quadrangle the next year that paid a monthly stipend on top of room and board, and became director of West Quadrangle my last two years in Ann Arbor. That last assignment—presiding over 1,000 students, seven houses, and a staff of about sixty-five—paid a decent wage. I found it possible to write a dissertation while handling that position. I even used the dorm library as my study when the dorm was closed over the summer. That position also created the possibility for a better-paying job than that offered to a beginning assistant professor—if you wished to become a dean of students somewhere. I did not pursue that option.

Back to the issue in question: close encounters on the ground with the troubles, hopes, anxieties, and disciplinary issues of college students for five years also taught things by osmosis about teaching. When I arrived at Ohio University, I was eager to teach. I soon found it to be the most scintillating activity in the academy. Anyone who does not love teaching probably should avoid a career in the academy. Otherwise, you may either find yourself constantly doing something you dislike or assuming an administrative career in which you could easily slide into telling those who do love teaching how to do it. Either route is a recipe of discontent for you and for authoritarianism in your relations to students and faculty. The best administrators I have known try to set aside some time for teaching, partly for these reasons.

My course schedule was two classes a day on a Monday/Wednesday/Friday routine and two more for longer periods on a Tuesday/Thursday format. I would teach during the day and return to our apartment on the edge of campus in the late afternoon. Quality time with my son, David, then less than a year old—more about him later—often meant lying on the living room floor, playing with him until I dozed off, and then letting him entertain himself by crawling all over a zoned-out daddy.

Then after dinner I would prepare two more classes for the next day. The theory classes, which grew in number and importance after my first year, were my favorites. I would teach courses on the history of thought and, periodically, a seminar course in contemporary theory. Textbooks on the history of theory by others provided a lot of stimulus for the lecture courses at first. I recall that Plato, Hobbes, Rousseau, Tocqueville, J. S. Mill, M. L. King, and Marx were among canonical thinkers I taught. Neither Sophocles, Lucretius, Augustine, Spinoza, Kant, Nietzsche, Wittgenstein, William James, James Baldwin, Michel Foucault, Gilles Deleuze, nor Marcel Proust had yet found their way onto my syllabi. Nor had others whom I pursued later in even more amateurish ways, such as Sankara, Wangari Matthai, Gandhi, Lynn Margulis, Anna Tsing, Catherine Keller, Jan Zalasiewics, Stuart Kauffman, Judith Butler, and William Apess, the latter being a Pequot of the early nineteenth century in New England who was perhaps the first Amerindian to write in English. He offered scathing critiques of how Harvard University treated Amerindians on lands it "owned" on the Cape.

•••

Later, as some of the latter figures became important to me, I waged a more active curriculum war against any graduate theory program organized tightly around "the canon." Canons change more rapidly and radically than canon defenders acknowledge. New events periodically press changes upon a canon rather suddenly, as those active in feminism, race studies, the dangers of fascism, and climate change have come to see. Indeed, vibrant intellectual programs need room for students and teachers to interrupt the canon of the day, so they can explore new dangers and possibilities. Few canonical thinkers in the *major* humanistic Euro-American traditions, for instance, prepared Euro-Americans to study how European empires live off exploitation of foreign regions. Some figures in the elided *minor* European traditions, however, come closer, particularly when they are carried into dialogues with decolonial thinkers outside Europe. Debates about the canon wax and wane in the fields of English, history, philosophy, sociology, anthropology, comparative literature, global politics, and political theory, as they must. Today, as the Anthropocene rattles a set of assumptions in the Euro-American canon, we are pressed to think anew about how the politics of regional exploitation and accelerating climate change intersect.

• • •

The canon issue came into play in a small, perhaps revealing way during my first year at Ohio University. The chair of the Department of Sociology informed my chair, Wid Elsbree, that it was poaching on their territory to include Tocqueville in a history of political thought course and Mannheim and Roberto Michels in contemporary political thought. He joined a strict field boundary between sociology and political science to the authority of a senior professor to confine my teaching within disciplinary guardrails as he saw them. I was required to justify my use of those scholars in class to a school curriculum committee. Wid handled much of the pressure. I composed a letter to show how all three figures are prominent in political theory. (But what if they were not, up to that time? What if new issues suggested the need for new field crossings?)

Junior colleagues in several fields found that intervention into a young professor's course by a senior colleague to be outrageous. They were not as surprised by it, though, as I was. My hope was that by launching a quiet campaign against the hubris of the sociology chair a senior scholar or two might ridicule him for erecting such rigid disciplinary boundaries. Some professional academics model field boundaries upon the trope of territorial walls.

The enforcers of a guild mentality are easy to detect. They are, for instance, quick to intervene in department meetings to say, "This is not political science"—or, as the case may be, "This is not sociology, philosophy,

English, or anthropology." I once had a chair of a Philosophy Department at Hopkins chastise me for teaching Nietzsche because Nietzsche was not a political theorist. (What *was* he, by the way?) To such bureaucrats, guild loyalty trumps other considerations: the guild mentality is a power strategy to guard professional practices and assumptions through appointments, department priorities, professional organizations, journals, curriculum rules, and tenure decisions.

•••

Here, then, is another rule: If you seek to be a critical intellectual anchored in a university, spend a third of your time on exploratory teaching, a third on exploratory writing, and a third cultivating political connections to other intellectuals in and around the academy. The third task is as important as the first two.

Moreover, three/thirds is not quite enough: you need to pursue a fourth task, too: to engage scholars who are open to it, emphasizing how these two role definitions do and can draw upon one another. For intellectuals need to draw upon scholarly study, and scholars do their work best when they appreciate the significance of intellectual engagement in the public life of a democracy. A fifth task is to become active in institutions of university governance.

It takes five/thirds, then, to carry out these tasks in the company of others. Some statisticians may pronounce that to be impossible. Perhaps it is. But I note how Whitehead, the great logician, emphasized how futile it is to pretend that every type of accumulation is the same. Two plus three, he says, does add up to five blocks. But two plus three drops of water may add up to one big drop. We do not inhabit a world only of solids, though many professionals committed to hubristic models of explanation pretend we do.

The life of intellectuality can be highly rewarding. That turns out to be the clincher. At the close of an academic career, it is too late to be asked, "What, hast thou not lived?"

You may need to do some more work on your math. These last few paragraphs almost sound as though you seek a unilateral role definition of the liberal arts academic as an intellectual and that you do not really respect people who serve as chairs, deans, provosts, etc. Is that what you mean to say?

No, I was chair of the department at Hopkins for seven years; we pursued a pluralistic model of field intersections during that period. Moreover, one sometimes encounters administrators and faculty who traverse multiple role assignments well. I will note a few instances as this text proceeds; we have already encountered one example in Wid Elsbree. It is also true that intellectuals require scholars to inform their work and that they must fold scholarly skills into that work while adding a public component to it. I guess I really want to assert that while divergent role priorities are needed in the academy, the threats periodically posed to intellectuality by professionals, administrators, and trustees require constant vigilance.

I soon realized that writing time and energy would be crunched if I taught such a heavy load at Ohio University for too long. The teaching itself was delicious and invigorating. You can't defend an idea well if you can't make it lucid and pertinent to students in the classroom. Ohio University thus had plenty of attractions. The size of the teaching load, however, became a reason to seek a position at the University of Massachusetts. Fascination with the prospect of participating in a lively graduate program provided another incentive.

$$\bullet \bullet \bullet$$

To this point, I had read neither Immanuel Kant nor Gilles Deleuze, and Nietzsche served as a private pleasure unratified by others I knew. Nonetheless, something was stirring. A theme was beginning to crystallize—through accumulating events of heterogeneous sorts. The idea: Thinking and periodic jolts by new events can become unruly partners, like lovers from different sides of the track who can neither let go of one another nor consummate their relation within the established order. If you give prominence to the effects of events in life and politics, it becomes important to become attuned to how the jolt of an event can trigger new thinking and how new thinking can enable you to better respond to unexpected events. Attentiveness to the event now becomes more important than the quest to complete a system.

I was thus becoming predisposed toward one side of a fundamental debate between Kant and Deleuze that later consumed much of my teaching and writing. Respected American scholars during this period in the humanities, philosophy, and political theory were often neo-Kantian, with Rawls and soon Habermas embodying noble exemplars of that tradition. Gilles Deleuze, a philosopher of the relative autonomy of the event, expresses acutely a counter-impulse then stirring in me, though I was not then prepared to articulate it: "Something in the world forces us to think," he says. "This something is an object not of recognition, but of a fundamental *encounter*. It may be grasped in a range of affective tones: wonder, love,

hatred, suffering. . . . The sign or point of departure for that which forces
thought is thus the coexistence of contraries, the coexistence of more and
less in an unlimited quality of becoming."[18]

You might find that a surprising event places an old accord into jeopardy—
an accord, say, between established habits of perception and your theory.
The discord or discrepancy may jolt you until a new adventure of thinking
and action is launched. You might now give more priority for a time to
cultivating new sensitivities, experiments, and inventions in relation to those
time-honored tasks of discovery, recognition, judgment, and explanation.
Old balancing acts now become rattled. You may thereby appreciate creative
possibilities that arise periodically, not only from the concord between the
faculties in a settled regime of thought but from discordances arising between
them in face of a new event. Less recognition, more experimentalism. The
double character of thought now moves to the forefront, with the consolidation of judgment and explanation gaining priority during some periods and
cultivation of new sensitivities and experiments at others.

To be clear, I do not end up defining the logic of the event in exactly the
way Deleuze does. I define the event, as we shall see, to be a surprising
obtrusion that places old thoughts, expectations, and habits of conduct
under new pressure. But the debt is there.

* * *

It was not inevitable that my judgment about the essentially bifocal
character of thinking and theory would take such a turn; the conclusion was
not implicit in an internal logic of thought itself. I was not on a path of
dialectical ascent required by the implications of my initial starting point.
But accumulating events—and previous forks already taken—opened windows
to such a possibility. To prize and pursue the power of thought, I was beginning to think, means to attend closely to periodic jolts posed by events that
ruffle, confound, or shatter some cherished habits. Moreover, such events
never stop coming while you are alive, even though their arrival is not
evenly paced.

At first, I thought a dialectical approach could do the job. Thinking,
however, is sometimes neither smooth nor dialectical. It does not always sink
more deeply into a path carved out for it nor follow an implicit trajectory of
progress. Even "negative dialectics" is not sufficient to it, though it opens a
door. Critical intellectuals, rather, seek to become worthy of the events they
encounter.

Some events are minor in import, others significant; some joyful, others distressing, others yet catastrophic. Some start small and burgeon into huge events. A pandemic unsettling the whole world, for instance, may start small when a microscopic virus jumps to a pangolin and then, in a fresh-meat market, crosses to humans. Three events, each larger than the preceding, with asymmetrical effects on classes, races, nonhuman species, and regions. I am told that the birth of Jesus started as a small event, unnoticed by many at its inception.

To work in this key is to affirm the wonder, precarity, and periodic choppiness of the world and to pursue critical thinking, crowned by strategic moments of experimentation and positive role adventures. Or at least such thoughts were percolating and simmering amidst others then in play. It does not take a quantum leap to move from the pragmatisms of Mead, Mannheim, and Mills toward what Gilles Deleuze and others call the "minor tradition," merely a viral crossing.

2

A Fifty-Yard Dash

It may be timely now to review your early years in a working-class family in Flint, Michigan. Again, we are interested in events that may have infiltrated into or touched your later intellectual life, teaching priorities, and political commitments. We know that you are not always a sure guide to such things, and, indeed, that your best recollections are not always perfectly reliable or complete. Indeed, recollection, as we have glimpsed, forms a crown on top of visceral memories that exceed recollection and carry strange efficacies of their own, particularly when a new situation is encountered. They may enrich, intensify, or disrupt conscious thought-imbued feelings. Still, you are a guide of sorts; you are interested in yourself; and your readings of shining moments in life—I mean events that are especially memorable with respect to the thinking and sensibility you have developed—remain pertinent.

It has become rather uncertain what relation I am to take to you. Are you a double, as Iago was to Othello, relaying an insidious, soft voice within that the official voice in Othello tried so hard to resist? Or are you a future voice returning to interrogate me as I report events from the past? One thing is clear: you do interrupt the smoothness of these reports. It seems clear that the self consists of multiple voices in conversation imbued with different degrees of clarity and force; shifts in the relations between these voices can be triggered when new events activate slumbering memories. Some voices may be cloudy or weak for a time and then gain momentum under the pressure of events. I will try to capture some relations and events in my early life that may have played a role in *prompting* later thoughts, political decisions, and intellectual projects. Thinking is too complex, however, simply to be determined by such events. Also, some recollections feel rather distant and detached, almost as if you are watching a newsreel of someone's else's life, while others become affectively rich and intimate—more your own. It is perhaps better to present the first type in the third person.

•••

Billy was born on January 6, 1938, to working-class parents in Flint, Michigan. His dad, the son of Irish and Scottish immigrants, had broken with the low-level managerial career of his own father in General Motors to become an assembly-line auto worker and to join the 1937 sit-down strike at Fisher #2 in the heart of the city. Other GM plants there were also part of the strike. It had to be a sit-down strike, otherwise the owners would pull unemployed Depression workers in by the back door as the strikers marched out through the front.

Billy's mother, Pluma, whose own mother was an orphan of unknown descent and whose father was of mixed French and other heritages, participated in the Women's Brigade as an eighteen-year-old during that strike. She was not strictly a subordinate woman in the family unit, as the typical story of a white working-class, nuclear family goes. The Brigade, you see, tossed food up to the strikers and sought to protect them from police attack by forming a ring around the factory at key moments. It was thought that police and/or company thugs would hesitate before beating the women in public view. The Brigade thus deployed established norms of patriarchal life against the authorities in this eruption of class struggle. Pluma also handled the family finances, such as they were.

William T., who was interviewed about this historic strike several decades later by a Flint UM professor, became a minor celebrity as a young guy who would periodically sneak out at night to run to his wife only to return to the cause before dawn. He was asked in that interview why he kept returning to the fray when so many others stayed away after fleeing under cover of darkness. "I guess because I am Irish," he said. His father was proud of being Irish. William T. was alone in that large clan to break from the Catholic Church at a young age because of its conservatism.

Much later I fantasized that perhaps Billy was conceived during one of those passionate nights when the nineteen-year-old William T. slipped into the house under cover of darkness. There is no evidence that this is true. But I enjoy the fantasy.

Billy was the second in a family soon to have four children. The Depression was in full swing. His early memories are set in a neighborhood on the outskirts of town when his dad worked briefly for Charles Mott, a rich guy

who later funded the founding of Flint UM. Mott hired Dad to work his
farm and gardens on weekends. On some days the boy would ride on a small
tractor with his dad, rather bored but happy enough to be with him.

•••

They soon moved to a country house close to Flint where Dad and
Mom kept a small farm. Dad was back in the factory by then, also working
part-time for the owner of the estate house in front by tending the owner's
fields. The latter job covered the rent. He was very energetic and, to a young
boy, larger than life. He also negotiated a life with two jobs, low income, a
small, ramshackle house, and three kids—with another child to arrive later.
The relatively high pay for auto workers arrived later as the union acquired
more muscle. The little family farm was equipped with a garden, cornfield,
pigs, chickens, and a goat. Billy was constantly warned to stay away from the
big sow in the rickety pen who displayed an ugly personality.

His older sister, perhaps not that happy to have a young brother taking up
so much space, led him out one winter day to the woods where there was a
pond. She coaxed the boy to walk on the thin ice. He hesitated. Finally, as
he did do so, the ice gave way and he fell in the icy water up to his shoulders. The girl panicked, quickly found a long branch, and heroically pulled
the terrified lad to dry ground. He was ice-cold and soaking wet. She
instructed him in strong terms to tell their mother that he had fallen into a
puddle they had not noticed.

He never completely trusted Sue after that event; perhaps his mother did
not, either. The word "ambivalence" was not yet in his lexicon, however. It is
clear that the event occurred, but I am less confident whether the element of
distrust amid emotional connections was forged at that moment or later and
projected backward. Sue was often troubled. She was haunted in later life by
resentment against getting married young, making it impossible for her to be
the first one in the larger, extended family clan to attend the community
college. She took pleasure in her children and having plays she wrote
performed in the Flint area later in life. Was she, as first child, the result of
an unwanted pregnancy? Was her mother particularly hard on her during
the first few years? Those things later seemed probable, since we never saw
pictures of a grand wedding, and Pluma's childrearing practices with the
three younger children were exemplary.

I recall as a young adult seeing a scratchy film that had been shot by our
grandparents, with adults sitting in the living room trying to watch TV
through the "snow" that obscured the images. Three-year-old Billy scampers

into the room, hat askew, glances at the boring scene, and bounces out again. The adults laugh. That is the sum of Billy's career as a film star. That little film strip underlines how early memories are often received later as events observed on a screen. The "he" and the "I" can easily get confused or mixed together in reflections about the early going.

Another event seared into memory was the day Billy played with matches in a dry field of weeds between the family home and the manor facing the road in front of it. He might have been four and a half, or even five. He was held back from kindergarten until the age of six, only partly because the available school was far away by bus. In a dreamy mood he lit a small fire in the grass between two sets of rocks, perhaps to protect a fort from marauders. The fire rapidly spread out of control, soon raging over a large, dry expanse. He tried to resolve the issue himself, doubtless to evade the displeasure of his beloved mother and to turn back his own sense of stupidity.

Finally, he raced into the house to tell her. She rushed out with a large broom, and he watched the woman frantically put out the flames from the front window. Eventually, the fire was quenched. Pluma made it very clear to him, without yelling, that he must not play with matches again.

Corporal punishment—and indeed any draconian punishment—was frowned upon in that family. Sometimes you were ordered to sit on the basement stairs for a while to ponder what you had done. To form a con-science. The absence of physical punishment did not strike the boy as unusual until a year or so later, when they moved to a working-class neigh-borhood in the middle of the city; there he witnessed a vocal group of fathers who were punitive, authoritarian, and sometimes abusive. They were definitely a minority in that neighborhood—most factory men eschewed such a demeanor—but the minority did suck the air out of life when they returned home after a hard day of factory work.

● ● ●

By 1942 our dad was either to be drafted into the infantry or volunteer for another branch of service. The war was in full swing, and he was at risk, even though there were by now two young children in the family. He opted to join the Seabees, spending two and a half years moving between Panama, Hawaii, and the Philippines. His squad faced several raids at the last location.

The now fatherless family moved to the middle of the city to live with my great-grandmother. Her house, 13 Cottage Grove, was located within a block of the Flint River and the Chevrolet and Fisher Body factories. The river served as a mobile dumping site for General Motors, a use that returned to haunt the city seventy years later, well after the old factories had been closed and stranded workers had been left to fend for themselves.

The sensitive boy, accustomed to playing alone in the woods and fields, was ill-prepared for the rough-and-tumble life of the white working-class evangelicals sprinkled through that neighborhood. They contended against the union-identified families there. The hard-livers, who had recently migrated from the south, were tough on the country boy at first, to say the least. He was not a good student, either, until the fourth grade.

An elderly neighborhood couple would sometimes call him into their yard when he was six and ask him to pronounce the word "pepper" over and over, enjoying inordinately his inability to pronounce the r and imagining that he did not notice the pleasure they took in that failure.

• • •

One day during the second grade, when the boy returned home bawling with a bloody nose and bruised body, his mother insisted that he tell her what had happened. He obeyed under surface protest, on the firm promise that she would not report it to the school. He had been beaten up by a big guy who had been held back for a year and was living a rough life in one of the shanties on the edge of the Flint River, lower on the income scale and housing quality than Billy's family enjoyed. Every few years those riverside encampments would flood over in spring, with the families somehow returning to reclaim the plots and shanties a few weeks later.

Two days after the beating, the two boys were summoned to the principal's office. She told them that a student had reported "their fight." She did not tolerate fighting, she announced with principal severity; they either had to promise not to fight again or face suspension. They promised. As the two boys walked out, it became clear that his fighting buddy had been taken in by the ruse. The big guy smiled at the smaller lad for the first time, saying, "We're lucky this time." That "we" was music to the lad's ears. Billy's mom was smart and relentless. The relentlessness showed in her conduct more than in things she said. She was gentle, yet few wanted to cross her.

• • •

On a beautiful summer day in 1945, the children were summoned by their mother to the front porch. They were fed potato chips and a Coke, smiling and waving at other neighbors as they did so. The Pacific war had just ended, and it was time to celebrate. None of the celebrants—mother included—had a clear idea about what the horrific nuclear bombings of Hiroshima and Nagasaki meant. That knowledge came later. They were simply delighted that William T. Connolly was returning home.

When Dad returned, the parental bedroom smelled to Billy as if a strange man had invaded the house. So masculine, hairy, and sweaty. Billy approached him politely and warily at first, in what the boy assumed was a discreet manner. Then the two began slowly to reshape a relationship. One weekend morning the boy started to crawl in bed with his dad while he was still asleep, eager to commune with him. The man awoke with a jolt and grabbed the boy. "Don't Ever Take Me by Surprise, Boy!" he bellowed. That set back the reunion a bit. The man was walking around with a mild case of postwar trauma.

The boy's mother had worked in the tank plant for a year during the war. And though the boy barely knew it at the time, she was not happy to relinquish that job after the war—as working-class wives were authoritatively called upon to do—so the men could take them back as the factories were refitted to car production. First stay at home as a good wife and mother; next work in a wartime tank factory as a patriot; then relinquish that job to men again during peacetime . . . a yo-yo syndrome.

•••

The larger-than-life man detested the fact that his son was more feminine than several other boys in the neighborhood. He could not stand his son to be bullied, either. So, after another rough fight (for the boy), the war veteran decided to train his boy in "martial arts." Billy's mother paced back and forth during the "training" sessions, clearly disapproving. When the next kid on the block showed up to harass him, Billy flew out the door in attack mode. The boy was Billy's size, and the new devotee of martial arts wrestled the boy to the ground.

Billy was strangling the lad when his dad rushed out to halt the fight. The veteran had forgotten to teach the cadet how to finish with grace. He brought the two boys inside to tell them they could keep fighting or become friends. He couldn't care less which, so he said. They decided to become friends. And the boy invited Billy to come play with him and others down the street.

After the erstwhile nemesis left, duly impressed with Billy's dad, Billy ventured outside. But now, two girls living in houses nearby suddenly seemed to enjoy his company. So, he hung with them for a bit, glorying in a

new aura of urban acceptability. The Commando called Billy back in, asking
if he was in fact more stupid than the war veteran had assumed. "Do you
want to get along with those boys, or not?" he asked, relaying the only
correct answer in a military tone. The bewildered boy wandered down the
street and was invited to join a softball game.

• • •

During this period Billy was mesmerized by a Saturday radio program
entitled "It Pays to Be Ignorant"—TV was not on the agenda yet. The
raucous contestants would compete to see who could give the most stupid
answer to topical questions about science, culture, and politics; the others
would then riff on the first answer. The boy, to the mild dismay of his
parents, would laugh hysterically about this or that answer. Sometimes it
contained a pearl of insight within its blatant ignorance. Very funny. I sense
remains from that early program bubbling up again during joyous bursts of
laughter today—though I prefer the resonant laugh of Kamala Harris to my
own.

Old commercials stick, too. "For a treat instead of a treatment, try Old
Golds," was a jingle endlessly repeated on the radio. Bill and Pluma each
smoked a pack and a half of those treats a day. That is one of the innumerable small ways capitalism infiltrates the soul. If you wish to look hot while
inhaling that treat, go to a film starring Lana Turner or Burt Lancaster.
Watch them light up the screen.

Memory never stops bubbling. When you rummage through the debris
for little gems. . . .

• • •

One day when he was eight or so, he and his buddy, Jimmy Ruther,
became enchanted with the bolo knives Billy's dad had brought home from
the Philippines that hung in holsters on the bedroom wall. In a daylight
trance, they hung two each over their shoulders and marched in warrior
style down Third Avenue. Perhaps they sought to impress some older tough
guys in the neighborhood. A cop stopped them, asking where they got those
knives and why they were walking around with them. He then drove them to
13 Cottage Grove and subjected Billy's dad to sharp interrogation on the
issue. We promised never to do that again; the knives disappeared, anyway.

• • •

Life now began to change, as a boyhood fog slowly began to lift. Billy became a better student in several classes. Winning spelling bees, being a class clown, walking Jacquie Stracka to the local movie house on occasion, and so on. He kissed her on the nose the first time he made the valiant attempt in a dark theater. The giggles and embarrassment were soon ironed out.

Then in the fourth grade Bill won the regional race for boys of that grade in the fifty-yard dash. He became a local celebrity at Durant Elementary School! Bill thus left Billy behind. Older boys at the school challenged him to races on the spot. He kept winning. He was soon invited to play third base on a Little League team composed mostly of older boys. More kids wanted to play with him. He realized the source of the rapid change in status was ridiculous but wallowed in it, nonetheless. He no longer needed those bolo knives.

I was thus born a second time in the fourth grade. That birth was accompanied by the gradual lifting of a fog that had up to then permeated my experience and school performances. An abiding sense of the unfairness of things accompanied the second birth, however, as I pondered how the move by a young country boy to the city could be tough and then be reversed by a single sports event. I later opposed the bullying rituals that junior high and some high school athletes enact; most teammates opposed them too. I became something of a leader at school, becoming class president the next year. I continued, however, to see athletics as a key to the good life. Perhaps I would run in the Olympics someday.

● ● ●

Several neighborhood boys in the fourth and fifth grades loved a contest called "Capture the Flag." We would walk to a stream a half mile away, choose teams, and plant a flag on each side of the creek. (We pronounced it "crick.") You had to capture the opponent's flag and carry it to your side of the creek without being caught in the attempt. Deception, patience, boldness, and speed were skills needed in that game, each at precisely the right moment. We loved it.

Occasionally after exhausting ourselves in the contest, we would gather where the creek spills into the Flint River. A large pipe on a ridge next to the creek jutted out discreetly from the woods, stretching a few feet over the river. It was large enough to sit on. We would lounge on it for a while, watching the river roll by and reviewing our recent adventures.

One afternoon as we sat on the wide pipe, we felt intense vibrations, then heard a roar emanating from the pipe, and finally watched in shock and disgust as a green, bluish avalanche poured into the river for several minutes—toxic waste dumped into the river by an auto company, gushing from a wide pipe secreted from public view.

That is the same area of the river where the younger boy used to hunt arrowheads before becoming one of the accepted, popular boys. He was not supposed to go anywhere close to that river, of course. He would relieve his boredom during the hunts by conjuring stories about Amerindians who left arrowheads behind as they hunted or waged war. That small collection of arrowheads was lost when the family moved away.

Capitalism still lives on the acceleration of growth and the concealment of waste, as Cara Daggett shows so well in *The Birth of Energy*.[1] And, of course, the accumulation of wastes of multiple sorts eventually takes its revenge, whether it be CO_2 emissions, pollutants poured into rivers, or the rise of wildfires. Decades later, when the Flint water supply became toxic after a neoliberal governor compelled the city to shift from Lake Huron drinking water to Flint River water, I woke up with a shudder in Baltimore during several nights, hearing, tasting, smelling, and seeing that toxic brew again. The boys never again jumped off the pipe to cool off in the river after that toxic event. We were foolish boys, but not utterly stupid.

• • •

William T. now rose to greater influence in the local union. He was a fiery speaker. He wrote incendiary articles for the union paper, sprinkling around italicized words as if his voice happened to be recorded on paper. By the time I was thirteen I wanted to caution him against the overuse of italics—as copyeditors have done to me later in life. But I never did. He became a committee man who dealt courageously with worker grievances against management on the spot and, soon, president of Local 598. I have a video on my Facebook page of an interview with him decades later about how he was brought into the office one day to be fired after writing up the grievance of one complainant on the line, an outcome only stopped when Charlie Shin (one of his union buddies to be discussed soon) walked into the office to tell "management" that labor would go on a "wildcat strike" if he were not returned to the line *after* completing a review of the worker's grievance. Management backed off in the face of that threat.

Dad once ran as a protest candidate against Walter Reuther to be president of the national UAW itself. He also brought me along to walk picket lines with strikers from time to time. I enjoyed the banter and respected the determination of those guys as they sought to wring concessions from a potent corporate foe. Nobody anticipated that GM would flee town to find cheaper labor elsewhere two decades later, leaving workers and the city behind to hold the bag. Much later, Dad won the Walter Reuther award for his early union leadership.

• • •

The UAW was one of the few labor unions then bent on racial integration, so African American workers were invited to the house when I was young—an uncommon event in that white neighborhood. Sometimes other labor celebrities showed up, too. Two or three times, the radical, vivacious Genora Dollinger visited with her husband, Sol. She had organized the Women's Brigade; she also gave a fiery speech during one of the thug attacks on strikers, encouraging resistance and calling upon wives and sweethearts to support men in the sit-down strike rather than staying home or heeding city-corporate propaganda. She was beaten with a lead pipe by thugs while asleep in her house because of that labor activism. Several years later the Kefauver Crime Committee confirmed that these attacks—there were several of them against labor activists, as well as shootings of the Reuther brothers who were UAW leaders—had been instigated by corporate officials in collusion with the Mafia. So, the killing of Jimmy Hoffa years later was not that surprising to me.

Anyway, I made certain I was in the living room whenever Genora graced the premises, clinging to each word and gesture emanating from the charismatic woman. She told me she read the *New York Times* all the way through every day (even though it then arrived two days late). Once, decades later, when Jane Bennett told me that she was reading about a fascinating Flint labor activist and feminist named Genora Dollinger, I impressed her by saying, "Yes, Dad and I were taken with her whenever she visited our house." That was the kind of understatement I did not master until adulthood. I failed to check out what Mother thought about the visits from Genora.

• • •

Father was an atheist who had grown up Catholic, Mother an agnostic who had grown up Protestant. They allowed their kids to experiment with churches in the area. At the age of eleven I started attending a Sunday School sporadically with some evangelical boys in the neighborhood. Some of the boys would not only assert solemnly that the Jews had killed Jesus, their families very often carried from the South a virulent racism against African Americans. Many northern working-class whites were themselves prejudiced, but the perspective of white evangelical migrants from the South and border states was definitely more extreme. There are several severe legacies of slavery in America; one on the list is how the migration of white evangelicals to the north to gain factory jobs helped to propel racism more widely and deeply into northern states.

One day the Sunday School teacher at the local Baptist church told me that if I stepped up the pace, I would win the boys' contest to recite the most verses from the Bible; if so, I would win a free week to a Christian camp on a lake. I loved to swim. So, the competitor stepped up the pace. I won, though the highest score in the boy's group would have earned merely fifth place overall if the girl and boy contests had been lumped together.

• • •

Camp was hell on earth. The young boys were ordered to wear loose T-shirts while swimming so our nipples would not be exposed. During large assemblies each morning the few of us who had not yet been saved were placed under immense pressure to confess publicly our lack of grace and to accept Christ. Twice, two of us were held late and called to the front of the room to explain to assembled preachers why we still resisted the love of Christ. Under intense pressure I started to cry—perhaps bawl is the word—during the Second Inquisition of Love. I was released. I ran to the cabin in a fit of anger and anguish, grabbing my baseball glove to take my rightful place in the game at hand. But the tear stains clinging to my cheeks when I reached the field convinced my teammates that I had indeed been saved. They gathered round to celebrate. I could not win for losing. The only thing was to wait it out until the week ended. That ordeal was severe, but not as prolonged as attempts during my adult years in a political science department by the evangelists of behavioralism to convert an entire department to its faith.

The tenacious pressure that many working-class white evangelical children face from infancy to the late teens was condensed for me, as it were, into one week of divine love and hellfire. And I had safety valves and outlets to draw upon. One was to gut it out at camp until the long week ended. Little wonder that many young evangelical boys and girls confessed total allegiance to the faith in public and devised secret ways to slip out of the web when outside adult supervision.

Racism, anti-Semitism, and misogyny readily sank into the soil of life here. There were escape hatches, but they were full of potential traps. Indeed, streaks of disavowed self-loathing still run through the culture of the white evangelical working class. It renders many susceptible to authoritarian lures from the right, makes them hypersensitive when liberals talk down to them, and very often encourages them to project the source of their real grievances onto African Americans and other minorities, particularly when an economic or military crisis explodes. Simply accusing evangelicals of being racist or misogynist, however, exacerbates rather than cures the malady. In a highly stratified system, it is often more tempting to look down than to look up when insecurities intensify. My close attention to such questions, however, was deferred to a later date.

• • •

A few weeks after the camp ordeal, I informed my dad causally one day that I was now an atheist. I was twelve. Fine, he said, just don't tell your teachers. I waited, I think, until the ninth grade to announce it in class one day at a timely moment in front of a favorite teacher, Mrs. Fletcher, who taught English and who had once chastised me for speaking one dialect on the playground and another in the classroom. "It is self-contradictory to be an atheist," she announced in a testy tone to everyone. I fell out of favor in that class. My dad had been right.

Decades later, however, she informed me at a class reunion that she and her daughter had recently begun to read Nietzsche. Any thoughtful Christian, she now announced, must engage Nietzsche with respect even if they do not embrace his philosophy. The little boy still rumbling around in Bill took that, first, as a sign that she knew something about his adult life and, second, as perhaps an apology of sorts. Or as much of an apology as a confident English teacher could marshal. The child in the adult accepted both eagerly.

My atheism has passed through permutations over the years. But Kierkegaard's leap of faith has never captured me, nor have other noble professions of faith in divinity by those reworking earlier, more bald convictions. I decided to see how much depth, insight, experimentalism, and presumptive care for the potential diversity of being could be mined from a nontheistic orientation to the world. The world in this sense includes human cultures, natural assemblages, diverse vectors of temporality, and the manifold imbrications between them.

My stance on those "immanence/transcendence" debates, in which I later participated with relish, has probably been inflected by residues roaming around from a long week at that evangelical camp. The idea became to find as much richness, vitality, and creative potential in the premise of a non-divinized world as possible, and then to fashion positive relations with others of different faiths if and when that was possible. I also feel confident that impressions and remainders from the joyous theater of the absurd pedaled by Jonathan Winters when I was a tweenie continue to rumble in my soul, too, though I no longer recall the actual skits. And my later wariness of those charges of performative contradiction issued against this or that theory? Perhaps it, too, is inflected by those minor school-day scars, remains, and skits, including a shaming from my beloved English teacher. Thinking becomes intense through the pressure of encounters and jolts even more than by ironing out minor discrepancies ("contradictions") in a pattern of thought felt to be on the very verge of completeness.

• • •

The encounter with McCarthyism is a case in point. It was in full swing by the 1950s, fueled by those hell-bent on inflaming resentment against the film industry, labor, the State Department, and the academy for being "fellow travelers" of communism. One day, after the family had moved just outside the city to a working-class neighborhood divided roughly between antiunion white evangelicals from border states and union loyalists, I saw in the newspaper that Charlie Shin—my dad's friend and a Marxist member of Local #598 who attended rump labor meetings at our house—had first been severely beaten by a group of enraged factory workers and then tossed into the street in front of Fisher Body #2. A picture of him sitting stunned on the street, posted on the front page of the *Flint Journal*, shocked and unraveled me.

It turned out that the House Un-American Activities Committee had arrived in town a few days earlier, exposing Charlie to have been a member of the Communist Party when he was young. My dad found a lawyer for him; Charlie soon moved next door to us. He was able to return to work about two years after the beating. My earliest exposure to Marx was through Charlie: "From each according to their ability to each according to their need," he would announce to me from time to time.

Our family now felt obligated to go to the dentist-brother of the impressive young lawyer who defended Charlie gratis. The lawyer was unfortunately more talented than the dentist. The McCarthy purge of radicalism from organized labor was highly effective, as it was from film studios and universities. Years later, during the funeral in Flint for my dad, who died at the age of 76, Charlie Shin drove down from the Upper Peninsula to honor him and to placate us. He told me he had read *The Politicized Economy* at my dad's suggestion.

• • •

The family of six, after moving from the city, lived in a four-room house on Ellis Park Drive on the outskirts of town. The house was small, but regular bathing, sleeping, and chore routines were quickly worked out by Mother. So it did not seem too cramped. Or perhaps the fact that during the school year I left the house at 8 A.M. and, when football, basketball, or track season was in swing, returned home at 7 P.M., mitigated any cramped feelings, doing so for my two younger sisters, too, who soon played sports at that school. After the house had been "fixed up," we sold it and moved next door to one with an extra bedroom. As the only boy, it was given to me.

• • •

From the age of twelve through fourteen, Bill's dad would take him on ice fishing trips to the Saginaw Bay with two of his dad's brothers and their younger boys. These were long days. Sitting around watching the men drink and joke was the order of the day for the youngsters. The induction rituals were all-male affairs. After the first experience or two, the boy decided the next time to help hack holes in the ice, set up lines, and then lace up his ice skates to roam for a few hours over the large Bay. "Hey, Billy," his uncles chided as he laced up, "too good to hang with us and catch the pike you love to eat?" "Let him be," his dad said. "The boy likes to skate. . . ." Today there is neither ice fishing nor skating on the Saginaw Bay. . . .

• • •

One summer, when I was around fifteen, Mother took the family on a three-week camping stint to a stunning state park in northern Michigan, close to Traverse City. We would pick cherries at a small orchard during the day to earn enough money to stay there, stopping around 3:00 P.M. to return to the park and enjoy the Traverse Bay beach. Nirvana! One Saturday, when Dad drove up to spend the weekend, he announced in grand style that he would make "mulligan stew." He bought good meat and numerous fresh vegetables; we all began cutting up the ingredients.

The fifteen-year-old soon noted his mother sitting quietly on a log, away from the celebration. "What's going on, Mom?" he asked quietly. "*He* drives up here *larger than life*, throwing money around like a big shot, while I've spent every day trying to make a go of it on a string so we can be here." Oh. . . .

The boy finally stuttered, "He *is* larger than life, Mom; you, um, are *full* of life." She smiled and seemed to glance at the awkward teenager differently for a mere second. Then the two strolled over to the royal cooking event, the boy now careful not to celebrate the festivities too much. Today, I sense how a brief, unexpected smile burned that little event into a recollection summoned up every now and then; it can sometimes spawn a reverie. So many other recollections are buried in sand.

•••

To channel your mother or father? *That* is the question. And which one on what occasions? I have not been that good at resolving these issues or in allowing a synthesis to emerge as two shadows slip and slide around in the recesses of an adult soul. Unless, perhaps, the later idea of "agonistic respect"—as a noble ethos to pursue across multiple differences in a pluralistic society—somehow embodies a composite of these two adults. There is no doubt that each contained traces of the sensibility prevalent in the other. So perhaps there was the concept, sitting in plain sight.

Many years later, when Jane Bennett and I would gather nineteen or twenty kids, grandkids, and adults together in northern Michigan for a week to commune with my ailing younger sister and to inhale the sweet surroundings, I would recollect again that lovely time camping with the nuclear family in a state park on Traverse Bay thirty miles to the east.

•••

Life was very good to me at Flint, Atherton, a small school on the outskirts of the city. I played quarterback in football and point guard in basketball, serving as captain of both teams my senior year. I also ran track and played third base on the baseball team. Immersion in sports, still inhaling those sweet fumes from a fourth-grade race.

One day when I was a freshman the news that my grades were slipping popped up at the family dinner table. "Do you worry about those grades?" Mom asked. "Not that much," the student/athlete announced officiously, "there is time to catch up later." "He has nothing to worry about." Dad intervened, adopting the grand voice of union orator. "I'm *sure* he'll get into *barber* school. He may even get a *scholarship.*" The table broke up in laughter. My grades began to pick up. Humor was my dad's best tactic of child rearing, whenever he focused on the task. . . . I may have followed him in both respects.

• • •

When I was sixteen, slated to become starting quarterback as a sopho-more in the fall, my dad and mom became excited in the spring about a new opportunity. Dad had accepted a white-collar job in the UAW; the family would move to southern California in late summer where the new job would be located. I was of course terrified. But nothing could be said or done about it. It was too big an upgrade in work and income for the family, and it spoke volumes to a man who was tired of the assembly line. A large group of Atherton students held a lovely going-away party for me, replete with gifts and expres-sions of beautiful teenage feelings. I attended the party in a state of shock.

Late one night in June, two weeks or so after that party, loud pounding at the door rattled the house. My older sister, Sue, and I stumbled up to answer, wondering why our parents had ignored the ruckus. "Your mom and dad have just had a terrible accident," the ambulance driver announced. "Your mom will survive, but your dad is going to die. She asked me to bring you to the hospital now." We left immediately in an ambulance driven by this noble man, leaving two young girls asleep untended in the house.

Mom did recover soon. But Dad had lapsed into a coma. At the hospital we were told again to prepare for his probable death. One of my grandfathers pulled me aside to tell me it was now time for me to quit school and become the family breadwinner. In the depths of that coma, however, the man smacked his lips in a kiss when his wife leaned over him two days later to show him that she was alive. Some of us began to think that the death sentence had been pronounced prematurely. I retain, after that night, a vague sense of foreboding when I hear a loud knock on the door at night.

• • •

It was June; the sturdy man's recovery was slow and uncertain. First, a serious coma, followed by scattered periods of semi-wakefulness, then a new plateau weeks later when he could speak a little but did not know where he was. He soon became paranoid, periodically ordering me to organize an escape from the prison ship on which the two of us were now captives.

The war had returned. I would try to talk the sailor out of his demand, adopting the sycophantic tone I later heard Haeman assume to his daddy, Creon. But, as Sophocles would have anticipated, the soothing tone only exacerbated the prisoner's anger. The charge of cowardice once again wafted through the air. Billy had never loved the label "Sally Boy" his daddy applied to him from time to time.

So, one evening the paranoid dad and the sixteen-year-old son plotted an escape. I was to lock the nurse into the closet the next time she entered the room; we would then scramble down the hall together with a wastebasket full of his belongings. That was as far as the plan proceeded. How would we find a lifeboat to carry us away on the open sea? That question was shuffled aside. Dad also had suffered a broken pelvis from the accident, so the escape would proceed at a hobbled pace.

When the nurse strolled into the room, I opened the closet door and stepped toward her with a sharp look and determined gait, throwing my dad the foolish sideways glance we shared when we were teasing the girls as we promised to obey them. He burst out in a full-throated laugh. The escape was aborted. I also sensed that my dad could soon make a decent recovery.

The war prisoner engineered an escape on his own a few nights later. I rushed to the hospital to search for the escapee. The staff had located—or captured—him just before I arrived. He was found holding a wastebasket full of belongings and hovering in a stand of trees on the edge of the hospital grounds. Nobody could figure out how the wounded commando had slunk down the hall, walked down a few flights of stairs, and slipped out a side door undetected. He became a bit of a staff celebrity after that. We were also informed, however, that someone had to remain with him every night until he was ready to return home, or else the staff would be compelled to bind him up at night.

I thus spent innumerable all-night stints at the hospital during that summer, watching and pondering as my father slowly improved. Others took turns, too. My later interest in the evolution of neuroscience and its possible contributions to political thought were surely triggered by those nightly experiences. It is probable that my dad suffered damage to the hippocampus, the small, delicate brain region that plays such an important role in the consolidation of short-term memory.

• • •

Dad came home in the early fall; he was unable to return to work for two or three more years. We thus lived on a string. Union members collected money for the family from time to time. And when he became more mobile the Local gave him a part-time job as janitor at the union hall. I took over that job when I attended Flint Junior College. He was able later to return to factory work for a decade until securing an early disability retirement at the age of fifty. That disability program was the fruit of intense labor negotiations, too, though not all workers were alert to this fact. Every time a new benefit was negotiated with "management" under threat of a strike, GM would send out flashy brochures a few months later saying how they had given it to members of "the GM family." Fake News has expanded immensely in recent years, but it has deep roots in old corporate practices.

One adolescent crisis for me was how to return to school after that definitive goodbye party, which was marked by a flood of gifts. But there was nothing to it. Word travels fast in a small school; everybody knew what had happened, though few mentioned it to me. Nobody cared that I was now wearing shiny new shirts to school, loot from the grand party. Well, maybe the guy who had hoped to become quarterback that fall did. That did not become a topic of discussion, either.

• • •

Dad, when he finally returned to work with damaged short-term memory, now began to enjoy the assembly line as never before. Several coworkers helped him make a go of his assignment on the line for the next decade. The task was to pull a cloth seat cover tight over the seat frame and tack it to the frame every minute or so. A sixty-pound pull, over and over, all day. The Marx I read on alienated labor thus came alive to me a few years later as I pondered how assembly-line regimentation that once had felt degrading to a vibrant man became a source of satisfaction and scene of fellowship after his memory and intellect had become blunted. He became a loving grandfather, full of tenderness for everyone. He also had a large supply of sayings to repeat to his grandchildren, to their pleasure and to the dismay of adults. One always brought a laugh: "I do not think I'm that good lookin', but what's my opinion amongst millions of others?" I have tried that out with my grandchildren a few times, to less effect. Perhaps my timing is off.

He somehow was also a fount of wisdom from time to time, when counseling a young parent, for instance, how to help his own young son negotiate a period of shyness and low self-confidence. "I remember a boy who was shy," he said to me once, "and that worked out okay." I never told the sweet old guy how I had decided to eschew applying the "Sally Boy" handle to my son. Some generational traditions are best broken.

•••

At no time during my youth did the family run out of food or forfeit the mortgage on the house on Ellis Park Drive. Sure, most houses on that block were made of "Modern-Crete," a weird concoction of cement and crushed corn cobs that crumbled after about forty or fifty years. So, the house had not been an astute investment. But wages had now become decent for workers; the local union was loyal to the family during its period of duress; and my mother worked as a housekeeper while her husband recovered. The fragilities held.

It became clear that I would need to earn tuition money to attend Flint Junior College, but I could live at home as a commuter. I also felt little desire to go through teenage rebellion, since I now became both an older brother and a surrogate father of sorts to my two younger sisters. And my sweet father was no longer an alpha-male figure of authority against whom rebellion was even imaginable. The rebel in Bill had to be stored for future targets.

•••

Things became tough for Pluma, however. Her thirty-five-year-old husband had lost his capacity for sex. She had to cope with this startling fact amidst adjusting to his other incapacities. The first issue was discussed only in whispers in the family, but the others found expression in her periodic bouts of impatience joined to our efforts to smooth things over. The guy would be sent to buy a quart of milk and return with bread and eggs. She no longer had a husband with good short-term memory or refined intelligence to entertain her with startling humor, commune with her about a great film, share a political project with her, or conspire about how to raise wayward children. Of course, he was no longer tempted to launch an affair, either. Some of these issues were relieved a bit later as the recovery kept advancing until it settled onto its final plateau. The former firebrand with jet-black hair and blue eyes became gentle and generous during his later years.

I did not develop enough maturity to discuss those issues with Mother during the most difficult period. But three of us—Judy, Kathy, and I—did try to provide support and psychic compensation. My two younger sisters, indeed, excelled at this task after I departed town for grad school a few years later. Our mother had always been the rock of that nuclear family; she was now even more so.

•••

I trust you are not an amateur psychoanalyst. That is why I hesitate to report the secret crush I had on the pretty young married woman living next door to us when I was twelve or thirteen. She needed to be saved from her mean husband, I surmised so clearly. The infatuation terminated suddenly one day when I noticed that she looked a hell of lot like a younger version of my mother. But I am already saying more than needed. I do not deny the role of Oedipal experiences. I prefer Freud to Lacan, however, and Nietzsche to both. I also prize the wisdom of Jocasta in *Oedipus Rex*, when she advises Oedipus to treat those childhood dreams casually rather than dwelling on them morosely. Every boy has them, Jocasta says, before she is drawn by her husband/son into the next phase of the maelstrom. . . .

Lots of people today have a little psychoanalyst roaming around in them, especially when it comes to interpreting the lives of others they do not know well. And I appreciate how you try to identify rocky encounters that may have helped to spur elements in your later thinking. Such an encounter can sometimes open up a new line of thought, even though it is seldom possible to identify just how that line is ignited or to know where it may turn next. I sense that you resist psychoanalysis because you think it too often forestalls activism. Fair enough. But remember that sometimes internal binds created, say, by a severe trauma run so deep that therapy is needed to loosen them. So, even though you later seek to replace the psychoanalytic theory of drives anchored partly in memory traces of a primal horde with an image of drives anchored in living intersections between events and social disciplines, don't allow that ambition to depress awareness of how traumatic events can overwhelm the pursuit of creativity you value so highly. The dissonances you prize in life pass into another realm when they spawn trauma. But, again, we run ahead of ourselves.

Tell us a bit about your high school and college years. Did you know in high school that you wanted to become a professor? Were there specific things about the high school or college years that prepared you for such a future? Or made it difficult to pursue it? Was it not a strange ambition to pursue, since there were neither academics nor professional people in your larger network of kinship relations? Did, perhaps, you simply want to cling to school as long as possible? Seeking a new home away from home?

It is perhaps already clear that I had few major interests in high school: excelling in sports, getting good grades, making classmates laugh, spurring friends into mild bouts of rebellion, and landing a steady girlfriend. The last item took care of itself shortly before my dad's accident. Inez Caon's parents had migrated from southern Italy; she was born in the States. She attended a Catholic school nearby. When we began to date in the ninth grade, I was told that a few white kids at my school defined her to be "colored." I found that inordinately amusing.

Her father owned a small tile and terrazzo company, and he was highly skilled. He was also brutish. The third or fourth time I knocked on the door to take Inez out, Emile rushed me like a bull. He and I had never even talked before. Inez and her mother tackled him, Inez high and her mother low, screaming threats at him as they held on for dear life to stop him from making it to the door. The fraught scene shocked me. (Maybe that is why I later came to love Lina Wertmuller films. . . .) Things quickly settled down, however.

Sometimes when Inez and I were about to go to a movie in her mother's car, Inez would bounce downstairs and return with three or four dollars in fifty-cent pieces. Her parents, refugees from Italy and the Great Depression, were suspicious of banks, even though they used them. They stored extra funds in big buckets sunk into the sparkling terrazzo floor that graced the basement. There were silver dollars in other buckets, too, but Inez never touched those. She was apparently untroubled about those treasury raids, so I soon decided to enjoy the periodic injections of bonus money.

I later began to suspect that Inez's father had abused her when she was younger. That bull rush at me was one hint. . . . He would also make leering comments in Italian about her in her presence to adult male friends visiting their house. She would brush them off with disdain. And she often seemed to avoid him like a pariah. When it became clear that our own intimacy was about to reach a new plateau, she told me a story about how an uncle had coaxed her into the woods for an hour one day when she was thirteen, carrying her out on his shoulders an hour later. I received the cloudy story—I never heard a word about that uncle again—to be a way to intimate that she was not a virgin.

But why worry so much about that issue with me? I was not Christian at that point. Virginity was nothing positive in my book—though it seemed inordinately important to several male high school friends who wanted their girlfriends to "give it up" only to them. Indeed, I had been on a futile campaign to escape the dire state of virginity myself from the age of fourteen and did not prize it in either girls or boys. Inez seemed not to know that—or perhaps not to believe it. My atheism and adolescent orientation to sexuality seemed to support one another—though not to require each other. Besides, I think I had digested Bertrand Russell's congenial book on sex and marriage by that time, or if not by then, within a year. The dozen or so drive-in theaters sprinkled around the perimeter of the car-centered city now became essential escape hatches for us in the summer—as well as to other teenagers who had enough money and parental tolerance to commandeer a car in the evening.

I did not transfigure the term "atheism" into "nontheism" until much later, after I absorbed how dogmatic the first handle can appear to others—and often be—and how the latter term could be crafted into an invitation to agonistic respect between spiritual constituencies rubbing shoulders together who pull different onto-theologies into everyday life.

• • •

The Atherton high basketball team won the school's first league championship during my senior year, and we advanced rather deep into the state tournament. Before the most important game of the season, one that would secure the league title if we won it, we were about to file onto the court when the coach asked me if I, as captain, had any words to say to the team. That had never happened before! "Yes, coach," I replied in sarcastic teenage style. Eyeing the cadre of tight teenagers, I broke into a robust verse of "Yes, Jesus Loves Me." My teammates, knowing my proud atheism, exploded with laughter at the irrelevance of it and roared onto the court loose and ready to play. It turns out that my camp experience contained gems to draw upon now and then, after all.

I was certainly not a scoring machine—the all-state player Dale Keller took care of that assignment brilliantly—but I did have one or two things to offer. Now, as Dale and I commune on the phone regularly, he sometimes says, "We have won the lottery of life, sweet William," because we have both survived past the age of eighty. I occasionally divert him from the trials of Parkinson's disease with which he now struggles by exaggerating my contributions to our high school teams and reviewing our true brilliance as comedians in the eighth and ninth grades. A win-win situation. We recall how we had promised one another in high school that whichever of us was dying first the other would laugh with him about the humorous absurdity of life. That pledge has morphed more recently into a summons to review old times together as Dale's struggle with Parkinson's proceeds.

• • •

One story Dale and I love to review is the day in an eighth-grade class we kept whispering and gesturing hysterically to each other across the aisle, laughing too loud and gesticulating too blatantly. Our behavior became unbearable to the teacher in a way I now grasp a bit better. . . . She said, "You two should just look at yourselves in the mirror and see just how ridiculous you are." But we could not stop: we were overwhelmed by our own humor. We were indeed mimicking Jonathan Winters, the brilliant, close to crazy comedian who enacted whacky characters and utterly entranced us. So the poor teacher kicked us out of class for the day. "Where are you two going?" she asked as an afterthought as we sauntered to the door. "To the bathroom to look in the mirror and see just how ridiculous we really look," I blurted. The class enjoyed that retort, though the studious girls we sought so much to impress had found our behavior impossibly immature up to that moment. We raced to the bathroom, pointing over and over at ourselves in the mirror, laughing hysterically for twenty minutes at how ridiculous and immature we truly were.

A shining point in a shared bank of memories. The positive element in the theater of the absurd was relayed to us through life experience and filtered through the bizarre humor of Jonathan Winters and Sid Caesar well before Nietzsche and Camus appeared on the scene. We sensed that to disavow the absurd after experiencing it is to risk folding too much existential resentment into life and then to seek unjust revenge against others for the very feeling you seek to suppress. But such thoughts were not yet well articulated. At that time, the feeling for life often found expression in antics and bursts of laughter we could not contain.

Of course, the shimmering event cost us a couple of weeks in detention hall. Strangely, neither of us recalls details of *that* experience. We were, as polite adults would say, teens coping with hormonal excesses. You could also say we were foolish boys gripped by the exuberance of life, if you prefer. Our continued bouts of laughter together over several decades—as we have kept in contact for the following sixty years or so across large distances and different careers—have been infused with a sense of the abundance of the world and the absurdities coursing through it. Dale's parents were half Chippewa, a people now mostly residing in the upper peninsula of Michigan; the national archery champion, now living in Arizona, has remained attentive to the condition of Amerindian peoples in Arizona.

•••

On May 9, 1958, an exuberant busload of high school boys pulled into the schoolyard. We had just won the state regional track meet. Dale had won all four events he entered. He and I were on the winning relay team. And I slipped into second place in the "low hurdles" just behind him, barely nosing out the lumbering hurdler from the north whom the papers had favored to beat Dale. Now in the locker room, one bloke pointed to a strange dart pointing down from the sky a distance off. "That's a tornado," we shouted. "Let's get the hell out of here." We collected the coach from his office and rushed to a ditch behind the school, throwing aside large timbers piled there in preparation for new construction. When the onrushing tornado tore up the baseball backstop two hundred yards in front of us, we dived deep into the ditch, listening in fear and horror as a whirlwind bounced above us with the body-wrenching sounds of ten trains packed with a horde of angry white evangelical preachers.

A family of seven in one house a mile past the school died when the tornado took a random dive to earth before bouncing up again. The roads around the school were now blocked. A barn a half mile east of the school was leveled. The Connolly house, a mile and a half away and in the track of the whirlwind, had half its roof torn off. Dale and I returned three days later to the ditch behind the school; we could now barely lift timbers we had recently tossed around like toothpicks.

An event seared in recollection. I did not read the book of Job until decades later, when I started teaching it in a class connecting classical myths of good and evil to contemporary issues. In that book the "Nameless One" bellows out of a whirlwind, er, tornado, to Job, setting him straight on how little he knows about the larger world of hippos, whales, hurricanes, and deserts and, perhaps, how the wild, multifarious grandeur of the cosmos does not bestow divine primacy upon human beings. The tornado and the later reading of Job are now welded on a sheet of memory for me: two events from disparate times vibrating together. The track meet may sometimes pop up for review, too. Resonances between disparate events placed on a non-chronological sheet of time can crystallize a mood or ignite a new thought under novel circumstances.

• • •

Lying on my back in a field for hours to watch the aurora borealis in northern Michigan; lying exhausted on a remote California beach after engaging in a life-and-death struggle with a rip tide; the humpback whale I tracked swimming full speed as my Oahu plane hovered just above it on a landing run; subterranean relays between early experiences with Jonathan Winters and later engagements with Friedrich Nietzsche; seeing the stunned look on the face of a friend of the family in the newspaper who had been beaten and tossed onto the street by frightened, angry workers; the first sight of a loved one's leg amputated above the knee; feeling the surge of a wave carrying you fifty yards on its crest as you body surf on a Pacific shore; watching clouds billow below us as friends perch on the 14,500-foot peak of Evans Mountain in Colorado, after having attended a boring conference in Denver; stepping gingerly as a lad onto thin ice over a pond in the woods; coping with a man crawling slowly and unevenly out of a coma; two young boys laughing wildly at themselves and the world as they stare for twenty minutes into a bathroom mirror at school; a woman squeezing your hand while dying; jumping in horror off a large pipe as toxic waste pours into the Flint River; hearing again the deafening roar of a tornado while discussing the book of Job in a class on politics and the Anthropocene; playing spin the bottle in the eighth grade and joining others in nervous laughter when a spin by one boy points at another boy—a bare instant before the bottle is spun again; watching and gauging the rhetorical strategies of Donald Trump as you recall in rapid sequence the Mafia, Joseph McCarthy, George Wallace, and the people who have fought against them; working to alter the alpha-male gait picked up by osmosis in high school football after a sweet musician at a music camp where I was counselor told me it might not fit the kind of man I sought to become. Your gait both conveys an identity to others and helps to shape what it becomes.

Multiple forces and agencies impinge upon and filter into life. Some may bubble up again as memories in the wake of a new event, as when a veteran with posttraumatic stress bounces into a series of painful memories upon hearing the blast from a tire blowout across the street. Or how a look one second too long from an attractive stranger incites romantic fantasies. Some events are nonlinguistic, teaching us about the limits of language, the recesses of agency, and the bandwidth of ingressions that must be synthesized for agency to be. Several memories are implacable, labeled by some thinkers to be absurd and others to be sublime. They may suggest how imbricated we are with a multifarious world that enables us to strive and to absorb but is not destined to be our oyster—a world striking at the very heart of Anthropocentrism.

A new event may trigger another sheet of memory tomorrow—as when, for instance, an outbreak of Covid-19 makes you think in a new key about those plagues in the plays of Sophocles, or—because Covid-19 involved a jump from bat to humans with a probable intermediary in between—how recent theories of horizontal gene transfer scramble the arboreal theories so recently sacrosanct in evolutionary biology. A newly distributed sheet may inflect your thinking and, as if from nowhere, prime you to run a new experiment.

• • •

Those high school basketball games—the strategic planning, calling defenses on the court, freelancing a fast break, the thrill of a key victory, the wounds of a loss, the team solidarity—formed some exhilarating moments in my life to that date. You might make a steal, stretch out to lob a pass over defenders to Keller streaking down court, and then hit the floor as you watch him juke a defender and lay the ball in gracefully for another basket. You might lie there a split second too long, absorbing the moment, allowing it to pour into layers of memory. The spiritual element of basketball. . . .

So, I resolved to become a basketball coach when I grew up.

• • •

Shortly after enrolling at Flint Junior College, that ambition unraveled. First, I now began to appreciate the intellectual quality of some courses. Second, I injured my upper ankle severely as a minor reserve early in the first season, making it unlikely that the coach at a two-year college would give me a chance the next year. And, third, it soon became clear that the "phys-ed" major I had adopted was fraudulent, created to keep star players in school for a brief two-year stint before dispersing into an uncertain world. As the first college student in the family, I had not selected a wise major to kick off a college career.

It was also clear that the coach followed an unstated rule in that league: do not allow more than two Black players on the court at the same time. This meant that one highly talented player from Detroit languished on the bench far more than he should have done. A surface sign, among many others, of the white triumphalism that cut more deeply into public culture than I then knew. The belligerent, racist forays by George Wallace into Flint and other parts of the Midwest during the late 1960s brought that lesson home starkly.

• • •

I held several jobs during my high school and early college years—setting pins at a bowling alley, picking cherries for a few weeks one summer in northern Michigan, digging holes to install car speakers at a huge drive-in theater under construction, drilling hinges eight hours a day at a tool-and-die shop during one dreadful summer, working on a short assembly line for a summer at a soda pop factory, hauling loads of topsoil in a dump truck one summer, working on housing construction during a couple of satisfying summers, being janitor at the local labor union during my college years, becoming director of intramural sports at Flint UM, and so on. In cumulative effect they provided money; a few helped to keep me in shape for sports during summers and off-seasons. They also taught me what I did not want to do or be for the rest of my life. The GM auto factories—several a half mile deep and stretching alongside the road for almost a mile—beckoned many young men in Flint in those days, tempting them to grab the wages, the "benes," a quick start in life, and the future stability they promised. The prospect filled me with dread. I was becoming a stranger in my own town.

In the *Misfits*,[2] "Gay" (Clark Gable) and his buddies discover that the wild mustangs they had chased down on horseback, lassoed, and sold for kids to ride were now being hauled to factories to be cut up into dog food. The chase and capture remained adventurous, but the enterprise had lost its glow. "It's better than wages," Gay asserts plaintively several times, deferring reckoning with the hourly wages, strict orders, and regimentation staring back at them from the future. The saying held for a while but lost its sway when "Roslyn" (Marilyn Monroe) bitterly pointed out the cruelties of the enterprise to them when she was enlisted to accompany them on a hunt. She loved the energy and strivings of the horses who were being tethered. They, too, had become misfits roaming the desert; the fragile cowboys tried desperately to think of them as wild mustangs, forgetting how they became commodities the next moment.

The erstwhile cowboys loved the sensitivity of this earth mother, but they could not tolerate her interference in their adventures. They thus placed her in a box, as she forced them to admit how their livelihood was doomed. There was no other place for them to go, either. That was their box, one that fostered profound resentment in the Eli Wallach character as he felt a lid closing on top of him. The stark scenes, filmed in black and white, underline the diverse modes of alienation portrayed: cowboys from their livelihood, mustangs from the wild, and a sensitive woman from a world of stubborn cowboys.

Arthur Miller, the author and still husband of Marilyn when the film appeared, later said that the director, John Huston, shot the scenes on vast moonlike vistas in Nevada to accentuate the stark condition of the misfits. Only later did I realize that it was shot on the Paiute Reservation close to Lake Paradise. Miller and Huston had failed to dramatize entire peoples rendered misfit by white settler America. Well, there is one scene when a probable Paiute member quietly watches white gamblers stream past him on the way to the rodeo. But that is it. Amerindians, mustangs, cowboys, a wounded divorcee—all placed in boxes by the institutionalization of dreams that ruled each out in turn, each new box displacing the old. The film marked one of the best performances by Gable, Eli Wallach, and Montgomery Clift and, I believe, by far the best by Monroe. She was, after all, synesthetic—a person who combines disparate perceptions in experience, such as sound and touch or melody and color. She shared that capacity with van Gogh, Cezanne, Kandinsky, Jimi Hendrix, and others. We now know that she drew upon it to perform specific scenes. I suspect that the earthy dance around the old tree and her response to cowboys lassoing those mustangs provide two such instances. Synesthetes sometimes absorb two-toned experiences too vivid to handle.

The film absorbed me as I started grad school and started to think about how old dreams can lose their moorings through dramatic power shifts in the worlds of Amerindians, settler societies, cowboys, vulnerable women, and auto workers. My grad student friends who attended that film with me in 1961 were not similarly gripped by it, however. The binds portrayed felt unreal to them, while I was beginning to translate the message about one dream ground into dog food into another of an auto industry living on borrowed time. The film was a commercial flop.

• • •

I, too, was searching for something better than wages during my high school and college years. One job pointed in a different direction from the others. I worked for six summers at the National Music Camp in Northern Michigan during my college years and first two years in graduate school— thanks to Dale, who had landed an assignment in the sports program there partly because he had become national archery champion at such a young age. He recommended me to the high school counseling division. I advanced over a few summers from cabin counselor to athletic director, to assistant director of the high school boys division. There I encountered several people whose intellectual pursuits were woven seamlessly into their lives. One of them, Dick Davis, gave me a book by Karl Mannheim, *Ideology and Utopia*, after one of our stimulating conversations; that book later played a large role in my dissertation. Another, Bob Luby, was twenty years older than I. He folded athletics, intellectuality, and musical interests into his daily life. We often ran wind sprints together, followed by stimulating conversations. When he became director of the High School Boys Counseling Division, I used to make fun of him at counselor meetings because of the names he gave to his array of counseling techniques. One was called "Antiseptic Bounce," for instance. I would twist it into a grotesque thing to tease Bob. Then, as a "unit leader," I would practice the technique and commend it to others. Bob found this paradoxical stance to be amusing, if juvenile. He became a role model to me. Perhaps Inez had sought such a model, too: a fraught venture for girls in a misogynistic world.

•••

Inez and I were in our second year at Flint Junior College, and she had become an accomplished gymnast, when at twenty years old she threw me over to start a relationship with her gymnastics coach. Bertrand Russell had not prepared me for this! Indeed, he might not have been on my side, since he favored young boys getting initiated into sex by older women and young girls by older men. It distressed me, too, how I found it strangely exciting to imagine them in carnal embrace and then have that feeling become transfigured into extreme jealousy.

While suffering this loss and indignity I began to feel more palpably how abusive fathers muddy the lives of their daughters. Many years later, Inez and I met again in New Jersey to review our current lives and interests. She now managed the inventory of a large hardware store. It was a delight to see how interesting she had become, how difficult teen events do not always circumscribe too severely parameters of the future. That afternoon of vibrant conversations resounded again for me several years later when I was informed that the lovely woman had died of cancer.

My little sister, Judy, ten years my junior, took gymnastics classes with Inez and that coach when she was an early teen. She eventually became an accomplished gymnast herself, winning some meets in tumbling. One day my mother, who drove Judy regularly to those classes, asserted with studied casualness, "I suspect Inez and Herb are having an affair, Bill. What do you know about it?" "Nothing," I said. She knew that I knew, and I knew that she knew that I knew. Such was the mode of communication between a working-class boy and a mother who doted on his woes more than she was supposed to acknowledge. My doubles can make of that what they will. Doubles need room to breathe, too.

•••

By my second year at FJC, I was thus without either a girlfriend or a basketball team. That is, without moorings. So I tried out for the debate team. It turned out that you made the fledgling team if you tried out. Still, I was a raw newcomer; the others had debated in high school. The topic for the year was "right-to-work" laws, the kind of law that—in the name of individualism—allows each worker to decide whether to receive union-negotiated benefits without paying union dues. In the warm-ups I performed much better at arguing against than for those laws. That was partly because the law's celebration of individualism was so slender, not applied to dating across races, to tolerance of wide religious diversity, to appreciation of atheism as a legitimate faith, even to respect for a diversity of dress codes. The other men on the team strongly favored those right-to-work laws. There was only one woman.

The best debater by far was an African American student. She had gained debate experience at Flint Northern High. Shortly before the first debate tournament—there were only in fact a few—the speech teacher/debate coach asked each of us to write down who they would like to have as partner for the year. We were to list choices in rank order on a secret ballot. I picked Amanda at the top, of course, scrolling down reluctantly to place others lower on the list.

A week later, the debate coach called me to his office. "Are you prepared to be Amanda's partner?" he asked. "I would love to," I said. "Okay, she wants to work with you too." I felt certain at that moment that no one else in the club had chosen the best debater on the team to be their partner. The need to call me in for private confirmation signaled that in this club white guys stuck with white guys. The coach himself was delighted that we would be partners. But, apparently, the whole thing had to be handled with delicacy.

We became a strong debate duo: she experienced, smooth, and deceptively gracious in rebuttals of the opposition; me green, intense, knowing something about labor history, and occasionally stuttering out useful points. After a couple of sessions, I was increasingly drawn to the attractive, articulate student. If she felt such tremors, they were sublimated into debate rehearsals in empty study halls. The pressures against interracial friendships across gender were pervasive and intense during this era at that school. I knew that, of course, but the knowledge surely sank more deeply into her bones. "The white man, as well as the Negro, is bound and barred by the color-line, and many a scheme of friendliness and philanthropy of broad-minded sympathy and generous fellowship between the two has been dropped because some busybody has forced the color-question to the front and brought the tremendous force of unwritten law against the innovator."[3] Skin color as an unwritten law of separation.

I learned things from my debating partner. She maintained composure and timing under pressure during a debate, comparable, perhaps, to a point guard on a fast break unleashing a split-second pass at the last nanosecond without conscious deliberation. Conscious thinking creates tells and interceptions. She could hold a compelling rebuttal point until an opponent had been softened up and then strike suddenly from nowhere, politely.

• • •

I enrolled at Flint UM my junior year, now eager to continue an intellectual career beyond college. Classes, in the main, were highly stimulating there, especially those in history, philosophy, and political theory. The school itself had only been in existence a couple of years. (Another instance of positive *Fortuna*, for me.) As I settled on trying to make it into graduate school to focus on political theory or philosophy, a few professors in different fields decided quietly to help me meet that objective. Paul Bradley was the only political scientist at the school; he taught a large variety of courses in effective ways I later came to appreciate even more. Dorothea Wyatt was an amazing teacher of American history, folding explorations of race and feminism into her courses during a period when they did not often gain prominence. She may even have been gay during a time when no whisper of such an orientation was permissible in public. Elston Van Steenburgh taught impressive courses in philosophy, even allowing me to nurture atheism in one course on the philosophy of religion as he himself took a different direction. I turned out to be the first Ph.D. from that young school, I believe.

The faculty nominated me for a Woodrow Wilson Fellowship, but I did not make the cut. No grad school offered me money, either, though I was admitted to a few. Only that secretary, stopping to order me to attend a meeting later the same day with a professor from UM Ann Arbor, turned the trick. I quickly reversed course and determined to make the most of graduate school. An academic career had to be better than wages.

It turned out, though I was not told until later, that four professors had driven to Ann Arbor to persuade the political science department to work out some funding support for me through a residence hall position. I owe a lot to those four and to that secretary. I try to meet the debt by paying forward, particularly by supporting undergrad and grad students as they become intellectuals during a difficult time and/or negotiate the strange world of graduate school.

3
The Pioneer Valley

How did you land a position at the University of Massachusetts after the three-year stint at Ohio University? Did the new setting encourage you to change your thinking? It seems clear that you had now become alert to the interweaving of teaching, writing, and politics, even though the obduracy of the event was probably not yet important to you. So, how did teaching, writing, the academy, family life, and politics intersect during this period?
A fellow grad student at the University of Michigan had recently secured a position in American politics at the University of Massachusetts. The school was looking for a young theorist, and George Sulzner urged me to apply. Unbeknownst to me at the time, the Amherst College political theorist George Kateb had read my book, and he recommended me after my application was submitted. I made sure this time to be ready when the interview took place. That was my contribution.

The move to the University of Massachusetts in 1968 was a dream come true for me, though it posed new difficulties for my then wife, Judy. David, our son, was three when we arrived. He was a delightful ball of energy who eventually became highly successful as a consultant and devoted himself to his wife, Jeanne, and four children. After a brief rough period in junior high school, he found himself and became inordinately successful in both his professional and personal ambitions. He is now a vice president at Ernst and Young. As an impressive public speaker—I have watched his talks on the internet—he brings news, ideas, and humor to high-tech audiences. Today he displays a wicked sense of humor, often making his daddy an object of it. He speaks to the absurdity of the extreme gap today between the richest and poorest in America in that humor. He and his family now breathe the acrid air flowing from the wildfires that increasingly disrupt life in California. I am impressed with how intelligently David and Jeanne have raised four wonderful and diverse children, always entering into the perspective of each before coming to a judgment about things. I am also pleased that David does not vote Republican. . . .

Debbie was born in Amherst in 1969, a year after we arrived in Amherst. She was a vivacious, bright little girl who would wiggle her legs frantically when she was thinking. She excelled in school early and went on to earn a Ph.D. in Anthropology. She is singularly impressive today in raising three boys with her husband, Jim, maintaining a good marriage, and holding a demanding career together as commissioner of Social Services in Newton, Massachusetts. Her book *Homeless Mothers: Face to Face with Women in Poverty* was in a sense a prelude to her current position.[1] It deploys sensitive ethnographies to explore a variety of gaps between the lives of poor single mothers in difficult straits and the public images formed of them.

I persist today in claiming inordinate credit for the achievements and sensibilities of these two remarkable adults, also informing my grandchildren from time to time that they too must never take any credit for their own achievements. They love those admonitions. It may be that such insistences replicate today—in their own way—the theology of Calvinism in Holland and England during the intensification of industrial capitalism. You tell people they cannot *earn* their way to salvation by good works; only divine (or parental) predestination can do that. Nonetheless, good works are ambiguous *signs* that you may have been *chosen*. Somehow, that paradox turns the trick for those who succeed. It also doubles the injuries of those who find themselves in abject positions. Luckily, my grandchildren do not believe me when I insist that only their parents are responsible for their achievements. Did devotees of European Calvinism and American Puritanism entirely believe those ministers?

Today I regularly detect diverse glimmers of the child in each of my adult children; they are two apples in their daddy's two eyes. When they were youngsters I used to "entertain" them with stories about my other, more enjoyable nuclear family in Texas. The vivacious wife and two children in Texas were terrific fun; the children were always obedient and yet highly industrious and entertaining. Names and ages were given. Rough spots in the narrative, whenever clarifications were demanded by the skeptical duo, could be ironed out until they disappeared.

These games also provided—though I was not sharply aware of it—warm-ups for theory panels I participated in at conferences. During that era almost everyone in theory—including me—was hell-bent on convicting opponents of "performative contradictions." The procedure is to first "tighten up" the alternative theory and then show its devotees how other assumptions they necessarily enact in daily life contradict their own theory. An entire version of critical theory was forged around that master tool. It was not until later, under the influence of Nietzsche, Wittgenstein, Proust, and others, that I really learned what a fool's game it is. If you come to terms with first, internally complex cluster concepts; second, the breakdown of the analytic/ synthetic dichotomy; and, third, the layered character of memory, thinking, and communication, such games give way. Because such a charge now loses much of its power, its assertion can now become an occasion to explore problems of the binary logic in which argument and the organization of evidence are often set. Logical empiricism and rationalism both depend on such binaries, though advocates of the former often profess that evidence alone assumes priority for them. In fact, it is evidence molded to fit a problematical logic that does much of the work.

Nobody I know has actually dropped a theory after others have "cleaned it up" and issued the charge of performative contradiction against them. Often, a minor clarification or change dissolves the power of the accusation. I thus take back a few early critical reviews and essays I wrote, invoking the performative contradiction as my own master tool of critique.

A year or so after I had dropped those stories and contests about the Texas family—because the kids had lost interest—the dynamic duo pressed me to talk again about that idyllic family in Texas: "What were their names again, Daaad? Where did you take that great vacation? We worry that you are neglecting them today while you spend so much time here playing basketball." Now, that's a good critique. As the Amherst crew well knew, I am bad at name recall. . . .

Much later, I came to love the week the extended family clan would spend together in the summer on one or another pristine lake in northern Michigan. Jane, Judy Beal (my sister), her husband, Bob, David, Debbie, and I would gather our spouses, kids, and grandkids together to spend a week of kayaking, cookouts, evening pontoon rides, visits to the Music Camp, and jaunts to Great Bear Sand Dunes on Lake Michigan. Each summer provided a delicious time to catch up with children, nieces, and grandchildren—the clan numbering around nineteen in all.

Judy Connolly was a superb mother of both children in Amherst when they were young. Both are devoted to her today. The rigors of academic life in a university town (as I saw it) were hard on her, however, and hard on our relationship, too. We were two rowboats pulling in different directions. By the time the children reached adolescence it became clear to both of us that

we would divorce after Debbie graduated from high school. Events hastened
the date a bit.

•••

The University of Massachusetts opened new vistas for me. First, there
was a growing graduate program, and I worked with others there to build a
strong field in political theory. Jane Bennett, Joan Cocks, Michael Gibbons,
Christine di Stefano, Tom Tierney, Robert Parks, Bob Higgins, John Buell,
Tom Deluca, Mark Weaver, Paul Shepard, Zillah Eisenstein, Wade Sikorski,
Louis Howe, Dwight Kiel, and Romand Coles are a few of the accomplished
theorists who came out of that program. Second, the Pioneer Valley—with
its five schools and ample space for countercultural life—became a gathering place for left-wing politics during the Vietnam War, the surge of feminism, the renewed struggle for civil rights, gay rights struggles, and
consolidation of an enemies list by Richard Nixon.

After a couple of years there I became president of the New Politics
Coalition, a faculty-community organization devoted to opposition against
the Vietnam War and resistance to Nixon. It flourished for a few years and
then declined as the local Left lapsed into disappointment during the later
Nixon years; the monthly voluntary contributions that sustained it faltered. It
snowed on the ice-cold October day we scheduled an art sale on the Amherst Green to keep finances for the coalition afloat. That did not help,
either.

•••

In 1972, when the coalition was thriving, a meeting of faculty members at
UMass was called to decide how to respond to the sudden escalation of the
Vietnam War by Nixon. I went to the rump meeting in the old field house,
attended by perhaps 300 faculty members. Someone proposed that I chair
the meeting, which left me with few options in case I found myself at odds
with the collective decision. After a long debate—in which some people
proposed more militant actions—we decided to join an illegal sit-in also
being planned by faculty and students at Amherst College. It would take
place at Westover Airfield Base. The next morning 1,300 faculty, students,
and community members were arrested at the base.

While we were being held in an open-air, fenced-in zone at the police
department in the small town of Chicopee, a batch of flyers was tossed down
anonymously to us. The flyers announced that Russian ships were breaking

the new blockade against North Vietnam, that Nixon was preparing for WWIII, and so on. Many protesters under arrest in that pen called for a breakout from the weakly guarded camp.

Near panic set in among the quarantined protestors. A small group of faculty from different schools gathered in the middle of the fenced enclosure to discuss what to do. I recall that George Kateb, the political theorist from Amherst College, was a key voice in the group. He commanded considerable respect. I had come to know his work and to commune with him across our differences on various intellectual issues. I especially respect *The Inner Ocean*,[2] a later study that explores how vague outside influences become infused into us to help contour the "individuality" that informs and distinguishes each of us. Kateb is a theorist of diverse individualities rather than, say, the regular, market-oriented individual that informs the work of Frederick Hayek or the hostile individualism inspiring Ayn Rand. The latter version of predatory capitalism is described by proponents, such as the Koch brothers, to be "libertarianism. . . ."

Anyway, the ad hoc council concluded that this was very probably a fake flyer and counseled the restless inmates to stay in place. We knew the charges filed against us would be draconian if we staged a breakout while under arrest. That, indeed, was the point of the flyers. A splinter Left-wing group at UMass, it turned out, had prepared and delivered them. They were too radical to join the anti-war protest—just radical enough to manipulate others to take dangerous action that would backfire against the cause as well as the protestors. Fake news.

Mark Rudd, a leader of the Weather Underground in the late 1960s and early '70s, embraced violence and manipulative tactics from the Left during this period. Today, based on sad experience, he contends that such tactics threaten to destroy the Left and detach it from the possibility of inspiring others. In a *New York Times* piece entitled "Political Passion Turned Violent," he says, "Over the decades I've reversed my understanding of social and political change: I now recognize that non-violence is the one essential strategy to achieve positive social change, an ironclad fact that the black civil rights movement understood well." And, "Violence is once again threatening our social fabric, this time from the far right."[3] I accepted the first point as a strong presumption during the period in question and concur on both points now. There are cases when the strong presumption must be overruled, as when the police staged a military attack on the Black Panthers in Chicago and when violence was the only way to overturn Haitian enslavement. But I do give considerable weight to the presumption, particularly during an era when the police and the right wing hold most of the weapons.

To me, the presumption against violence, however, must not be stretched so far that it automatically rules out nonviolent disorder itself. I resist attempts by the Right to call any protest the Left enacts violent.

Some protestors were conservatized after that intervention by a manipulative section of the Left in Chicopee. Others of us, rattled by the event, nonetheless continued on a critical course as we looked askance at groups who strive to manipulate others into violent action, especially if they themselves continue to sit on the sidelines waiting for the true revolutionary moment to arrive. As Elaine and Jerry decided one day on *Seinfeld* as they wondered whether it was time to restore intimacy to their platonic friendship, "Maybe a few simple rules are needed." Here are two:

"Do not commend political actions to others you would not undertake yourself; do not trust others who do so to you."

Those nonviolent protests in the Pioneer Valley were matched by other spontaneous protests sprinkled throughout the country. In cumulative effect they intensified pressure to wind down an ugly, racist, imperial war.

• • •

During the early years at UMass I started work on a second book, entitled *The Terms of Political Discourse* (1974). I wanted to extend and revise some themes pursued in the first study. Theorists such as Ludwig Wittgenstein, Stuart Hampshire, Charles Taylor, and W. B Gallie now augmented my earlier list of influences. The role of language in life and politics had been given short shrift in the first study. Questions about possible pulses of real creativity in politics and culture now began to percolate, too.

One purpose of *The Terms of Political Discourse* in 1974 was to draw political inquiry closer to humanistic thinking and further from the image of the natural sciences then attracting many social scientists. At the same time, it sought to pull the humanities two or three steps away from the neo-Kantianism that informed many practitioners. Several things had to be dismantled: the sufficiency of the designative theory of language, in which concepts are said to be sound if they fit the objects to which they refer; the sharp distinction between vocabularies of description and those of evaluation or ethical judgment; the dichotomy between analytic statements and synthetic statements, in which the first type is said to be purely conceptual and the second to be purely empirical or synthetic; and the idea that the terms of political inquiry can be distinguished sharply from concepts and practices that help to constitute operative cultural life.

The key move, perhaps, was to show how operative terms of description in cultural life often describe from a moral, or sometimes more loosely, judgmental point of view. Diverse terms such as "mistake," "normal," "rational," "delinquent," "hysterical," "relativism," "murder," "freedom," "subject," "rigor," "interests," and "democracy" all invoke multiple criteria of description, and yet the point of gathering each internally complex cluster together into one concept is to encapsulate a presumptive judgment as to how to respect, care, treat, repudiate, accuse, change, or punish the people and institutions so described. Of course, a new theory could seek to revise some of those criteria, but that would mean it seeks to alter presumptive ethical judgments, not to eliminate them. Since political discourse cannot eschew such terms without losing touch with the life-world it seeks to grasp, this means that to explain or interpret an aspect of political life is also to forge presumptive judgments about it. The presumptions might be overcome by other considerations. You might, say, develop a theory in which the pursuit of freedom is no longer an aspiration but a danger. But even here the dichotomy between explanation and evaluation, so beloved by professionals of the day, now bites the dust.

If a series of tight transcendental arguments could establish a closed, universal morality, they could marshal a mode of rationalism to replace the images of neutral empiricism in play in the social sciences. But that possibility is cast into doubt, too. So, the text soon revolves around exploration of "essentially contestable concepts," particularly concepts such as interests, power, freedom, democracy, agency, and responsibility, that play significant roles in both political life and political inquiry.

A concept is contestable if either its point or criteria are susceptible to challenge through a combination of debate and political enactment. To be contestable, however, it must also be imperfectly shared by the parties involved, so something will turn on the contestation. It is *essentially* contestable if there is reason to suspect that a social settlement drawing upon it during one period is unstable and could fall out again after a new turn in science, or a surprising event, or the rise of an unexpected political movement. The later transfiguration by Michel Foucault of the term "normal" into the verb "normalization" constitutes a radical example of such a mode of contestation. The move helped to energize a series of movements in the domains of incarceration, gay rights, gender, and sexuality. Any theorist who tells you to accept his or her definitions before starting inquiry has already settled half the issues before the inquiry officially gets off the ground.

Politics itself involves both imperfect conceptual settlements and the susceptibility of an unruly world to new encounters that could unsettle things again. Political struggles thus incorporate conceptual elements into their very constitution. The dream of conceptual closure, on the other hand, is treated as a nightmare. Such a dream would purge the element of messiness from which new modes of creativity emerge. The politics of purity is a disciplinary politics.

The issue of creativity is posed in this book, though it is both underdeveloped and confined to political and artistic life. The last chapter of *The Terms of Political Discourse*, entitled "Conceptual Revision and Political Reform," remains my favorite. To make its point about live relations between creative enactment and conceptual change, analogies of the day drawn from chess are forsaken. Players in chess are too fixed in their potential range of movement, and creativity is concentrated in the chess master. The chapter illustrates, rather, how experiments with new bodily skills, strategies, and conceptual revision work together in the game of basketball. The term "foul," for instance, acquired additional complexity after the jump shot was rapidly introduced by players themselves into the game, as if from nowhere. Coaches and referees then had to adjust their rules and norms to a creative shift they did not invent. Now we are in a better position to think about the role of bodily performances and the creativity of social movements in politics, as the text begins to do.

It sounds as though the book is organized around a self-refuting thesis. You claim to know that some concepts are essentially contestable, but that very knowledge is incompatible with the certainty of the assertion of essential contestability. Please show us, if you can, where such a charge goes awry. Also, since many terms describe from a moral point of view, does this awareness now orient you to seek a community in which a normative consensus becomes absorbed deeply into organic unity? How well, looking back, do the themes of that book stand up today?

The book received a fair amount of attention, some of it critical, especially in the early going. In 1999 it won the Benjamin Lippincott Prize, awarded every two years to "a work of exceptional quality that is still considered significant after a time span of at least 15 years." I continue to cherish that award, thinking of it as a testament to the arrival of a boy from Flint into the academy.

The most common objection, yes, was that it advances a self-refuting thesis. But the idea was not to *prove* the theme, but to assert speculatively that it may well be so, to provide as much preliminary evidence and argument as possible to support that contestable judgment, to show how the work of others was already saturated with more contestable judgments than they acknowledged, and to express and support (contestable) positions on the key concepts in question. To engage in the conceptual dimension of politics.

An internally complex concept, indeed, often becomes more contestable when it sinks roots into life and is entangled with others in active use. Then, new events, protests, or encounters may jangle some of those entanglements, creating pressure for conceptual revision. For example, introduction of the concept "non-theistic reverence for the fecundity of being" fills a previously vacant space between two common notions: one that identifies spirituality only with faith in an omnipotent divinity and another that restricts secularism to cold analysis without spirituality. The new concept may, by squeezing in between these two, open a door to new negotiations between spiritual constituencies of different types. It may help to widen the ethos of pluralism.

I in fact concurred with a theme Whitehead had advanced in the 1920s, though I did not yet know his work: he projects the probability that a speculative element will never entirely disappear from science or philosophy, even though the cutting edges of speculation are apt to shift over time.

Politics itself dries up, *The Terms* argues, if too much contestability is purged from cultural discourse. So, no, the quest governing that book was not the pursuit of community; it was pursuit of a positive ethos of engagement between multifarious partisans that encourages contestation to proceed without violence and allows new majority assemblages to form. The closure of politics, indeed, was a dream inhabiting behavioralism and later modes of scientism, too: you best install a predictive mode of inquiry if you make the human objects of inquiry themselves more predictable. A potential alliance between academic behavioralism and corporate state politics of social control is woven into the epistemology behavioralists adopt.

Moreover, retreat into skeptical withdrawal—the academic desire to wait until each issue is settled before making judgments or taking action—often does not work well, either. The stakes are often high, and the need to act amid uncertainty can be pressing. The mass sit-in at Westover and the quick decision to treat those flyers as fake merely represent two minor examples of the need to decide amidst uncertainty. It arises often in politics.

Those who resisted the Vietnam War, in part through creative, nonviolent illegalities, also supported an expansive, *bifocal* image of democracy itself. We insisted through enactment that democracy consists of both elections *and* periodic social movements that press against specific electoral and corporate settlements injurious to other regions and/or to specific constituencies in this regime. The latter troubles often fester below the threshold of electoral attention before becoming articulated and pressed through social movements; when they succeed the established terms of discourse become altered, too.

The idea, then, is neither to sink into a simple individualism, nor to pursue organic community, nor to assume with confidence that positive change is impossible without revolution. It is, rather, to forge a positive pluralist assemblage in which diverse constituencies negotiate a positive ethos of engagement between them. That theme receives more development later, particularly in relation to promoting economic egalitarianism and expanding pluralism. Such a thesis is not a species of relativism, either, at least if you take that (contestable) concept to mean that each territorial culture consists of specific notions that are internally settled and resistant to periodic jostling from inside or outside. No culture is that centered or settled; most are marked by significant crosscurrents, both across constituencies and within selves. And besides, those who support the theme of contestability and creative pluralism both pursue evidence for and against their themes and draw sharper lines of unacceptability whenever others press belligerently to create, say, a narrow White Christian nation.

Some critics of the idea of essentially contested concepts seemed themselves to be captured by a two-slot model of analysis: you must be either a neutral objectivist or a relativist—an Either/Or that dumbs down discourse. They also remained too inattentive to the variable quality of the public ethos that informs conceptual contests, ranging from quests for radical domination on one edge to a receptive ethos of pluralist engagements on the other.

As the text argued in the company of others, the analytic/synthetic dichotomy in which such a two-slot model is set forms the linchpin of a positivist method in the human sciences that is indeed open to powerful critique. That dichotomy, treated by many professionals as a neutral rule of method, is in fact a contestable norm that supports closed conceptions of culture and method. Wittgenstein, Quine, and others had already charted the path of its critique. Some elements in a complex cluster concept are rather loosely attached to it and others more tightly so; the result is that several fit neither the tight "analytic" relation demanded by the dichotomy in question nor its purely "synthetic" or empirical twin.

As a concept evolves in the face of new events, some dimensions may be tightened, others loosened, some dropped, and others yet added. Concepts evolve with life. Conceptual contests are struggles over which evolutions become legitimate. That is why setting a regime of "neutral," simple definitions to guide inquiry before it starts can easily become a recipe for authoritarianism. The second edition of that book, in 1983, contains replies to critiques that had arisen.

• • •

There were things, however, about the first edition that eventually began to trouble me. For instance, the book had drawn upon Peter Strawson's view of the centered agent as a common resource to draw upon to mitigate and inform the terms of conceptual debate. His centered notion of the universal subject—even one with somewhat porous qualities—increasingly seemed exaggerated to me.

A. H. Adkins's study of Homeric Greek culture in *From the Many to the One*,[4] for instance, contends that the "I" was more lightly experienced in the Homeric world; there and then micro-voices within and around the I exercised impulsive powers themselves, with diverse voices often jostling against one another. Sometimes they overwhelm the I. At other times some slide into it, rendering it more than a singular unity. On his reading, subliminal dimensions of modern European life make it possible for us to engage Homeric culture, if imperfectly, but these engagements also rattle the centered notions of subjectivity and moral agency sustained by the Cartesian and Kantian traditions. The modern subject is more of a multiplicity than official accounts of it acknowledge, even if the multiplicity supports agency. That judgment eventually encourages those who imbibe it to explore an ethic of cultivation to contest those that *derive* morality from a singular god or the unity of the subject.

I only later began to interrogate seriously the human exceptionalism inhabiting that book, however, moving then through an engagement with Foucault's genealogies of the subject (to which that book had carried me to the edge) to explore pulses of creativity in multiple beings and forces that are both nonhuman and variously entangled with the human estate. Bacteria, viruses, hormones, and fungi embody significant instances of the latter sort: such micro-agencies in the gut also play roles of importance in helping to compose one's own macro-modes of agency. Those nano-agents, further, contribute to horizontal modes of species evolution, the evolutionary changes that upset the tree-like model of slow evolutionary progress that prevailed in Euro-American thought after the advent of Darwin. Moreover, coronaviruses periodically cross from animals to humans; they can threaten to bring down entire societies.

Finally, though there were a few hints, the text did not address closely cultural processes of affective contagion through which cloudy processes below clean conceptual representation slide, slip, and bounce into the mores of cultural life. The danger of fascism was not firmly on my radar, either. More about those issues later.

• • •

During this period, I became close friends with a young economist at UMass by the name of Michael Best. Both of us had fathers who had been active in labor movements, something of a rarity in the academy. Indeed, his dad had been harassed relentlessly by the FBI as he scrambled from town to town to avoid agents after being exposed as a former member of the Communist Party. One thing Mike and I shared—besides interest in playing together in adult basketball leagues—was a visceral sense that some upper-middle-class academics who jumped from that tier of life straight into Marxism did not grasp well the richness and travails of white working-class life, especially pressures facing many in it to slide toward the right under economic duress. Many Marxist academics had never met a worker or, perhaps, studied closely how fascism had defeated powerful movements of social democracy and communism in Germany upon the advent of the Great Depression.

Mike was a charismatic teacher preparing to be considered soon for tenure at UMass in the Economics Department. I had recently received tenure, though the provost informed me casually one day shortly after the event (I was on the Faculty Senate where such short conversations occurred) that the former Ohio University president, who was now on the Massachusetts State Board of Regents, had pulled my tenure file up to the state level for a week to peruse it. That had not occurred before, he told me. It was returned later without comment, the provost said, emitting one of his characteristic chuckles.

If junior faculty members had good teaching records and were publishing articles, their reappointments before the tenure year were considered a mere formality. But, because the Economics Department took a turn to the neoliberal right shortly after Mike's appointment, it began to look as if the executive committee might not wait until the tenure year to dump Mike. We decided to develop a counterstrategy.

First, we decided to accelerate the book project we were working on
together on political economy, launching the project by coteaching a class
in the program of political economy (STPEC) in which we participated.
Second, we engaged students who were dissatisfied with the rigidity of the
department and who very much admired Mike's teaching. Third, I alerted
Dean Alfange, the dean from political science who was a person of great
integrity, about the high quality of Mike's work and teaching and the
strangeness of the peremptory rumblings against him. His teaching record
and evaluations were stellar. We soon had to climb a small mountain to
figure out how to respond to this rapidly unfolding situation.

• • •

The Holyoke Range overlooks the Pioneer Valley, flowing in an unusual
pattern from east to west. It juts up from the valley, prominently visible from
the house I inhabited on Potwine Lane for several years in South Amherst.
Yes, Potwine Lane, its road sign stolen innumerable times to be placed over
the doors of dormitory rooms at Hampshire College, a few blocks from our
house.

Route 116 cuts through the notch dividing Round Mountain to the east
from Bare Mountain to the west. Round Mountain, like the rest of the
range, formed itself a few million years ago from volcanic eruptions. It has
been blasted to smithereens over a few decades, hollowed out by years of
intensive quarrying to mine basalt for road pavement. When you drive
through the notch the hollowing out of that mountain is barely visible. But
as soon as you climb Bare Mountain to its west, the blasted-off top, hollowed-
out middle, and battery of cranes and trucks mining basalt become starkly
visible.

To view and smell that mess is to suffer traces of what Glenn Albrecht in
Earth Emotions calls *solastagia*.[5] If nostalgia is a sense of loss and yearning
for a place you have left behind, *solastalgia* is the loss of the place while you
are still there. If and when the feeling of loss becomes severe because of
extensive strip mining, or an expanded drought zone, or a polluted aquifer,
or more extreme storms, or a radical reduction in the bird population, or
new bouts of extreme heat and blight in urban centers, or the demise of
other familiar species, or the bleaching of coral reefs, or several such losses
together, it can spawn a mood of melancholy that infects everything you do.
Already during this period, the sight and smell of that open-air mine took a
toll on those roaming the Holyoke Range as we hiked on it and absorbed the
vistas it opened to the north and south.

Immediately to the west of the notch, then, is Bare Mountain, about 1,000 feet high, overlooking the Pioneer Valley to the north, Holyoke College to its south, and the hollowed-out Round Mountain to its east. The latter should now be called Concave Mountain. The rock summit of Bare Mountain provides a stunning view of Amherst College, the town of Amherst, and the University of Massachusetts sprawling just north of the town center. Apparently, the Strategic Air Command also prized Bare Mountain, since it built a bunker twenty feet below its base during the 1960s to protect air force personnel in the event of a nuclear attack.

A bit further north of Amherst you see Mt. Sugarloaf jutting out on the edge of the Connecticut River—the very summit where the brilliant King Phillip made his last stand against white colonialists in 1675, a defeat that allowed European settlers to pour into the area in ever-growing numbers. The history of that battle and many other things is delineated in *On Our Ground* (1992), a set of superb essays edited by Barry O'Connell at Amherst College and written in the early 1800s by William Apess, a New England Pequot who was perhaps the first Amerindian to write in English.[6] Amerindian peoples occupied and sustained that land for over 10,000 years, after they fanned out from the Bering Strait 15,000 or 16,000 years ago to migrate south and east until they occupied the two American continents. Let's see, 10,000 years for Amerindians in the Pioneer Valley and 400 years so far and counting down for European settlers, as the fragility of things grows.

I stage a fictive dialogue between Apess and Henry Thoreau—his New England contemporary—in *The Ethos of Pluralization*.[7] The dialogue explores barriers and untaken possibilities of intersection during that period, untaken possibilities that could perhaps also help us to imagine a new politics of pluralization today—one that challenges tight equations between territory, land, property, and sovereignty officially in charge of white settler society. If it was too late for settlers to return to Europe by the 1830s, what were the possibilities for a distinctive politics of pluralization incorporating cultural elements from two disparate cultures? Low to be sure, but both Thoreau and Apess sought them . . .

The low mountain range overlooking the valley stretches to the west of Bare Mountain for about seven miles until it encounters the Connecticut River, with a Summit House built at the top of Mt. Holyoke as a small hotel in the early nineteenth century still standing at its peak. The public Summit House now allows hikers to rest, soak up the views, and ponder the histories lurking in them.

I hiked that range, with its stunning vistas, several times during our twenty-year sojourn in the Pioneer Valley, sometimes with others and often alone. I knew then I loved those hikes: working up a sweat, pausing on this or that ridge to view the valley from a distance, slowly sinking into a reverie, and then trekking on again. The numerous ridges jutting out have been forged by a discrepancy between the slow rate of basalt erosion and the faster erosion rate of sedimented rock on the range.

Today, recalling the hikes, friendships, and events across a halo of time and place, I know better how vital they were to my sense of the world, its dangers and possibilities, experienced the first time as activity, the second as memory, with a shining point arising through resonances across the times.

• • •

One afternoon in the early 1970s, the day after the executive committee had voted against Mike's renewal, five of us joined Mike at the top of Bare Mountain to console him and to devise a new response. Neoliberals in the department, of course, showed little appreciation either for the importance of the Holyoke range to life or for ideas emanating from this dedicated ecologist and egalitarian.

The cluster of Mike Best devotees, once the short, steep clamber was negotiated, oscillated between smoking some weak cannabis of the day, absorbing views of the valley, and pondering the new circumstance. We reviewed carefully what the chair had told Mike about how he did not fit into the future plan of the department—a new plan the chair devised well after Mike had been appointed. Those words did not sound like things the chair had said to others about Mike, since the pronouncements to others had not noted a shift in departmental plans. And faculty hired under one set of plans were not supposed to be punished if those plans suddenly changed. I had kept an ear tuned to the circulation of such judgments, listening to the gossip that animates the currency of administrative life more than college administrators care to admit, even though they are among its leading purveyors—the hierarchical terms of political gossip in the academy. Mike had consulted other sources, as well.

We agreed that Mike would ask the chair to put his reasons for denial in writing to Mike; then Mike could forward those comments to Dean Alfange. Any discrepancies between the department report to the dean and the account given to Mike by the chair might create a wedge. We needed something.

During the period our plan was put into motion an outside committee came to town to evaluate the department. It issued a critical report saying the department was too narrow in its structure and planning. I reminded the dean that this is exactly what several of us had been saying all along. Mike was now receiving quiet encouragement from other voices in the administration, too, and a large cadre of students was campaigning actively on his behalf. Alfange himself had become concerned about the narrowness of the department.

That concatenation of disparate events—along with the book—somehow converged to create a new opportunity for Mike. The dean recommended reappointment, and a few years later the department unanimously recommended tenure. The college-level committee agreed; the outside committee evaluation of the department found receptivity with students and upper levels of the administration; and the chair of the department and a few others resigned to go elsewhere.

Shortly thereafter Sam Bowles—a radical economist with populist tendencies who was, I believe, being blocked for promotion at Harvard—was offered a position in the Economics Department at UMass by Dean Alfange. He said he would come if he could bring a few dissident economists with him, subject, of course, to academic review.

So: a fortunate convergence of several events, many of which stretched far beyond the influence of the young mountain strategists. Mike received tenure. And soon the Economics Department took a distinctive turn to the left, an unusual turn enabled by a singular concatenation of events. The book Mike and I wrote together played a modest role in that scenario, particularly in the tenure decision. It played a much larger role in our ethico-political trajectory. And Mike has continued to write fascinating texts in political economy.

● ● ●

I was now coming to appreciate more richly how the contingency of events and timing—good, bad, and horrific—helps to shape political and personal life. An outside report, say, might arrive just in time or too late to make a positive difference. The dean at one moment may be a neoliberal, locked into a narrow image of the future, or an exploratory thinker. A mountaintop coterie might seek to drive a wedge at a timely moment between the chair and the dean. Or it may give up under the onslaught of administrative advice to face reality. Good and bad luck. Good and bad timing, too.

My boyhood experiences, strange conjunctions during this period, and soon, new encounters with Sophocles, Foucault, and Nietzsche, helped to consolidate such an outlook. That is why I later found it amusing when a few critics linked my exploration of the "globalization of contingency" to an image of world mastery. What a joke.

The *Politicized Economy*, by Michael Best and me, was published in 1976, followed by a larger, revised edition in 1983. Its purpose is to show how the demands of capitalist growth, the narrowing institutional structure of consumption options facing workers and the racialized poor, the growing stratification of income and wealth, the alienated, authoritarian character of menial work, expanding capitalist assaults on nature, and intensifying resentments by white workers and others against the state were bound loosely together in an interfolded set of connections. There are, however, elements of slack within and between the interlocking institutions that—depending in part upon the force and quality of social movements—can press things in one direction rather than another. It is thus a *politicized economy*.

One animating fear of the text was that unless tensions of the day were engaged in progressive ways, a new political movement on the right could pull resentments of disaffected segments of the white working class in increasingly repressive and racist directions. We warned of "neofascism." The text also continues an argument from *The Terms of Political Discourse* about how each explanatory theory generates distinctive prescriptive presumptions. It deploys the diverse perspectives of Milton Friedman, John Maynard Keynes, and John Kenneth Galbraith to display how such presumptions work.

Workers, the text says, are increasingly caught in a bind. As the official site of electoral accountability, the state is held responsible for their growing grievances. And yet the private corporate establishment remains free to initiate actions on its own that simultaneously increase these troubles, displace most responsibility for them onto the state, and make it more difficult to mobilize progressive state alliances to overturn them. While the text thus concurs roughly with theorists such as Jürgen Habermas (*Legitimation Crisis*) and James O'Connor (*The Fiscal Crisis of the State*) in that thesis, a few distinctive themes emerge as well.[8]

First, it shows how a history of corporate/state actions to shape the "social infrastructure of consumption"—public arrangements and expenditures that slant consumption possibilities in some directions rather than others—makes it increasingly difficult for working-class families to make ends meet even when their incomes grow modestly. It pursues that task by comparing a regime engaged in an uphill battle to generalize "exclusive goods" to one that generalizes "inclusive goods." The former agenda increases side costs, congestion effects, and environmental destruction as it becomes extended to more people, while the latter becomes less expensive per capita, more ecological, and more satisfying as it is extended. An automobile/road/expressway/truck/air/gasoline system vs. one based more on mass transit, biking, trains, and walking trails provides one example of the difference, with the state's priority to build highways and subsidize fossil fuel shaping the infrastructure in which consumption transportation choices are made. General Motors, Royal Tire, and Standard Oil, indeed, had together launched a campaign during the 1930s to eliminate trolley service in twenty-seven cities to render the auto/road/highway system indispensable. This was a systematic political project. People thus "choose" cars under a system rigged in advance to foreclose other choices. Choosing between carriers of private health insurance vs. the opportunity to participate in socialized medicine provides another example. And massive public subsidies of suburbs and white flight vs. extensive public enrichment of urban areas denotes a third. The text delineates, too, how liberal drives to generalize exclusive goods exacerbate the racism already plaguing the working class. Fred Hirsch came out with a fine book, *The Social Limits to Growth*,[9] a year after ours appeared; his insights into consumption binds were incorporated into the next edition.

The chapter on "Nature and Its Largest Parasite" addresses links between capitalist modes of growth and patterns of environmental destruction; it also explores how income, work, and consumption pressures facing the working and middle classes contribute to that result, too, as they struggle to keep afloat in an economy whose priorities and instabilities repeatedly set them back on their heels. Finally, the text contends that liberalism will have difficulty protecting itself against future "neofascist" pressures unless it redesigns its current orientation to political economy. We urge pursuit of a new kind of democratic socialism, one that changes public/private orientations to growth, work, pollution, consumption, and mastery of nature to become more just and to relieve the ugly politics of displacement in play—one that also works to maintain a high degree of autonomy in the media and institutions of education.

We experimented with a cluster definition of the working class, one that draws together a dependent position in the mode of production, relative educational opportunities, yearly income, low degree of job security, typical pattern of consumption, low lifetime earning prospects, retirement opportunities, health insurance, and relative susceptibility to environmental assault into the notion. Such a definition improves one's ability to probe political tendencies of the working class as its position evolves.

Does this book, too, soon become a study you decide needs considerable revision? Or did it, finally, settle more things for you? It certainly moved political economy to front and center in your work more than had the first two books. Are you above all, then, a political economist?

The book sold well for several years, being taught in college classes on critical political economy. I remain attached to its accounts of consumption and the political element inhabiting social and economic institutions. That makes them rather less susceptible to tight structural explanations than many on the Left had assumed.

There are several things insufficiently pursued in that text, however. For one, we did not probe the potent connection then gestating in the U.S. between white neoliberals and white evangelicals. Each of these constituencies was soon altered by its engagement with the other; the combination intensified white racism and transformed American politics for the next forty years. Our own inheritance of secular categories—meaning, roughly, the idea that social explanation invokes only nontheological elements as causal factors and treats spiritual forces as derivative effects—may have diverted us from that formation as it was gestating. We seemed to buy into a then common assumption in social theory that secularism was fated to expand over the next several decades rather than to be rattled and punctuated by new events and activism from the theological right. That failing produced a large crack in the middle of the mirror we held up to the future.

For another, we did not deeply explore the value and sources of cultural pluralism, almost falling into the trap of construing cultural pluralism to be only a mirror reflection of a market economy. We thus did not take ample measure of new movements of *pluralization* then surging in the domains of faith, sexuality, race, and gender nor discern sharply enough how our own wariness of unmediated models of collectivity suggested the need to revise established models of pluralism rather than to bypass them.

For yet another, the text folded ecology into its analysis of capital, fossil extraction, the organization of work, and the infrastructure of consumption. But it did not overcome the tacit assumption of planetary gradualism—the assumption that on their own, large planetary processes such as glacier movements, drought zones, atmospheric CO_2 levels, ocean currents, climate change, monsoon patterns, and species evolution always change on long, slow time. That assumption continued to plague most Euro-American perspectives on the right, center, and left in literature, philosophy, and social sciences during this period. Our text was no exception. Those issues would command attention later.

• • •

During this period, I also taught a couple of graduate seminars with Glen Gordon, a colleague in American politics who eventually moved through being chair of the department, to dean, to provost, to being fired as provost by the system president for refusing to make the draconian cuts the latter demanded, to becoming dean again after the faculty rebelled against that firing. He was a Madisonian who contested several of my views. The issues in one of our seminars eventually found expression in an edited book called *Social Structure and Political Theory*.[10]

We occasionally formed a potent alliance in the Faculty Senate across our differences, as when he, as secretary of the senate, broke a tie by voting in favor of my motion to withdraw academic credit for ROTC courses. There was no academic merit to those courses. Credit was reinstated, however, a year after we both retired from the senate. When Glen was chair of political science and I blurted something wild in a department meeting or bar, he would chant, "You can take the boy out of Flint, but not Flint out of the boy." I saw and see his point, while valorizing it in a slightly different way. Glen serves as an exemplar to me of how a faculty member can move into university administration and work to fend off its manifold pressures to become another adversary of critical intellectuality in the university. The great honor the faculty bestowed upon him at his retirement indicates how appreciated those strengths of administrative character can be by a faculty. He became a model for me of what a university administrator should be, one that I tried to emulate, however imperfectly, during the seven years I was chair of the department at Hopkins. He died in the spring of 2020. We have so far been unable to organize a proper memorial because of the Covid-19 pandemic.

I also became involved in the valley with the work of Mort Schoolman, who taught in the political economy program at UMass for a few years; with Jean Elshtain, a political theorist; with Michael Shapiro, who visited UMass for one delicious year; and with James Der Derian, a new appointee in International Relations then with whom I have since kept in close touch. The latter two soon helped to foment a veritable revolution in the study of global politics, starting with a book they edited together, *International/ Intertextual Relations*.[11] I continue to be indebted to the work of these two scholars. Jean Elshtain was also a force to contend with, but I later began to miss the Jean I had once known when she took a turn to the Christian right, initially blaming gays for the appearance of AIDS and supporting the horrors of the Iraq War because Iraq was a "failed state."

Mort Schoolman had been appointed to the Social Thought and Political Economy (STPEC) program at UMass with the understanding that he would remain for a three-year term. At the end of the first year, however, the faculty director announced to Jean, Mike, and me that he was going to replace Mort. Why? we asked, The only point, the director said, is that I have the authority to make that decision. We told him that he had the authority, all right, but that when we resigned from the program he would be directing an empty shell. There would be few faculty or students to direct. He relented. Mort finished his term at UMass. He has had a distinguished career at SUNY, Albany. His book, A *Democratic Enlightenment*,[12] poses contemporary issues about time, memory, and the partial incorporation of identities of others into your own.

•••

I met the social philosopher Steven Lukes when he paid a week's visit to Amherst College in 1975. His lectures were superb. Our work converged around a couple of themes, most notably the exploration of essentially contested concepts and efforts to examine anew the concept of power. He suggested that I apply for a fellowship to visit Nuffield College in Oxford—with his support—and I jumped at the chance. The application succeeded. The year 1977 was thus the date of my first trip outside the American continent at the ripe age of thirty-nine. We arrived in Oxford with two young children and—with help—found a nice house to rent in Summerville, a mile-and-a-half bike ride to the Oxford Colleges.

Soon Steven, Sheldon Wolin, Charles Taylor, Alan Montefiore, and I formed an intellectual cohort, joined by Ronnie Beiner and Michael Sandel—two graduate students in theory at Balliol. Sheldon was visiting Balliol as Eastman professor for a year and Chuck had just started a longer term at New College as Chichele professor. The whole venture was exciting and stimulating, even beyond my expectations.

During this period, it was still pretty much a male world of faculty in theory at Oxford and most other places. That began to change soon, under pressure from feminist movements. The same was true during my early days at UMass. Soon thoughtful grad students at UMass such as Zillah Eisenstein, Joan Cocks, Christine di Stefano, Susan Risch, Shane Phelan, and Jane Bennett helped to change that culture as the institution and Pioneer Valley responded to the upsurge of feminism.

I note that Wolin's magisterial book *Politics and Vision* had already informed my lecture courses in the history of political thought before the

Oxford visit.[13] Taylor's explorations of how ontological, epistemological, ethical, and theological dimensions of politics and political thought work back and forth upon each other had also begun to influence my thinking before I arrived; it has continued to pose challenges to me from that date forward. To contest Taylor on a single dimension of his thought presses you to make corollary adjustments in other dimensions of your own thinking, too. Besides *Sources of the Self*,[14] Taylor's later essay, "Overcoming Epistemology," drives several of these lessons home. The contention is that no epistemology escapes entanglement in a larger ontology, so epistemological debates spill into ontological ones.

It was not always smooth sailing at Oxford for me. One day early on when I was making my first presentation to a large seminar on theories of the state that Steven and I had convened, I turned to page 4 of the carefully prepared text, only to find it missing. Everybody important to me happened to be in the room that day, for faculty members often sat in on each other's seminars. When we departed the seminar room I asked Ronnie and Michael just how clumsy that moment had been. As they reassured me, I studied their faces intently for furtive signs to the contrary. They were impressively impassive, so it seemed probable they were covering. Of course, that ripple dissipated soon.

Another time when Jacques Derrida came to town for a week to lecture on his newly translated book, *Of Grammatology*,[15] I eagerly announced after the first day to Alan Montefiore, the organizer of a term-long seminar on Derrida, how humor is essential to Derrida's philosophy. After Derrida left town, Montefiore announced my conclusion to the large assembly. The pronouncement amounted to a summons to speak. As forty or so heads turned toward me, I studiously scratched a few words on a pad in front of me, with my head down in elementary school style, until the pressure lifted. My "insight," in fact, was exhausted by one sentence.

The vibrant theory ensemble at Oxford broadened my thought and bolstered my self-confidence as we explored issues about ethics, the subject, political activism, political economy, and the state. Ronnie Beiner and Michael Sandel, gifted graduate students who soon carved out notable intellectual careers, also organized us into a theory reading group. We invited Stuart Hampshire, Michael Oakeshott, and Isaiah Berlin to speak, all sparkling moments. Full immersion in intellectuality was the order of the day there, with no apologies to administrators who may doubt its value or to a few colleagues who dismiss unfamiliar ideas without bothering to examine them before doing so.

A sense of intellectual self-confidence, as well as consolidation of long-term relations with Sheldon, Chuck, Michael, and Steven, in particular, tarried after that term. I was later lucky to gain a year at the Princeton Institute of Advanced Study, another at the Stanford Center for Behavioral Studies, several months at the Humanities Center in Australian National University, and a term at the University of Exeter—all superb experiences. At Exeter, in 2003, for instance, Jane Bennett, Nathan Widder, and I organized a study group on politics and time featuring Bergson, Proust, and Deleuze. Nathan had been a scintillating undergrad at Hopkins. His book *Political Theory after Deleuze* is illuminating.[16] Nonetheless, that year at Oxford was definitive for me, opening horizons and instilling new tasks.

One risk of a historical review such as this is that it too easily slides over false starts and dead ends to identify high points. You have become wary, by the time of this text, of smooth stories about planetary change and species evolution, but your own stories often seem rather smooth. Are there paths that became dead ends? Sure, you have noted a turn away from predictivism and other items like it. But recall what Nietzsche says about evolution, including both patterns of species evolution and the evolution of a pattern of thought. "The 'evolution,' of a custom, an organ is thus by no means a progressus toward a goal . . . but a succession of more or less profound, more or less mutually independent processes of subduing, plus the resistances they encounter. . . . The form is fluid, but the 'meaning' is even more so."[17] The question now is this: What dead ends were pursued during this period, what issues stumped you?

I suppose that during the Oxford gig I underwent, under the magnetic influence of Charles Taylor, what might be called a communitarian temptation. I was already critical of the links between neoliberal individualism and social ruthlessness, and such a critique could readily slide toward a communitarian ideal. Taylor is a charismatic thinker, writer, and speaker who then espoused a version of it. I was not tempted by the theistic variant he pursued then (only to modify later), but by what might be called an immanent version. Immanent because it was grounded in a naturalistic image of evolution and harmonization that broke with mechanistic images of culture and nature, communitarian because it sought to promote a new political unity. That tendency found overt expression—albeit with hesitations—in *Appearance and Reality in Politics* in 1981.[18]

However, enhanced attention to the noble politics of pluralization in the early '80s in the domains of race, creed, gender, sexuality, and ethnicity, combined with my encounter with the work of Michel Foucault, interrupted the communitarian temptation. I began to see how the individualist/ communitarian debate (and its kissing cousin, the liberal/Marxist debate)— debates that more or less dominated Anglo-American thought in the 1970s and '80s—did not exhaust the possible terms of engagement. I became increasingly wary of popular critiques of Foucault during this period, critiques that charged him with amorality, or claimed his morality lacked a proper grounding, or convicted him of radical individualism.

The common sense of the day was that if critics from disparate traditions converge in their critiques of Foucault, then it is highly probable that they are right. Another possibility, however, is that the critics were marked by complementary assumptions and existential demands cutting across these differences, complementarities themselves in need of challenge. Foucault was not merely an alternative voice operating on the established checkerboard of thought; he jostled the board and melted down some of the pieces on it.

●●●

As I began to address Foucault's work old habits of thought at first prevailed. I read *The Order of Things*, with its separation of modern European thought into *epistemes* in which each period housed some regimes of thought and debate while foreclosing others. The book made me dizzy. As I was about to launch a dialectical critique of it, however, I happened upon a strange little memoir Foucault had uncovered in the archives and published as *Herculine Barbin*.[19] That book consists of essays by nineteenth-century French journalists, jurists, theologians, physicians, and biologists, all puzzled and distressed over a child and orphan who had been raised in a convent as a girl and was later pronounced to not fit that category of nature by priests, scientists, and doctors. Those tortuous commentaries are followed by a memoir written by Alex/ina, bemoaning the suffering an entrenched set of dichotomous gender categories had imposed upon her/him. Alex/ina committed suicide shortly after the memoir was completed. So much suffering imposed by cultural disciplines upon bodies to sustain a gender/sexual dichotomy. The text gathered dust in the archives until Foucault unearthed and published it alongside the commentaries it inspired at the time.

"Must we *truly* have a *true* sex?," Foucault asks in the brief Introduction to the collection, pressing readers to think again about the forces, institutions, and pressures of "normalization" that sustain the gender binary.

Disturbed, I began to glimpse and feel how normalized categories of gender, sexuality, biology, time, theology, and nature are both insinuated into our bodily prompts and more problematical than I had heretofore realized. Conceptual disciplines reach deeper into bodily tissues and the world than detected in *The Terms*. I now sensed, then, how conceptual *normalization*, through the politics of discipline, *cuts into* bodies, modes of punishment, binary logics, judgments of morality, and images of nature. Note, too, how Foucault transfigured the noun "norm" into the verb "normalized," doing so to highlight multiple practices involved in producing and maintaining norms. Normalization invokes disciplinary powers in schools, churches, families, medicine, prisons, work, the military, and scientific practice, where these institutions often collude with each other consciously and unconsciously. They also encounter resistances that might either foment change in them or engender new intensities of punishment and normalization.

The book jolted me. It was time to study Foucault relentlessly. There is no social life without disciplinary practices, but the shape and intensity of modern types can create subjugated injuries in need of genealogical exposure and political reshaping.

• • •

Judith Butler would soon revolutionize the then extant Anglo-American readings of Foucault as she nurtured a rising field of gay and queer studies and helped to reshape feminist theory, all this starting in 1990 with *Gender Trouble*.[20] Prior to the Butler intervention, however, most American feminists, Rawlsians, Habermasians, Wolinites, Arendtians, Taylorites, liberals, and Marxists were extremely wary of Foucault, to say the least. Because this coterie disagreed with each other on many fronts and yet converged in their critiques of Foucault, the convergence carried considerable cachet. How could they all be wrong?

Butler challenged that. Her later work, too, particularly *Precarious Life*,[21] continues to inspire me and many others. I particularly appreciate how she probes complex relationships between disparate experiences of vulnerability and possible consolidations of a generous cultural ethos across multifarious differences.

When Butler became a faculty member in the Humanities Center at Hopkins during the early 1990s, she exerted considerable influence on the Hopkins theory enterprise, including most definitely me. It was to my dismay that she left Hopkins for Berkeley in the mid-1990s, though several of the Hopkins crew, again including me, continue to follow her work.

We are addressing now, however, a period prior to Butler's protean engagements with Foucault.

•••

My first seminar on Heidegger and Foucault was organized at UMass in 1980. We read, I believe, large sections of *Being and Time, The Question Concerning Technology*, and later texts on language by Heidegger, as well as *The Order of Things, Discipline and Punish, Herculin Barbin*, and *The History of Sexuality*, vol 1,[22] by Foucault. The idea was to tap into affinities between these two thinkers while testing ourselves at the junctures where they jostled against one another. We were very impressed with Heidegger's ecological concerns and his attention to how the "essence of language" emerges when a new thought is on the verge of springing up and you cannot find a word or phrase to capture it: such an event discloses both the indispensability and insufficiency of the web of language to thought. It also reworks the meaning of "essence."

The seminar seemed to be going well when a student announced that Foucault would deliver a few lectures at Dartmouth starting the next week. He had already made a splash at Berkeley, soon inspiring a fine book by Hubert Dreyful and Paul Rabinow, *Michel Foucault: Beyond Structuralism and Hermeneutics*.[23] This would be his first engagement on the East Coast. The students organized two cars; we trekked up twice amid winter snows to attend the lectures.

•••

The two events astounded me. A new encounter. Foucault presented lectures in English with a remarkably light touch, displaying through humor and generosity how his perspective addresses real uncertainties in the world and inspires experimental action. I was hooked. He explored the early Christian "hermeneutics of the self," a theme that spoke to the Heidegger side of our own seminar. He then proposed that we spend less time deciphering our deep selves—deciphering *too* much neither the primordial instincts that are said to animate us nor cloudy connections to God said to be lodged in the depths of the soul. That we, rather, spend more time working artfully upon ourselves to become, through cautious experimentation, more thoughtful, sensitive, and creative beings. That we become *experimental* intellectuals, including ourselves among the appropriate objects of experimentation.

Foucault tapped a murky double percolating in my official self. I now sought to decipher that double a bit and to experiment upon it even more. "Don't explicate too much," Gilles Deleuze says somewhere. Neither he nor Foucault opposed "explication"; they, however, sought to redress established balances between explication and experimentation upon the self in intellectual life.

Foucault was very funny. The humor spilled out, for instance, when a Dartmouth analytic philosopher asked him a polite question about the self-consistency of his theory. "I am not an analytic philosopher," Foucault replied sweetly. "Nobody's perfect." The rounds of laughter, in progressively larger waves, showed how the crowd digested in turn several meanings embedded in that terse, light pronouncement. It showed how laughter can tap proto-thoughts not previously formulated. First, the colloquial phrase expressed a French man's awareness of a common American slogan, tossing it back to us lightly in a French accent at a timely moment. Second, it questioned whether the ambition of many analytic philosophers to express truths in sharp, precise sentences corresponds in fact to the layered complexity, multifariousness, and elements of openness in the linguistic world we inhabit. Third, it suggested that human normality is always an imperfect social formation ("nobody's perfect"), attaching that insight to an aspiration (fourth) to work upon the self to render it more open and presumptively generous in its encounters with shifting circumstances. Teaching through humor.

I began to understand what I had merely blurted to Montefiore one day a few years earlier. I repeated the line—"nobody's perfect"—for a year or two every time an occasion made it remotely possible to do so. This irritating habit continued until another phrase came along to serve as its twin: "Shit Happens." The two phrases together emphasize the place of contingencies of various sorts in the organization of subjects, collectivities, spiritualities, and economies, as well as in the surpluses that occupy each formation.

The seminar at UMass became a threshold experience for me, and for several students, too. However, several friends in the valley on the Left, especially in Marxist and feminist circles, became wary of my turn for that very reason. Those responses seemed to dissipate over time. Judith Butler had a lot to do with that.

• • •

By 1983 it became clear that Judy Connolly and I were going to divorce even before Debbie completed high school. Our relationship, though civil, had lost intimacy and close lines of communication. As the amicable divorce proceedings neared completion in 1984, she became involved with another person, and Jane Bennett and I launched our relationship. Judy now lives in Amherst with her partner of several years.

Jane and I now became very close. In 1985 I moved to Johns Hopkins and she to Rider College near Trenton, New Jersey, so we were merely a short train ride apart. She soon moved first to Ursinus College outside Philadelphia and then to Goucher in 1988, a school located just outside Baltimore. Eventually, she accepted a position as professor at Hopkins in 2004, where she soon was given an endowed chair.

We started teaching seminars together every couple of years even before she became an official part of the Hopkins constellation. We continue to do so today. One recent seminar was entitled, "Process Philosophies and Political Manifestos." It explored the vexed question of how—during a time of fascist danger and galloping climate change—to carry insights from Whitehead to manifestos calling for rapid political change and how to incorporate the urgency of manifestos into process philosophy during acceleration of the Anthropocene.

Jane and I have more or less digested Sophocles, Epicurus, Spinoza, Kant, Butler, Nietzsche, Gilles Deleuze, Alfred North Whitehead, and Cornel West together. I have inhaled fumes from her readings of Whitman, Kafka, and Thoreau and have perhaps carried Foucault, Tsing, Keller, and Proust to her. Her books on *The Enchantment of Modern Life*, *Vibrant Matter*, and *Influx and Efflux: Writing Up with Walt Whitman* continue to inspire me.[24] I am tethered to her intellectually and emotionally, all the more so as we diverge on a few issues.

We habitually read each other's work before sending it out for review. If she tells me something does not work I often get upset at first, only to take another look at it when I am alone. We are soul mates and intellectual collaborators. We also disagree about who has the best sense of humor. I insist that residues of Flint immaturity lodged in my adult self give me a slight edge. She says her sensitivity to the ridiculous does so. Humor, too, is a contestable concept.

Jane and her sister, both highly competent, must contend with a volatile mother, a brother with severe schizophrenia that has been untreatable for decades, and a father who was very ill for a decade until his death. To engage a brother's schizophrenia across several decades—including multiple evictions, legal proceedings, police cruelties, family crises, and jail terms—can deepen your sense of an element of unruliness woven into things. It thus amuses us sometimes when theorists who insist that critique must not be joined to positive agendas charge Jane with a rosy view of the world or "romanticism." I wonder whether they mistake determination for optimism. Or, more, whether they have not yet overcome their own disappointment that the earth is more volatile than they had once supposed it to be. Do they still feel that the nonhuman world they encounter is not good enough to live up to their previous aspirations for it? Who knows? It is clear, at least, that the shock of the unruliness of the planetary engenders multiple reactions today among intellectuals, scholars, and citizens. Perhaps new memoirs will clear these issues up. My responses to the planetary condition are reviewed in Chapter 4.

• • •

In 1983 a group of grad students organized a city league basketball team in Amherst. When I praised their talent and criticized their strategies after they lost the first game, they invited me to serve as coach. I said I would coach and play a little. We devised several defenses and a couple of offenses. During the games I would wait until the first quarter ended and then enter the game when things had slowed a little.

One of the stars, Steve Johnston, soon left UMass with me to attend Hopkins as a grad student. He now holds a chair at the University of Utah. His book *American Dionysia* is a superb reading of tragic possibilities in the United States.[25] When friends gather at his apartment for New Year's celebrations, he and I may pull out the second-place trophy we won in Amherst to review the key game and to allow the revelers to celebrate our feat one more time. We know they love those stories, particularly if they have heard iterations of them before.

• • •

In 1984 I was awarded an NEH fellowship to pull together a set of college and university teachers for a summer seminar at UMass. The seminar was entitled "Genealogy and Interpretation." Thomas McCarthy was teaching an NEH seminar on Habermas in Boston, so he and I agreed to have the two seminars meet jointly a couple of times, giving the then hot debates between Foucault and Habermas ample airtime. Kathy Ferguson, Stephen White, Kathy Jones, Thomas Dumm, Bill Corlett, Mark Weaver, and Alex Hooke were among the key participants in that seminar. We read Geertz, Winch, Taylor, MacIntyre, and Heidegger as diverse exemplars of deep interpretation as they joined that enterprise, often to the intellectual's pursuit of self-consciousness. Nietzsche, Foucault, and a touch of a new Connolly provided exemplars of genealogy.

The summer seminar stimulated vociferous discussions and debates as we debated the sources of ethics, the place of activism in democracy, the relations between theory and social science, the indispensability and dangers of disciplinary practices, the limits of established concepts previously burned into us, and the sources and capacities of human subjects. We debated with Tom McCarthy's seminar whether the "quasi-transcendental" arguments of Habermas were as powerful as he and they thought. Tom himself had doubts.

The seminar sessions were spiced up when several of us traveled to the Harriman Reservoir in southern Vermont during off days to talk and balance seven or eight bodies precariously during long afternoons floating on a small rubber raft I brought along. Maybe these balancing acts taught us more about how to go back and forth between periods of orientation and disorientation in intellectual life. The raft was called Cal II, after the name etched on it by an economy hardware and clothing chain.

I note a few books and essays that may have been touched by issues posed during that seminar. Kathy Ferguson's later book *Emma Goldman: Political Thinking in the Streets* ties the anarchistic themes in Goldman's thought to the character of the activism she practiced,[26] reminding one of parallels to work by Foucault on the "insurrection of subjugated knowledges." Kathy, during the midst of the G. W. Bush Iraq war, also posed a question for closer public discussion: "Is it time to call it Fascism?" The question elicited lively debates in academic settings, spilling here and there into the press.

Thomas Dumm, in *Michel Foucault and the Politics of Freedom*,[27] offers a scintillating reading of Foucault on freedom, crystallized through Dumm's critique of both positive and negative images of freedom—the pair that was thought by so many for so long in Anglo-American thought to exhaust the modern alternatives. It turns out, he shows, that it is not only the institutionalization of positive freedom that shapes and regulates people's wants. Isaiah Berlin, the patron saint of negative freedom, tacitly invokes a "normalized self" to anchor negative freedom, and indeed many of those norms have confined women, gays, transsexuals, Blacks, and other minorities in ways that too often slid under the radar of those protecting negative freedom. The way is cleared now to explore more richly experimental and creative elements in freedom, even to address the question of how to work upon selves and constituencies to become more responsive, self-experimental, and politically organized. Dumm's recent work, particularly *Home in America*, continues to elicit debts to Foucault.

Stephen White's *Sustaining Affirmation: The Strength of Weak Ontology in Political Theory* provides a highly stimulating entry.[28] White, engaging Kateb, Taylor, Butler, and me comparatively, uses the occasion to display the indispensability of ontology in each perspective and to make the case to come to terms receptively and reciprocally with the contestability of each amidst the shared incapacity of proponents to entirely shake off this dimension. He supports deep pluralism in politics. And, as we shall see later, he pursues a "two-folded" approach to thought in which genealogy and interpretation are both invoked at different junctures.

Jane Bennett soon wrote *Thoreau's Nature: Ethics, Politics and the Wild*,[29] drawing Thoreau and Foucault together to explore how "techniques of the self" can help loosen and rework some internalized role disciplines that harden sensitivities to the world and promote too much regularity in politics.

Alex Hooke, *Alfonso Lingis and Existential Genealogy*,[30] provides another entry into this gallery. While there are existential elements in Foucault's genealogies, Hooke explores how Lingis, the maverick thinker who fits no discipline neatly, plays this element out as he ushers us through a host of intersecting cultures that include both human and nonhuman types.

• • •

My first publication after that seminar responded to Charles Taylor's influential critique of Foucault, "Foucault on Freedom and Truth."[31] Taylor insisted that Foucault had lost any place for the subject, truth, and ethics. The essay attracted considerable positive attention. My response was entitled "Taylor, Foucault and Otherness."[32] It took issue with Taylor's charge that Foucault had dismantled the subject and was thus unable to ground an ethic. Rather, I proposed, first, it is possible to extract from Foucault a social ontology that contests both a world susceptible to mastery over nature and Taylor's own experience of a gracious God; second, it is also possible to forge an ethic of cultivation that foments presumptive care for actual and potential diversities of being in this world without grounding itself in either divine transcendence, derivation from transcendental arguments, or a fictive contract; third, a positive notion of the human subject as "an essentially ambiguous achievement" can be distilled from Foucault. That is, the subject is not an eternal formation but an achievement that takes different forms in different materialized cultures; moreover, there is more shade in its formation than is captured by dominant theories of the day. It is elaborated through distinctive bodily processes; it is capable of work upon itself; and political regimes can act collectively upon it.

What, then, is the source of ethics? Contesting a morality grounded either in divine transcendence, transcendental arguments, or a fictive (white, gendered) contract, I supported an "ethic of cultivation" as a source to put into contestation with the others. The latter is not entirely exempt from an element of luck (good or bad) because it draws and works upon strains already folded into life. A pluralist ethos of positive negotiations, I was beginning to see—when joined to a sense of planetary unruliness—may carry you both toward an acute sense of tragic possibility and inspire energy to fight against such binds as they surface. Of course, if you support "deep, multidimensional pluralism," you also seek to forge a public ethos that welcomes a variety of theological and secular creeds into the public realm itself when the issue requires it, rather than striving to encompass all secular and theological creeds under one public canopy. These themes were developed further in "Beyond Good and Evil: The Ethical Sensibility of Michel Foucault."[33] After a few years of polite coolness, Taylor and I revived our friendship when we agreed, during a day-long exchange at Rutgers University on secularism, that a relation of "agonistic respect" between us was well worth pursuing. That was a relief.

Did these adjustments in theory affect your personal or political conduct much, moving it in new directions or posing dispositional issues to address? I mean Foucault himself doubts that mere shifts in intellectual orientation—the beliefs and ideologies you profess—suffice to remold dispositional proclivities, habits of behavior, and ethico-political action. Freud would concur on that score. If "tactics of the self" are important to the quality of intellectual life, you may be under a dispensation to provide some sense of how they have worked in your case.
During the early and middle 1980s gay and lesbian rights movements intensified in the States. They became very active in the Pioneer Valley. I supported them. One summer day, however, as Jane and I attended a large gay pride parade in Northampton, Mass., I found myself eager to applaud on the sidelines and unable to step into the march itself as I had intended to do. My refined belief on that issue, it turned out, did not mesh with other visceral tendencies to conduct. Why? Was I embarrassed that *I* might be identified as gay by those on the sidelines? Was a visceral fear about disrupting a delicate heterosexual disposition incited by the event? One thing was clear: my legs did not step into the parade.

That event disturbed and distressed me. Not enough in my working-class background had primed me to engage this discrepancy—that is, to fold surface beliefs on the issue into more entrenched bodily dispositions to action. (This, of course, is exactly where an Augustinian invokes a will essentially divided against itself, but I sought to address such discrepancies without invoking the onto-theological machinery of soul and body, original sin, the need for divine grace, etc.) I started talking with trusted gay friends about the gap between my principles and conduct, though that too was not easy to do at first. They were rather less surprised by that discrepancy than I.

Soon, with light prodding from others and inspired by Foucault's work on techniques of the self, I enacted several small behavioral changes. I attended films that presented same-sex romances, which was easy to do in Northampton. I talked about these political issues more actively in classes I taught, listening to the words I spoke as I spoke them and attending closely to the verbal and facial responses in class. I wrote about the issues actively, thereby allowing my thoughts to find textual expression. I walked in the next march, with the knots in my stomach now more relieved. But not entirely dissipated.

Such repetitive, modest actions upon the self by the self can make a cumulative difference to proclivities of thought and action. My public behavior changed. Perhaps my official beliefs now became more securely hooked into the visceral register of being. Perhaps a disavowed sense of danger that same-sex relations posed to my own sensual orientation was relieved by these tactics. I did feel vaguely that the queasiness in my gut had been tied to the issue of heterosexual performance. Entrenched habits of working-class masculinity needed to undergo another adjustment. Indeed, new biocultural models of masculinity are very much needed today.

So many have had to work so hard for so long to conceal their sensual dispositions from public view to placate heterosexuals and then, later, to render them visible in order to propel a political movement under dangerous conditions. I merely had to rework a strange queasiness in my gut to bring it into closer alignment with my verbal articulations. Belief, again, is a manifold thing.

The books *Politics and Ambiguity* (1987) and *Identity/Difference* (1991) now explored questions of sexuality, race, and gender more closely than I had heretofore. They also began to test emerging views about the uncertain, real connections between tactics of self-experimentalism, adjustments to the visceral register of cultural identity, the quality of thought, and ethico-political commitments. The next step would be to carry these orientations into deeper engagements with how new political movements can and do slide and seep into the visceral register of cultural life.

● ● ●

In 1984 I was appointed editor of *Political Theory*, the flagship theory journal in America. George Kateb, at Amherst College, was appointed consulting editor, a new position added to that journal. George and I worked exceedingly well together. Only a few articles appeared during my six-year term discussing Foucault's work—including Taylor's (now) classical critique of him as a theorist whose radical skepticism was said to forfeit any notion of the subject, truth or freedom. Despite that, a few theorists did start calling it *The Journal of Foucault Studies*.

My main objective during that editorial tour was to open the journal to younger scholars and to increase the number of essays that moved beyond canonical theory—itself a noble activity—toward new explorations of democracy amid the shifting contours of capitalism. A decade later Jane Bennett became the editor, and, recently, Davide Panagia has been appointed, giving the theory program at Hopkins—discussed in Chapter 4—a strong voice in this journal over a rather long period.

A more pronounced experiment, with new concentrations on race, gender, climate, and decolonial thought, was launched a few years later. Over several months in 1996 several theorists met relentlessly to organize a new internet journal. Jane Bennett, Wendy Brown, Bill Chaloupka, Tom Dumm, Anne Norton, Mike Shapiro, and I wanted a journal that would encourage theorists to address surprising events of the day in ways that might jostle settled perspectives. I loved these meetings. When the founders of *Project Muse* at Johns Hopkins met at our house for a social event one day, they expressed interest in the idea. Now christening the journal *theory & event*, we agreed to join *Project Muse*. The journal's slogan was lifted from a saying by Gilles Deleuze: "The task of philosophy is to become worthy of the event." Its first editors were Tom Dumm and Anne Norton. It often sponsors special issues on topics such as 9/11 and the 2020 pandemic. Above all, it provides space for young intellectuals in the academy to find their feet.

• • •

The Foucauldian entry into American discourse jostled the hegemonic liberal/communitarian debate in America—a debate with George Kateb, Judith Schklar, Jürgen Habermas, and John Rawls ranged (with their internal differences) on one side and Iris Murdoch, Hannah Arendt, Charles Taylor, Michael Sandel, and Alasdair MacIntyre on the other. Alternative voices now emerged tethered to neither side of that debate. Indeed, our little NEH seminar in 1984 itself internalized larger social movements in feminism, Queer studies, and African American politics well underway. Those movements helped to press the academy in new directions; the academy in turn helped to propel such movements more actively into localities, corporations, unions, and churches.

During one conference at Yale a few years later, Richard Rorty and Cornel West strolled over to join Bonnie Honig, Chantal Mouffe, Stephen White, and me at our dinner table after a cohort of deliberative Democrats had accused our entire panel of nihilism. We were nihilists, they said, because we could not establish an authoritative ground from which to *derive* a public ethic. They perhaps had not yet encountered the theme of an ethic of cultivation joined to pursuit of a pluralist ethos of agonistic respect between constituencies who ground their faiths and identities in different sources. For our part—or at least mine—we needed to think more about the actual and possible relations between the conceptually crude visceral register of culture and more refined processes of cultural deliberation. We had a lively time at that dinner.

The official terms of Anglo-American theory were in flux again—just when a larger evangelical/neoliberal machine inadequately grasped by academic secularists was heating up to draw white Christian nationalists and a neoliberal economy of cruel privileges into a new assemblage. It is difficult now to recall how the individualist/communitarian debate retained hegemony for a decade in Anglo-American theory and philosophy. You could not publish an essay during the 1980s, for instance, without clarifying where it stood with respect to Rawls. Today that imperative has dissolved. A lesson lurks somewhere in that fact.

4

The Hopkins School of Theory

You doubtless skated over a few events during the last years in the Pioneer Valley, perhaps negotiating the shoals between good taste and raw truthfulness. You may, in your politeness—or even political correctness—underplay the relays between love and thinking so that a change in one zone resonates with those underway in the other. Shining moments in sensual life may suggest, for instance, how letting go can also open one to periodic moments of suspension in thought, moments where you become more like a seer than an analyst, moments in which you dwell in uncertainty under the pressure of new events to see if a new thought bubbles up for further reflection and possible assimilation. The minor traditions of thought you celebrate attend to such variations and moments. They often refuse the prudishness that can capture major traditions.

Moreover, a couple of your stories are tedious, to be honest. No matter. They are doubtless of interest to you, as events festering and accumulating to bump sooner or later into thought-imbued feelings. Those thoughts doubtless play roles in later encounters with new events, too. Remember, though, readers peer between lines as well as through them, partly in the light of your recollections of early experiences in Chapter 2.

Tell us about the transition to Johns Hopkins University, the intellectual alliances and enmities forged there, the place of periodic bouts of activism in your life within and beyond the university, and any significant shifts in thinking. In particular, attend to some impulses and events that prodded your thought, even tactics you adapted to disrupt old extrapolations.

It was tough to leave UMass, so many friends and alliances forged across twenty years. Jane and I soon settled into a row house on a street three blocks from the campus. She now taught at Ursinus College ninety miles to the north of Baltimore, renting a small apartment in Collegeville to live in three days a week. We continued to launch intellectual adventures together, perhaps, as you say, each of us periodically fomenting moments of suspension in the other.

Dick Flathman quickly became an intellectual buddy of mine, too: he inspired by Proust, Wittgenstein, Oakeshott, and Montaigne; I by Nietzsche, Foucault, and, soon, Deleuze. Both of us also attended to the work of Judith Butler, who soon became a valued colleague in the Humanities Center until she departed for Berkeley a few years later.

Dick and I disagreed on many things. The debates were persistent and lively, he contrasting liberalism, individuality, and skepticism to communitarian theories he resisted, I forging a position that was more radical without lapsing into Althusserian thought. The palpable authoritarianism embedded in the latter's sharp distinction between science and ideology was hard to take. Even he gave it up at a certain point.

One concern propelling me was how much of democratic theory remained one-dimensional, especially in its failures to punctuate common renderings of public deliberation, identity, and principle with genealogical explorations that challenge the sense of sufficiency in these formations. What would happen if you wove themes from Foucault and Nietzsche into democratic theory itself, working upon those two thinkers even as you drew sustenance from them to refine democratic theory?

Neither Dick nor I accepted the strictures advanced by "historical contextualists" or "the Cambridge School," led at Hopkins by esteemed colleagues John Pocock and George Kelly in the History Department and the Humanities Center, respectively. Nor did we embrace universalist and rationalist themes advanced by neo-Kantians. Kirstie McClure arrived later and became an active participant in these discussions until she migrated to UCLA.

Early on, Dick and I became de facto cochairs of a superb dissertation by Bonnie Honig entitled *Political Theory and the Displacement of Politics*. It drew upon Machiavelli, Nietzsche, Arendt, and Wittgenstein to promote its thesis and soon earned the political theory First Book of the Year award. The study displayed the thoughtfulness and boldness of Honig; it also helped to publicize the larger atmosphere of thought emanating from Hopkins. A later book of hers, *Emergency Politics*,[1] further illustrates the prescience of her thinking.

After an overwhelming departmental vote for tenure for Honig at Harvard a few years after she left Hopkins, some upper-echelon administrators decided that they did not want Honig, as a "post-modernist" (a misnomer, of course), on the faculty. They reversed the department's tenure recommendation. Dick and I wrote and publicized critical letters to the figures involved. Mine was addressed to the faculty member/administrator who, I was assured by trustworthy moles on the Harvard faculty, had engineered the reversal. I called upon him to launch an investigation, demanding in fact that he look into questionable things he had done himself. Harvey Mansfield—a Straussian in the department who had supported Bonnie—called to tell me that my letter was a fine piece of sarcasm. He said he had forwarded it to the entire Harvard faculty. Was he being sarcastic? I could not tell. We had had a public exchange a few years earlier when I responded to his ironic take on democratic norms with a sarcastic take on the role of the esoteric and exoteric in his mode of thought.

The two public letters from Dick and me, the stellar credentials of Bonnie, and a veritable tidal wave of letters soon flowing in from multiple sources spurred a minor whirlwind in the academy. It revolved around the question of whether faculty and administrators who misrepresented the work of younger scholars were really in a position to make such judgments.

Bonnie left Harvard and soon flourished at Northwestern and Brown universities. Years later, Bonnie helped to launch a similar protest after the University of Illinois trustees reversed the academic appointment of Steve Salaita, a thoughtful professor of Amerindian culture who had made critical comments about Israeli Palestinian policy they found unacceptable. Giving forward. At her behest, I participated in the public critiques of the school that followed.

• • •

A few years after my arrival at Hopkins, after considerable sparring, Dick and I decided to teach a seminar together on Nietzsche and Wittgenstein. The seminar moved back and forth between engaging Nietzsche for a couple of weeks and then Wittgenstein for two. The role of language in culture and politics became a major topic of discussion. One week I brought to class new findings by a young neuroscientist on the strange role the amygdala plays in emotional thought. The amygdala is a small brain nodule in each hemisphere shaped like an almond. They are rather simple nodules, also moving faster than the other nodules to which they are connected. The amygdala can ignite powerful fears and anxieties after, say, a blowout across the street incites again a flood of wartime traumas—involuntary memories invading the present. Or think about how culturally entrenched feelings of

THE HOPKINS SCHOOL OF THEORY

disgust can invade higher ethical judgments (though disgust bypasses the amygdala and passes through other circuits). Flathman claimed that to emphasize the triggering role of the amygdala—because it moves below the threshold of linguistic subtlety and clean, conscious representation—was to court reductionism. I insisted that this discovery offered a potential avenue to engage "the visceral register of cultural life," a biocultural register flowing into other dimensions of embodied life. By exploring its modes of infusion and expression in relation both to other conceptually crude brain regions with affinities to it and to more refined registers of deliberation, we could learn more about how constituency proclivities to affect-imbued perception and judgment are formed, how they bounce and seep into cultural relations, and how they help to trigger new social movements for better or worse.

The amygdala moves fast and mobilizes intense affective charges, but it is not aconceptual. It is merely more crudely or coarsely so. It is not entirely innate, either, so readings that reduce it to the inheritance of prehistoric harsh drives covered over by a thin veneer of civilizational reason really don't cut the mustard. Finally, it is not merely locked into the interior of the individual, either; constituency cohorts are consolidated in part through visceral modes of communication, as Donald Trump was to show us once again a few decades later. (Corollary attention to mirror neurons, gut/brain relays, and olfactory sensors soon followed in my thinking, along with attention to the complex circuits of exchange in which the amygdala participates.)

The seminar now began to focus more on brief things Wittgenstein said about the role of "training" and "nature" in discursive relations, as well as those Nietzsche said about how new thoughts grow up in you like fungus, you know not how. "One day they are there," he notes, perhaps generated by childhood neglect, or trust in your parents, or severe traumas, or a world event. No thought is utterly devoid of affect, the thinker insisted, and every thought has some efficacy. The thinking of entire constituencies, for instance, can be infused with predispositions to existential resentment. Concentrating on the individual thinker for a moment—rather than an entire culture— Nietzsche says, "Woe to the thinker who is not the gardener but only the soil of the plants that grow in him."[2]

One question, then, becomes how to work upon the visceral dimension when it incites doubles in you or us that a dominant voice seeks to repress, sublimate, or transcend. And, almost paradoxically, how to open receptive valves at other times to allow the visceral register of normality to become infused with influences heretofore alien to it.

The visceral register itself is often too cloudy, incipient, or intractable to be susceptible to close, reflexive articulation or revision. By cloudy I do not mean merely that which is clear in itself but opaque to consciousness. That would set the issue on an epistemic register alone, as rationalists tend to do, thereby seeking to render less opaque that which is clear in itself. Rather, the visceral register is often cloudy in itself, behaving as a diffuse cluster of pluri-potentialities on the way. A subset of empiricist academics, devoted to sharply defined concepts, definitive evidence, and clean proofs, display visceral allergy to this sort of exploration, clinging to the primacy of a binary logic and epistemology to ward it off. That is how they so often bypass those affective modes of cultural communication through which democracy can be nurtured and other modes through which fascist movements are activated.

Anyway, the visceral register of cultural communication, on my view, is both indispensable to creative thinking and agency and problematical to them. It now becomes even more apparent why arts (or "tactics") of the self are important to intellectual life itself, since they can help to unblock it in some instances to encourage new thoughts and projects to spring forth for more refined consideration. Arts of the self are one of the means by which gardeners of the intellect tend to that which has grown in them of its own accord, as they work to prune some affectively imbued tendencies to thought, to uproot others, and to refine yet others.

Dick advised me to study Proust if I wanted to pursue such a course without collapsing into a reductionism he saw looming on the horizon. I said, "Okay," though there was a delay of a few years before that order was obeyed.

Students such as Kathy Trevenen, Kam Shapiro, Davide Panagia, Alan Wood, Paul Saurette, and Jason Frank were indispensable participants in the seminar on Nietzsche and Wittgenstein. They are now sprinkled around the continent, excelling as teachers and writers.

● ● ●

Dick and I continued to pursue agonistic collaborations, even after a drinking problem began to get the better of him. As chair at the time, I tried to protect him from administrative action, so much so that some suggested I had become an enabler. I also participated in one intervention organized by his family and another organized by me that drew a few of his valued colleagues into the fray. It was dismaying, to say the least, to see a vital interlocutor and friend sink into trouble.

After Dick's death several years later, Paige Digeser, a former student of his, closed a memorial event in his honor at the APSA by letting the audience hear fifteen glorious minutes from an interview Paige had taped shortly before Dick's demise in California. It now all flooded back, how the timbre of his voice had slipped into my being alongside ideas I had initially approached warily or later treated with agonistic respect. Another Double. Dick noted in that interview how important the Hopkins School had been to him during those years.

• • •

What is the Hopkins School? It certainly is not a set of ideological agreements among theory faculty and students. Rather, as it has evolved, it has come to mean a general hesitancy to organize a theory program only around the historical and contemporary canon dominant at a particular time. Neither historicism nor neo-Kantianism provides its center of gravity for most faculty and students. By 1988 we began to organize qualifying exams around a list of thinkers each student wanted to place into critical conversation across regions and times. And we worked to consolidate intellectual connections with departments of anthropology, history, German, the classics, the humanities, and English.

Our seminars seldom follow a linear path. Rather, a theme or topic is selected and diverse voices are more or less wrenched out of historical context to confront one another, a pedagogy that sometimes pries open zones of uncertainty between disparate thinkers set in different times and places. Different voices, shooting across distance, time, place, and ontology, can sometimes provide launching pads from which thinking starts again. One seminar on Sophocles and Kant I introduced pursued such an agenda. Another on Augustine and Nietzsche did, too. Later seminar crossings between geologists, philosophers of time, and postcolonial theory induced similar effects. Seminars as intellectual adventures more than modes of canon induction.

Another way to put it is that I don't quite know what the Hopkins School was or is. Its ideological markings are diverse, but many students emerge from the school with creative energy and a desire to open up new zones of inquiry in response to emerging problems. It is a cluster idea, gathering together diverse elements, as Wittgenstein would say, into family resemblances. But alongside the list of former theory grad students from the Nietzsche/Wittgenstein class noted earlier, you may recognize its ethos in the work of Paige Digeser, Lars Tonder, Matt Scherer, Paulina Ochoa, Ellen

Freeburg, James Wiley, Chas Phillips, Simon Glezos, Douglas Dow, Nobutaka Otobe, Mario Feit, Steve Johnston, Karena Shaw, Char Miller, Stephen Engelmann, Nicholas Tampio, Sophie Michic, Alan Keenan, Jeremy Arnold, Corina Goulden, Mario Feit, Suvi Irvine, Ben Meiches, Mina Suk, Chad Shomura, Smita Rahman, Tom Kuehls, Matthew Moore, John Tambornino, Drew Walker, Andrew Ross, Kellan Anfinson, Jairus Grove, Douglas Dow, Adam Culver, Derek Denman, Mabel Wong, Matt Moore, Vicki Hsueh, Tripp Rebrovic, Zachary Reyna, Anatoli Ignatov, Jake Grear, Patrick Giamario, Nicole Grove, Dorothy Kwek, Katherine Goktepe, Nathan Gies, Cara Daggett, Chris Forster-Smith, Franziska Strack, Stephanie Erev, Jishnu Guha-Majumdar, Tim Hanafin, and John Masin-Peters, with more grad students now rambling across the rainbow trail.

Two things the theory faculty loves about this constellation are, first, how earlier crews step forward to engage and support younger ones and, second, how often former students boldly open up new projects. They continue to add new insights, references, and potential adventures to our thinking. Jane Bennett, Jennifer Culbert, Sam Chambers, P. J. Brendese, and I currently (2020) serve as the theory faculty, with scholars from other departments such as Paola Marrati, Naveeda Khan, Anand Pandian, Katrin Pahl, and Shane Butler providing the program with invaluable inspiration and Siba Grovogui (until he, sadly, left for Cornell), Robbie Shilliam, Lester Spence, Bentley Allan, Nicholas Jabko, and Emily Zackin providing sustenance from other fields in the department.

At the date of this writing it is uncertain how much longer this program will flourish and evolve. If or when a university president, dean, and/or chair become hostile to it, it becomes difficult to sustain, even when a large coterie of graduate students is drawn to it.

• • •

The pace of my writing now began to accelerate. *Politics and Ambiguity* (1987), *Political Theory and Modernity* (1988), *Identity/Difference* (1991), *The Augustinian Imperative* (1993), and *The Ethos of Pluralization* (1995) appeared in rather quick succession. *Political Theory and Modernity* sought to compose a history of modern thought that expresses themes dear to many in the Hopkins School. I focus here on the book published latest on that list.

The agenda of *The Ethos of Pluralization* is to revise and radicalize pluralist theory, to show how crucial a significant reduction in economic inequality is to production of a positive ethos of cultural diversity, to gauge

how struggles for new modes of pluralization involve both risky, creative formations of identity on the initiating side of political movements and "critical responsiveness" from receiving constituencies who may feel blindsided at first by a movement, to explore how both macropolitics and the micropolitics of media, churches, unions, localities, corporations, and universities is needed to sustain such movements, to appreciate the value of cross-state citizen movements during an era in which the pace of life has sped up and the scope of issues extends well beyond the reach of territorial state sovereignty, to probe severe barriers African Americans and Amerindians face with respect to pluralization, to show how new drives to pluralization are propelled in part by the demands of emergent constituencies and in part by larger forces that help to press them into being, and to warn that adamant indifference of vibrant pluralizing forces to a politics of egalitarianism could well incite voracious reactions of "fundamentalism." Too many themes; I focus on a couple.

Often, as a new constituency becomes consolidated, liberals say that others now recognize a cohort whose mode of being was already *implicit* in the order of things. The advance of women, African Americans, gays, or a new creed, it is said, involves rendering explicit what is already implicit in the idea of the person, or the text of a constitution, or historical precedent, or the will of God. This study contends, however, that the creative politics of pluralization often stretches and exceeds such dialectical movements. Indeed, the established thickness of concepts of person, God, constitution, or civilization can create barriers to the movements in question. That is why crossing the dicey threshold from illegibility or illegitimacy to legitimacy is so often uncertain, creative, and dangerous, as an emergent constituency struggles to shake up the normative order of things and overcome barriers of violence and blindness.

The bumpy politics of pluralization, while underway, solicits agendas that inform both the identities of the initiators and those of constituencies on the receiving end. Its politics also occupies several sites, including public protests, state bureaucracies, corporate policies, court challenges, university organization, local initiatives, temple politics, public elections, and cross-state movements in its orbit.

Augustine, Kant, Tocqueville, Hegel, Rawls, Habermas, Michael Walzer, Charles Taylor, and Seyla Benhabib, in different ways, insufficiently grasped the real uncertainties and creativities that accompany such dicey movements. A new drive to doctor-assisted suicide, gay rights, Islamic inclusion, or nontheistic reverence, indeed, might encounter barriers that some of those thinkers (and the cultures they represent) had unconsciously coded into the very thickness of the person, the logic of civilization, the dictates of God, the religious unity of the nation, the injunctions of the secular, or several of those together.

To perceive how such a dynamic works variously upon us, it is more insightful to probe a movement during its precarious middle of becoming rather than after victory or defeat "as when feminists proceed through the fight against discrimination with gender duality to pluralize gender performance itself. As when citizens risk the charge of treason or irresponsibility to extend citizen initiatives to movements exceeding the boundaries of the territorial state. As when carriers of post-secular, nontheistic reverence for the diversity of being struggle to pry open space between the conventional sacred/secular duopoly to place a distinctive ethical sensibility on the political scale."[3] The text closes with a critique of Tocqueville's reading of Amerindians as peoples who had to die off so that the advance of a white, Christian civilization on an "empty continent" could continue.

If you believe, as I did then and do now, that new proliferating drives often disturb and distress many white working-class people already struggling to make ends meet and to locate pegs upon which to hang their grievances, then it is also wise for pluralizing movements to relieve job insecurities, authoritarian modes of work, and wealth/income stratifications bearing down on that class across its regional and racial differences. It is also important to chart how the proliferation of relational identities helps to pluralize the working class, too. One chapter concentrates entirely on those issues. Even though there are real tensions between equalization and pluralization, it argues, both must advance together if either is to curtail the precarity otherwise facing it.

A key concept introduced in that book is "critical responsiveness"; it pairs with "agonistic respect," elucidated in a preceding book. If agonistic respect speaks to aspirational relations between constituencies who regularly rub shoulders together while, say, bringing different onto-creeds into the public sphere, critical responsiveness speaks to a positive ethos to negotiate between legitimate constituencies and those striving to make room for themselves by revising the extant terms of legitimacy. The fascinating thing about the politics of pluralization is how it sometimes alters the identities of participants on both sides of that threshold. When a new creed, for instance, is added to old pluralist balances. For example, a new celebration of nontheistic reverence for the deep ambiguity of being might encourage those Christians, Jews, atheists, and Muslims who do not revolt against its inclusion to clarify anew cloudy dimensions in their own creeds.

Indeed, one chapter in the text challenges the equation between territoriality, national identity, and democracy, arguing both that the attempt to spawn a world of nation states breeds repressive politics and that it is needful to forge activist citizen assemblages that exceed the territory of a state so as to act effectively upon numerous issues that roll across territorial states. Since corporate, finance, and state alliances already exceed the sphere of state-centered democracy, cross-state citizen assemblages must be active more often, too.

Pluralizing processes can place neoliberal capitalism under severe strain, but they do not suffice to transcend it. An interim agenda of egalitarian economic change is thus proposed, both because it is more just and because it provides a way to dampen the actual and potential hostility of many working- and middle-class white males to the politics of pluralization. The chapter in question thus wheels out new versions of themes first proposed in *The Politicized Economy*. It warns about the danger of "fundamentalism" if such actions are not pursued.

Did that book address the thesis of "intersectionality" developed by Kimberle Crenshaw and others? Her thesis, presented first in "Demarginalizing the Intersection of Race and Sex," is that often subordinate constituencies face double and triple burdens, combining the disadvantages of gender, race, class, sexuality, or disability into one subject position. And sometimes those multiple burdens can open positive connections across constituencies to press for radical social change.[4] The powerful work of James Baldwin, to take merely an earlier example, was undoubtedly informed by the multiple burdens he faced, such as urban poverty, being coded as Negro and homosexual at the same time, and having talents that fit neatly neither into the athleticism nor musical skills that then provided escape valves for Blacks.

The work on intersectionality did not influence me at the time, and it could have done so had I encountered it, since the two perspectives touch. Crenshaw concentrates on how some constituencies face double or triple pressures, such as, say, women who are black and poor people who are disabled. Her work is indispensable. I also remain concentrated today, after the advent of aspirational fascism, on a quest to find points of intersection between some segments of the white working class and diverse racial, gender, and religious constituencies. It has become more rather than less difficult today to enact such positive intersections—both more important and less probable. Even winning a presidential election may not be sufficient if Congress remains loaded with white, male officials from small towns and rural areas hell-bent on blocking pluri-egalitarian projects. It was also not until later that I began to appreciate how the literature on creolization could inform my work on the politics of pluralization and the corollary task of negotiating a positive ethos of pluralization.

●●●

The *Ethos of Pluralization*, after a slow start, attracted a fair amount of academic attention, particularly with respect to tensions and interconnections between established modes of diversity, new modes of pluralization, and egalitarianism. Some critics asked how pluralism could be "deep" if all constituencies are also called upon to embrace a world of deep contingency? (As I myself did.) But the pluralism pursued in that book does not demand such onto-unity; it, rather, solicits constituencies of diverse faiths to work upon themselves to acknowledge without deep resentment how their own deepest faiths may be *contestable* in the eyes of others with whom they interact; even more, of how traces of self-doubt may arise as a minor voice within any constituency. The effort is to build spiritual alliances across several minorities of different sorts.

Others claimed the book scrambles the very national unity needed to promote egalitarianism. The language of "fragmentation" was even invoked sometimes to describe my image of the tensions between pluralism and pluralization. Such critiques are based, first, on the assumption that it is impossible to mobilize a pluralist assemblage to support the needed objectives; second, that a unified nation would actually pursue them effectively; and, third, that given intense modern pressures to diversity on several fronts, you *could* invent a nation without introducing severe repression. The text interrogates those premises.

The study contended that even pursuit of a liberal nation is dangerous today. Such a pursuit opens the door during rough times—and rough times do erupt—for extreme national unitarians to run roughshod over liberal images of the nation on the grounds that they are too weak and unmanly. I also contended that critics of the new pluralism regularly underplay the collective punch and potential of *pluralist assemblages*. Negotiation of reciprocal ontological modesty between carriers of different faiths— including those of secularists and nontheists—thus becomes an essential virtue of deep pluralism. By "ontology" I meant the most fundamental presumptions an individual or constituency makes about the order of the cosmos and the place of human beings in it—whether it is, say, governed by a beneficent God, or subject to unruly gods, or containing a moral code susceptible to proof through transcendental arguments, or consisting of a pliable nature susceptible to human mastery, or composed of volatile planetary processes replete with intersecting temporalities exceeding consummate capacities for human control. To profess deep pluralism is to confess the ineliminability of ontology from cultural life while acknowledging without deep resentment the contestability of several candidates. Candidates with plausibility are apt to shift over time but never to be reduced to one or two. Or so the speculation goes.

Critics also emphasized how the politics of pluralization encounters deeper structural barriers for African Americans and Amerindians than a generic treatment of pluralism acknowledges. I concur. I wished they had attended to two chapters exploring the severe barriers faced by both, though Chapter 2 on "The Desire to Punish" and Chapter 6 on Tocqueville and Amerindians did not suffice to the issues posed. Later engagements with the white evangelical/capitalist resonance machine and aspirational fascism return to those issues.

Today I am drawn to work on race and democracy by Cornel West, James Baldwin, William Barber, Lawrie Balfour, Charles Blow, P. J. Brendese, and Adam Culver. Cornel West, early on, became a model for me—along with Judith Butler, Michel Foucault, and Charles Taylor—of how academics can work to become critical intellectuals, though I never achieved their heights of performance. West's *Black Prophetic Fire* explores a diverse history of African American activists who often combine organizational skill under trying circumstances with charismatic power.[5] West himself is a charismatic leader of the democratic Left in and beyond the academy; his embrace of Black prophetic Christianity, with its long series of encounters with Constantinian Christianity, is bracing and compelling. He helped me to rise above latent tendencies, drawn from parochial experiences, to equate most Christian theologies with conservatism and even with the white triumphalism paraded by many white evangelicals. Baldwin has been important, too. *The Fire Next Time* embraces the pursuit of existential affirmation amidst respect for tragic possibility, as it conveys a heightened racial consciousness into Nietzschean appreciation of noble multiplicities.[6] I was moved by that book when I read it upon its appearance; Adam Culver returned it to the forefront of attention in a fine dissertation entitled "Race and Vision: A Tragic Reading."[7]

Some Marxists thought my ideal of pluralism and pluralization, with its corollary pursuit of equality, deflates the goal of communist unity and is not hard enough on capitalism. It is critical of capitalism, however, without embracing either an (early) Althusserian ideal of science, or its critique of subjectivity, or an unmediated ideal of collectivism coming from any quarter.

According to the positive ethos of engagement pursued in that book, diverse constituencies, sharing partial connections across class, race, sexual, or religious differences, strive to negotiate a larger assemblage amidst appreciation of contestable elements in their own perspectives: above all, they coalesce to oppose dangerous "unitarian," authoritarian, fundamentalist, or fascist movements organized around the territorial singularity of a creed, identity, gender, race, or nation. Critical assemblages are needed in these instances, partly because highly centralized modes of opposition to such forces threaten to become too much like the thing they oppose.

And so it went. One symposium on the book was published in *Philosophy and Social Criticism* (Winter 1997). Another set of discussions appeared in *The New Pluralism*, edited by David Campbell and Morton Schoolman.[8] A third, wider-ranging symposium on those issues appeared in *boundary 2*.[9]

The text also argued that periodic cross-state and regional modes of citizen activism are now critical to a world marked by the tightening of global interdependencies and an acceleration of speed in several domains. To be a citizen today exceeds acquiring juridical status in a state, though that is important. It also means devising ways to affect decisions impinging upon you and us from a variety of sources, close or distant. We must construe ourselves to be citizens of the earth, then, as well as, when lucky, juridical citizens of a regime. Though that theme found ample expression, the assumption of planetary gradualism did continue to haunt this book.

• • •

Jane Bennett accepted a position at Goucher College in 1988, bringing our commuting era to a joyous close. Then, in 2004, she accepted a position at Hopkins after we had both been courted by another appealing school. As early as 1988 we began teaching occasional seminars together. In one seminar—taught in 1993—called "Metaphysics, Bodies and Politics," a graduate student from the philosophy department named Ben Corson informed us that we sounded even more like Deleuzians to him than either Foucauldians or Butlerites. I introduced a seminar with him on that topic the next term, and Deleuze soon appeared in seminars Jane and I taught together. An intellectual turn was gestating. Before it was launched, however, two themes that had been simmering needed more attention.

• • •

In *Why I Am Not a Secularist* (1999) I, as a nontheist, pose challenges to the hegemony of secularism in the Euro-American academy.[10] The dominant theme of such a secularism is a pluralist democracy in which believers confine their faiths to the private realm to leave the public realm free for deliberative politics rising above creedal differences. One goal of the theories by Rawls and Habermas (at that time) was to overcome the horrendous religious conflicts and wars that had both plagued Euro-American life for centuries and vindicated its imperial invasions. The adverse effects of such a modus vivendi, however, are to overestimate the role that neutral categories of deliberation can and do play in public life, to ignore contestable ontologies invested in liberalism itself, to strive to consign ritual modes of cultural communication to the private sphere alone, and to intensify festering resentments among several religious constituencies who feel the adverse effects the public/private quarantine imposes on them. The text labels the aforementioned themes "the conceits of secularism." These conceits foreclose attention to spiritual attractions and anxieties that inform much of the white working class, to the spiritual aspirations informing many African American movements, and it ignores how a generic idea of "religion" consigned to the private sphere unconsciously represents an idealization of merely one version of *Protestant* Christianity.

One alternative to the secular modus vivendi is to negotiate a positive ethos of public engagement in which diverse constituencies bring their onto-creedal orientations with them into the public realm when it is pertinent to the issue at hand to do so, anchoring negotiations between them in reciprocal appreciation of the contestability of those onto-orientations. Of course, the extreme right opposes just that mode of reciprocity, but the violence of those exclusions makes it all the more important to construct a positive ethos of engagement between constituencies willing to do so.

Most liberal and radical theorists in the States ignored this critique of secular conceits. But, to my surprise, a cluster of theological and anthropological thinkers engaged it closely. Charles Taylor, Fred Dallmayr, Talal Asad, John Thatamanil, Naveeda Khan, Anand Pandian, Bhrigu Singh, and Catherine Keller are notable voices in that regard. Asad, in *Formations of the Secular*, soon argues against the sufficiency of the secular, too, showing in subtle detail how recent anthropological definitions of "religion" in Europe both ignore the role that ritual plays in cultural life and translates the metaphysical diversity of their own public cultures into an invidious hierarchy.[11] These issues become clear, he argues, once you transcend the Protestant definition of religion commonly treated, even in European anthropology, to set its generic definition.

John Thatamanil, in *The Immanent Divine*,[12] places Sankara—the 800 BCE Hindu sage—into fertile conversations with Paul Tillich—the twentieth-century Christian who communes with an impersonal mode of Being above being. Thatamanil identifies points of contact between Hinduism and some variants of Christianity as he shows secular readings of both traditions to be one-dimensional.

Catherine Keller, in *The Face of the Deep*,[13] shows how early Judaic and Christian texts were almost as receptive to the theme of a limited God who acted upon a festering "Deep" already there as to the later Augustinian story of an omnipotent, omniscient God creating the cosmos from nothing "before" time arose. These adjustments, as she knew, open space for receptive modes of communication with theistic and nontheistic traditions beyond Euro-American circles. Her more recent book, *Political Theology of the Earth*,[14] draws diverse theological traditions into more intimate communication with one another and with festering earthy processes, preparing a diverse assemblage of those who care for the world to address temporal volatilities of the earth itself. I have been moved and informed by these texts, as I seek to advance nontheistic variants of themes they pursue.

• • •

I had by now become more alert to the intellectual need to move back and forth between positive formulations and genealogical inquiries that call into question selected truths and norms of the day wired into tacit proclivities of cultural life.

But *how* to prompt creative moments under the pressure of a new encounter? A few techniques to prime fermentation of the intellect in such circumstances are listed in *Neuropolitics* in 2002, a text exploring connections between new work in neuroscience, film technique, and tactics of the self to prime creative adventures of thought.[15] Some techniques on that long list are not those I commend but those that draw people into more destructive, resentful moods. The mix of two types on one list—even though readers were warned—turned out to be a tactical mistake, tempting a few people to pretend I commend the latter in order to disparage the entire list. Live and learn. I quote a few of the positive techniques, then, many of which continue to play a role in my intellectual life when I seek to allow a new thought to spring forth almost on its own in the midst of a quandary:

"You listen to Mozart while reading a philosophical text, in order to relax your mind and sharpen its acuity of perception."

"You go for a slow, long run after having struggled with a paradox or quandary that perplexes you."
"You underline passages in a text while reading it, and then outline the text you have just underlined, remembering as you do how close the relation is between hand gesture and brain processes."
"On some occasions you express in public one or two views you have previously tried out only in the shower."
"You read Proust to sharpen your powers of perception and memory."
"You introduce the phrase *nontheistic gratitude* into discussions with secularists and believers, knowing that it will sound like an oxymoron to many."
"You focus on some new adventure of thought just before going to sleep, in the hope that the dream work done that night will open up new possibilities of thinking in the morning."[16]

Though long slow runs, regrettably, no longer play a role in my life, I do follow an alternate workout routine that helps new thoughts to spring up on occasion; and I still practice several of the other techniques when a political problem, intellectual issue, or strategic dilemma perplexes me. Such techniques dilate the valves of subliminal reception, opening one to revised possibilities of affect-imbued thought, because no thought is ever free from an affective tone of some sort. Dream priming is perhaps the most productive of the lot, at least to me, in conjunction with teaching and writing.

• • •

Concepts such as agonistic respect, critical responsiveness, branded contingencies, nontheistic gratitude, pluralization, the evangelical/capitalist resonance machine, the visceral register of cultural life, emergent causality, deep pluralism, immanent naturalism, incipient pluripotentialities, theorist/ seer oscillations, sociocentrism, bumpy temporalities, a broadband ethos, entangled humanism, the politics of swarming, normality porn, and improbable necessity have percolated up for further review after immersion in relevant texts, the emergence of new events, and appropriate exercises. I now see that most draw diverse elements together into cluster concepts to highlight tensions and interdependencies between elements that belong together. Concepts as clusters, not identities. Concepts as living, mobile crystallizations that often change in their distribution of emphasis over time. Concepts with normative edges designed to highlight periodic modes of becoming amid a world marked by intersecting temporalities with diverse speeds and durations. The refusal to be bound by an analytic/synthetic dichotomy in *The Terms of Political Discourse* paved the way for such practices of concept elaboration.

Other tentative formulations, certainly, have not passed critical review after emerging for further reflection, though I no longer recall most of them. The critical thing, to me, is to respect those strange percolations spurred, first, by intensive review of a perplexing issue and unfamiliar texts and, second, immersion in these tactics of the self. Now a new synthesis might be launched as you seek to adjust old ideas in the light of a new event—the theorist and the seer, oscillating back and forth between analysis and seeking, not in ways governed by a dialectical logic but in more bumpy and uncertain ways. Thinking, in a world often punctuated by events, is a bumpy process, replete with joys and precarities.

You may now sense better how such tactics sometimes tap the third dimension of memory. But have you probed this uncanniness sufficiently? We previously noted, first, recollections; second, dispositions without recollection (e.g., embodying specific crystallizations of early caresses, periods of neglect, hits, a bloody nose, the deafening roar of a tornado, adult delights, an arrest, a shocking assassination). You now invoke a third element of memory, one that can sometimes be tapped but not known. This is perhaps how your recent engagements with James, Nietzsche, Proust, and Whitehead come into play. The last philosopher, for instance, speaks of "scars of the past"—those uncertain remains from a cloudy potentiality previously on the way that never reached fruition because another was consolidated. An incipience from the past may tremble again in the face of a new situation. Nietzsche calls such efficacies "remains," Whitehead "scars," Sophocles "tremors," James "litter," Michel Serres "noise," Freud "memory traces," Proust "vegetal memory."

Several of those thinkers also intimate that such scars, remains, traces, tremors, noise, or litter set preconditions for creative thinking, feeling, and action. They exert strange efficacies, comparable to how Oedipus felt a strange thud in his stomach after Jocasta—to reassure her unsettled husband— carefully described the crossroad at which her first husband had been assaulted and killed.

You and I both know that many logical empiricists and rationalists will oppose to the death the reality or significance of this third dimension of memory. They call evocation of it "irrationalism." Why? Because it threatens the explanatory control of which they dream? At any rate, you have a task on your hands—preventing misrepresentation of the theme by others to make it easier to kill. I suggest, however, that you face a demanding task, too. The list of tactics you have composed merely scratches the surface of how to tap and be touched by this third dimension. Buddhism, Daoism, Hinduism, and Native American cultures all contain practices that tap it profoundly. Have you encountered those traditions? If not, are you finally becoming ashamed of your Euro-American amateurism?

Ahhh, like slumbering bacteria in the gut, waging a bodily attack after receiving a "quorum call." I sensed at the start you would eventually pounce, delivering a blow difficult to parry. At least you do not resurrect the dialectic, sensing how it, too, makes things too neat.

My forays into the traditions you note have been amateurish, to be sure. One fascinating neuroscientist who was also a Buddhist—Francesco Varela—prodded me in this direction several years ago. His book *Sleeping, Dreaming, Dying: An Exploration of Consciousness with the Dalai Lama* opened new vistas.[17] That book convened conversations between neuroscientists and the Dalai Lama on pertinent topics, especially elucidating how neuroscience studies and Buddhist techniques could in tandem inform and prompt lucid dreaming. Such explorations pull one, certainly, further along this route than I have gone. Talal Asad's work, comparing Muslim and medieval Christian ritual traditions, opens similar doors. His book *Genealogies of Religion: Discipline and Reason in Christianity and Islam* is a marvel.[18] Eduardo de Castro, in *Cannibal Metaphysics*,[19] invites comparisons between Amazonian practices of cross-species engagements and techniques commended by Gilles Deleuze. Edouard Glissant, in *Poetics of Relation*,[20] also brings Deleuze and Caribbean thinkers into fertile intersections. The work of Nidesh Lawtoo, *The Phantom of the Ego*,[21] is highly suggestive, too. It focuses on the subliminal character of affective communication. And I have begun to tap resources offered by Daoism in an amateurish way. Finally, the recent book by Jane Bennett, *Influx and Efflux: Writing Up with Walt Whitman*,[22] percolates into my thinking and the ways I engage the aforementioned issues. Bennett's animating questions are: How do shifting atmospheric forces *ingress* into the sensorium, often below conscious attention? How can we respond to such ingressions in more sensitive, caring ways? She explores, for instance, how shifts in atmospheric pressure become intertwined with other thought-imbued feelings to help compose new moods. Influx and efflux.

But, hey, I am a boy from Flint who began fumbling around with these issues only after becoming dissatisfied with other characterizations of how new concepts, ideas, and themes spring up for review. I imagine you will say that such a background generates dissonances between it and life in the academy from which positive mindfulness could be enhanced. Perhaps so. But related tasks must be kept in play, too. For today we must revise an entire array of old political concepts and embedded cultural proclivities in the face of new encounters that shake them up. The urgency of time means that the exploratory side must be set in tense relation to the urgent need for new syntheses.

The issues you pose rise again when we turn to how aspirational fascists work on the visceral register of culture. An intellectual's cultivation of mindfulness, to me, must be intermittent; it must not devolve into withdrawal, though that is a temptation, too, as fascist movements proliferate and the Anthropocene gallops at an accelerating pace. My rather stereotyped "Western" worries about tendencies in Daoism and Buddhism to quietism, however, have been allayed somewhat by François Jullien, in *Vital Nourishment*,[23] as he promotes exchanges between a minor tradition of Western thought and Daoism. The Daoist focus on oscillating between inhaling and exhaling speaks to concerns posed here.

• • •

In 2002, the Bush administration and Fox News launched a virulent campaign to transfigure public outrage against the attack by a group of Saudi/Muslim extremists on the twin towers in Manhattan on September 11, 2001, into support for a massive American invasion of Iraq. A relentless use of fake news and constant pressure on liberal representatives took a heavy toll; it included, above all, the regime's bald insistence that Iraq had nuclear weapons aimed at the States. Jane and I joined several marches and protests against the war, some incredibly large, to oppose the invasion before it started. But Bush, the Republican Party, the neoliberal wing of the Democratic Party, and a media blitz machine overwhelmed all these protests.

Two thoughtful young faculty members at Hopkins organized weekly faculty and student noon-hour vigils in front of the campus library, with the events starting well before the invasion and continuing well after it. Each event was marked by an initial period of silence followed by brief speeches against war fever and the long instabilities this horrendous adventure would create in the Middle East. Undergrad students would often pass by the small crowd, hesitate, and then proceed on their way. Note the moment of hesitation.

Many faculty members found these vigils to be foolish or crazed, either because they believed that Iraq would be crushed and rebuilt or, often, because they concluded that such protests against a destructive, irrational war must be ineffective. Go along to get along. I had encountered that response before in graduate school as I watched Kenneth Boulding protest

THE HOPKINS SCHOOL OF THEORY

alone the early stages of the Vietnam War before most people had become attentive to it.

Of course, the protests did not stop the war. No participants thought they would. You can call the participants visionary realists. The potential power of such critical events, if and when they accumulate in several places, is often delayed. People may bypass them with disdain or hesitation at first; later, once a crazy war killing hundreds of thousands begins to unravel, as millions of critics anticipated, and the nationalism cools, many recall dim doubts earlier aroused. They turn against the war.

It is nonetheless difficult to get some academics—who often express high confidence in their analytical powers and corollary disdain for ineffective protests—to acknowledge that such soft influences could work on the visceral register of cultural life. Indeed, few academic supporters of the war I knew acknowledged later just how wrong they had been. Many simply wanted to move on, though doing so could leave them in the same place the next time a crazy, destructive venture is launched.

Tacit identification with habits and positions of the powerful encourages disdain for minority protests against reckless, ruthless state actions. Protestors—enacting vigils, national protests, and published critiques—act in part to publicize opposition and in part to ensure that they themselves do not settle into the grooves of the reckless and the powerful. It is when you partake in some prerogatives of the powerful that such dissident acts become particularly obligatory.

The two untenured initiators of the Hopkins vigils, one in history and the other in political science, did not receive tenure. A few of us wondered whether their antiwar activism had incited some of the opposition to them. That issue, of course, was never mentioned by the opponents of tenure; they, rather, invoked high standards of academic achievement, standards that challenge achievements of many scholars already tenured. I follow these two careers today, as they continue to write and act in interesting and evocative ways.

• • •

During this period I began to write more critical op eds myself about the endless Iraq war and related issues. One essay about the need to fortify protests excited the ire of a trustee, according to the provost. The provost assured him, he told me, that my opinion piece was okay because Hopkins also had Paul Wolfowitz on its faculty, an architect of that very war. I did not think until later how I should have responded: "Okay, but would it have been better

yet to celebrate the principle of academic freedom?" or, "Did you check with
him to ascertain whether a sufficient diversity of views is represented by
university trustees, the military, corporations, urban police forces and the
Bush regime?"

A few years later, Jairus Grove, a dynamic grad student at Hopkins,
proposed that I introduce a blog and that he handle the technical issues.
Jairus now teaches at the University of Hawaii and has published a powerful
book entitled *Savage Ecology: War and Geopolitics at the End of the World*.[24]
It explores the cruelties and trajectories of the "Eurocene," a Euro-capital/
military/imperial assemblage that imposed colonization and took the lead in
fostering rapid climate change.

I countered with another proposal: we start a blog together, inviting
numerous people to contribute to it. Jairus Grove, Derek Denman, and I
now organize *The Contemporary Condition*; several others have played such
roles on it in the past, too. Many people contribute. A timely post occasionally reaches as many as 10,000 people in and around the academy. It allows
us to test political thinking on the way or to warn about an imminent event
before it becomes a fait accompli. To put it in grander terms, terms elaborated by Foucault in his final set of lectures, such blogs—there are numerous
instances in play today—allow you to enact the "courage of truth" in the
face of fast-moving events and right-wing media/state/evangelical/corporate
avalanches.

Such interventions are not grand, but they may help in the company of
many others to prime thoughts, to forge new affiliations, and to strengthen
a readiness to episodic political action that can otherwise slide into resignation. A few of my posts are entitled "What Was Fascism?" (2010), "The
Fragility of Things" (2010), "Aspirational Fascism" (2011), "The Politics of
the Event" (2011), "'Melancholia' and Us" (2011), "The Dilemma of Electoral Politics" (2012), "Toward an Eco-Egalitarian University" (2014), "Populism or Fascism?" (2018), "Dietetic Capitalism" (2018), and "What Time Is
It?" (2021). Such posts, again, may accumulate with others to prime larger
discussions; almost as important, they also work upon the visceral register
of authors and readers themselves, fortifying their readiness to stand up to
power when needed. They perform, when joined with other such interventions, double duty.

• • •

It now became clear to me that it was time to think anew how American
capitalism works, in the light of recent events and the insufficiency of

secular categories to the world. An initial entry entitled "The Evangelical-Capitalist Resonance Machine" was published in *Political Theory* in 2005.[25] American neoliberalism, it contends, is not reducible to variants then finding expression in Europe. It is more extreme and virulent. Why? Starting at least by 1980 neoliberals who celebrate the primacy of capital and impersonal markets forged a creative assemblage with lower- and middle-class white evangelicals. White evangelicals who heroically contest these trends are discussed, too.

The formation mobilizes an affective resonance machine between neoliberal high rollers and less affluent white evangelicals, as each absorbs aspects of the existential spirituality most prominent in the other.

Here is how the spiritual resonance between these two constituencies is summarized in *Capitalism and Christianity, American Style* in 2008.[26] "Across these differentiations, the two parties are bound by similar orientations to the future. One party discounts responsibility to the future of the earth to vindicate extreme economic entitlement now; the other does so to prepare for the day of judgment against nonbelievers. These electrical charges resonate back and forth until they generate a political machine much more potent than its parts."[27] The upshot: "Today, resentment against cultural diversity, economic egalitarianism, and responsibility to the future whirl together in the same resonance machine. That is why its participants identify overlapping targets of demonization and marginalization, such as gay marriage, women seeking equal status in work, family and business, secularists, those of Islamic faith, atheists, and African American residents of the inner city who do not appreciate the abstract beauty of cowboy capitalism."

George Gilder is identified as a right-wing intellectual who helped to inspire this new machine. Its creativity is not to be depreciated, since earlier neoliberal heroes such as von Mises, Hayek, Friedman, and Ayn Rand were either atheists or casual about institutional religion. One key to the new assemblage is how a spirituality of *existential resentment* absorbed by one angry class of whites resonates with that of *hubris and special entitlement* exuded by another white class. Indeed, each now folds into itself tendencies already prominent in the other. The result is a movement that then exceeded European neoliberalism in virulence.

Chapter 4, "Is Eco-Egalitarian Capitalism Possible?," lists a broad set of interim policies in the domains of income, job security, housing, sustainable power, and the infrastructure of consumption that could curtail the threat posed by the Anthropocene and also relieve burdens of the working classes writ large. The interim reforms would not transcend capitalism but could perhaps prepare the way for future movements and practices that do. In focusing on the new machine, the book seeks to illuminate a series of grievances and insecurities in the white working class that have opened it to new intensities of racism, misogyny, and antidemocratic propaganda.

The book thus identifies "neofascism" as a turn the new resonance machine could well take if concerted efforts by pluralizing forces to siphon a larger portion of the white working class into egalitarian pluralism are not undertaken. It emphasizes "the volatilities" the machine spawns. It was published a few months before the machine manufactured the economic meltdown of 2008.

It sounds as though you think that book was prescient about events to come, as it explains how the machine captured large sections of the donor and white working class together, exposes crisis tendencies generated by the machine itself, identifies sources of its hostility to warnings about climate change, and articulates the fascist dangers it secretes. Are there not, though, things you would present differently were you to revise it today?

I remain pleased with how it challenged the economism of most Euro-American economic theory. Most economists of right, left, and center dismiss or deflate the importance of spiritual elements in both political movements and economic practices. Think, for instance, of how a collective spiritual demand that the future must be construed to continue capitalist practices of consumption disables attempts to reconstitute the infrastructure of consumption today to cope with climate change.

If I were to revise it today, I would focus more on how neoliberal escalation of a debt economy traps many poor and working-class families struggling to make ends meet in a consumer economy organized around the generalization of exclusive goods. I would also draw upon Lisa Duggan's superb book *Mean Girl* to probe again how *creedal differences* between neoliberal and evangelical cohorts are trumped by the *affinities of spirituality* between them.[28]

Duggan, focusing on how Ayn Rand inspired numerous American libertarians and neoliberals—the list includes Paul Ryan, Steve Jobs, Rand Paul, Ronald Reagan, Mitch McConnell, the Koch brothers, and Alan Greenspan—shows how the novelist spiced up boring neoliberal and libertarian stories by sinking market fantasies and hubris deeply into the visceral register of alpha-male cultures. Rand transfigured a dry neoliberal creed of capital entitlement into contagious stories of alpha masculinity, enchanting white women, lusty affairs, natural race and class hierarchy, market supremacy, and heroic atheism.

Duggan does not discuss evangelicalism. But notable to me are some affinities in narrative structure between the heroic stories Rand promulgates and theological stories absorbed by white evangelicals on the right. Each party dramatizes how a historic fall into a social quagmire of care for profligate losers will be followed by sweet victory for a ruthless few in a new world of winners. Each celebrates American exceptionalism as it disparages African Americans and those indigenous cultures that preceded the conquest of America. Duggan's account also invites comparison with a notable study by Libby Anker, *Orgies of Feeling*,[29] which explores the narrative structure of film, book, and TV melodramas that capture the imagination of so many Americans during electoral seasons.

The *Left Behind* series—so important to white American evangelicals— tells stories that resonate with the narratives reviewed by Duggan. In that series, read by over sixty million, conspiring non-Christians around the world—who often speak English in thick accents—are finally plunged into a molten sea of sulfur so that a victorious few can enjoy the fruits of a divine holocaust—the most violent holocaust in the history of the world. That story line—reviewed in *Capitalism and Christianity*—also makes another connection to the secular stories by Ayn Rand: it plays up how delicious sex can be between husband and wife in white, believing, churchgoing, heterosexual, nuclear families. The most extreme neoliberals and evangelicals today ridicule concern about climate change. Why? That concern undermines simultaneously the story of economic mastery over the earth demanded by neoliberals and divine mastery over it invoked by evangelicals. To the latter even to think that human institutions can influence the climate is to commit a sin of pride, falsely bestowing upon human agency only what God can do. There are more moderate neoliberals and evangelicals, again, who call these extreme stories into question.

I should note another study that augments themes in *Capitalism and Christianity*. In *Democracy in Chains: The Deep History of the Radical Right's Stealth Plan for America*, Nancy MacLean examines archives left behind by the academic neoliberal James Buchanan.[30] He supported a minimal state and strong market model in public pronouncements during the 1970s and '80s, all the while quietly joining the Koch brothers to devise strategies to lock in neoliberal changes by constitutional means so that a popular democratic majority could not reverse them in the future. The discrepancy between the public themes of Buchanan and the covert political agenda he supported helped to set up American neoliberalism for the even nastier things that happen later. Though Maclean ignores the evangelical dimension, her admirable book, too, is indispensable to updating and refining themes pursued in *Capitalism and Christianity*.

• • •

When *Capitalism and Christianity* appeared, some intellectuals with interdisciplinary interests were drawn to it. Marxists, Keynesians, and neoliberal economists, however, mostly ignored it, finding it to wander too far from secular terms of analysis. Where is the labor theory of value? Why fold religious practice and existential spirituality into the very sinews of political/economic institutions? Does not the very idea of a new resonance machine between heterogeneous constituencies undercut the possibility of rigorous analysis and clean policy prescriptions? What, anyway, do Nietzsche, Weber, Deleuze, Keller, Gilder, MacLean, and Connolly have to do with a rigorous analysis of political economy today—either to expose its internal rationality or to uncover its dangerous trajectory? Did not Weber himself— who uncovered spiritual/capital conjunctions during the consolidation of industrial capitalism in northern Europe—say that the spiritual element withered as the system condensed into an economic mechanism? Did not even Foucault, in *The Birth of Biopolitics*, presciently trace the rise of neoliberalism without needing to consult its spiritual dreams and affinities?[31]

To me, those who ignore the historical conjunction between evangelicalism and neoliberalism in America inadequately grasp how that assemblage overwhelmed movements on the Left in the early 1980s, how it exacerbated the distinctive *virulence* of American neoliberalism in the domains of race, gender, ecology, and income inequality, how neofascism can morph out of that machine, and how it is essential today to fight it off by negotiating alliances between several constituencies with affinities of positive spirituality across their different onto-creeds and social positions.

The book addressed new volatilities of capitalism during a period of rapid climate change. Nonetheless, it only began to address the twin assumptions of planetary gradualism and sociocentrism that continued to plague most political interpretations of the day.

• • •

The explorations of intersections between pluralism, capitalism, creed, and spirituality had found one expression, as reviewed earlier, in the pre-

sumptive ideal of agonistic respect. That concept encouraged some commentators to lump my perspective with that of Chantal Mouffe, the author
of books such as *The Democratic Paradox*,[32] placing both of us under the
rubric of "agonistic democracy." There are similarities, but the differences
between us are significant. She draws upon Carl Schmitt, and I find Schmitt
to subtract the element of respect from agonistic respect. She seems to favor
a centralized movement to oppose the Right, and I contend that such an
agenda of centralization is dangerous to a world marked by pressures to
minoritize culture along several dimensions. I focus on pluralist assemblages
to pursue that task. She remains sociocentric, and I, from the advent of
Capitalism and Christianity on, challenge that syndrome.

In a paper delivered at a 2019 APSA panel reviewing the NEH seminar on
Genealogy and Interpretation thirty-five years after its occurrence, Stephen
White addresses another key difference. The absence of a genealogical
dimension in Mouffe, he says, authorizes a "one-folded approach" to democracy and justice as opposed to a "two-folded approach" he and I adopt. "My
point here is not about citational niceness. Rather it is about a crucial difference between Bill's understanding of agonism and the Schmitt-derived one.
Only the former is rooted in a clear understanding of two-foldedness."[33]
The second fold involves periodic, genealogical investigations of notions of
democracy, justice, subjectivity, race, identity, capitalism, or sociocentrism
that have heretofore governed one's work and that of others. The most famous
genealogies are by Nietzsche on Christian morality and Foucault on modern
sexuality. The notion of "agonistic *respect*" also plays up a *presumption* of
respect to contending parties, unless and until they intensify economic
inequalities and racism or enact fascist drives.

• • •

It was with anticipation, then, that Jane Bennett and I looked forward to a
year-long visit in 2010 from David Howarth and Aletta Norval, two former
students of Ernesto Laclau and Chantal Mouffe teaching at Essex University. It soon became clear how the divergencies noted earlier had already
softened in their thinking. David and I taught a seminar called "Rethinking
State Capitalism." It placed Marx, Habermas, Polanyi, Deleuze, and Foucault
into discussions. Debates between us about the place of immanence in
thought were illuminating, too, since he had been attracted to how people
are impelled generically to pursue notions of transcendent unity that cannot
be attained, and I had been more attracted to an "immanent naturalism" to
be placed into competition with other onto-creeds in political life. His

humor greased these discussions, during class and at a nearby bar to which
the class often sojourned afterward. Affinities and differences between us
come out well in his essay "Pluralizing Methods: Contingency, Ethics and
Critical Explanation."[34]

Aletta Norval delivered a superb paper comparing Jacques Rancière and
Stanley Cavell. It folded a higher degree of positivity into actual democratic
practices than Rancière could accept in his then sharp distinction between
"politics" (the moment of radical disruption) and "the police" (everyday
politics in formal democracies).

Jane and I became attached to those two, sharing intellectual interests
and even taking a vacation with them in Lyon and Grenoble, France. I also
loved to spar with the brilliant young James Howarth. On a train ride to
Grenoble, the twelve-year-old reviewed with me the faults, as he saw them,
in the five proofs of God's existence. I had not examined these proofs until I
was twenty, learning only later how most theologians find such arguments to
forge an unproductive trail through which to explore the vicissitudes of faith.
One day I explained to young James what irony meant and why I preferred
sarcasm. He challenged me on that issue thereafter, often informing me that
what I had just said sounded like irony to him. David and I told the lad he
was too young to worry about this issue.

*Would you agree that your thinking took another turn at this point? Focused
now on "the planetary" more than before, folding work on the periodic volatility
of several planetary processes into explorations of capitalism, spirituality,
colonialism, race, politics, and ecology? Did you worry that such a turn could
overwhelm earlier insights into the spiritual dimensions of pluralism and
political economy?*

I had, certainly, long been devoted to "environmentalism." And in *Identity/
Difference*, I noted how (what I later called) periodic planetary volatilities
become intertwined with capitalism and precarious practices of state
sovereignty. The actual planetary condition was bouncing ahead of Euro-
American cultural theory: "Nonstate terrorism, the internationalization of
capital, the greenhouse effect, acid rain, drug traffic, the global character of
strategic planning, extensive resource dependencies across state boundaries,
and the accelerated pace of disease transmission across continents can
serve as some signs of this contraction of space and time."[35] So, now: "The
globalization of contingency is the defining mark of late-modernity."[36]
Covid-19 now cuts up the world and consigns people in many places to
lock-ins as I write this study. I was amused, then, when a few critics took my
rendering of the globalization of contingency to mean that such events are

readily susceptible to technical mastery simply because they are not subject
either to divine will or to implacable laws. The attribution, in fact, exposes
a problematic assumption of those who make it: the idea that without divine
ordination or closed necessity, contingencies are fluid things that can readily
be controlled. The opposite is of course more often the case. Some contingencies, like those listed previously, can plague and overwhelm. The
critics in question, perhaps, confused me with Richard Rorty, who did link
contingency to a prospect of world mastery in *Contingency, Irony and
Solidarity*.[37]

• • •

Contingency to me today contains several, often intersecting, dimensions. It is a cluster concept. It can involve, first, concatenations between
diverse, blind trajectories, generating effects either too fast or outside
established awareness before coming to attention. Complexity theorists often
fold that theme into the relative indiscernibility of "initial conditions."
Contingency resides, second, in lags between new happenings and the
resources of established theory, such as when accelerating climate change
rolled along below the radar of scientific attention until being widely
recognized late in the day or when viruses or bacteria spawned multiple
pandemics well before the best sciences of the day knew what they were,
how they worked, or what to do about them.

There are, third, pulses of real creativity in the world, in which subliminal resonances between heterogeneous agencies periodically usher something new into being that exceeds the intentions of the intersecting parties.
As when, say, resonances between a virus and human cells enable the virus
to attach to the cells, or when a new social movement arises out of resonances between white evangelicals and neoliberals. The two cases are very
different, to be sure—with the first inhabited by mere traces of agency and
the latter by more robust modes—but it is today timely to explore the diffuse
affinities across such differences. Or so it seems to me. The latter tack avoids
the human exceptionalism that is one source of so much global destructive-
ness today in the intersecting domains of capitalism, evangelicalism, and
imperialism.

There are, fourth, contingencies of timing in which a trajectory moving
at one speed encounters another proceeding at a different speed at just the
right time to upset things or to open a new, positive possibility. Closely related
to that are situations in which several contingencies follow each other in
rapid succession. For one example, the events of Trump's income tax exposure,

the death of Justice Ginsburg, the nomination of Barrett to the Supreme Court, and the Covid-19 infection of Trump followed each other in rapid succession during the 2020 election, making it difficult for many voters to digest the rush of events. Each of these events, indeed, arrived from a different place, converging to mark the chaos of an election campaign.

Sophocles, Nietzsche, and Proust are superb at displaying such untimely conjunctions. The secretary whom I bumped into at a key moment on a dim hallway provides one small example. Meeting a new lover while on vacation involves another. The Younger Dryas event, which rapidly closed down the ocean conveyor system, involved planetary contingencies of timing connecting disparate forces; it profoundly conditioned the life of Atlantic peoples and numerous other species for centuries.

Moreover (fifth), some contingencies, once folded into the drive structures of human beings, become obdurate (or "branded") while others are more tractable. Some constituencies resist acceptance of same-sex marriage obstinately, perhaps to protect a fragile sense of heterosexuality installed in them, while others are much more pliable in this regard.

An *event* is thus a contingency, or cluster of contingencies, that affects profoundly one or more constituencies—human and/or nonhuman. An event stands out in that it arrives unexpectedly, pressing those who encounter it either to change course or to become more obdurate in staying the course. Events are thus not history. Their arrival punctuates and turns historical processes, sometimes in large and sometimes in modest ways. An event sets off multiple vibrations that may resound in several directions. Its effects may even slumber for a while and then erupt in the face of another event. As when that cop, videoed with his knee pressed for nine minutes on George Floyd's neck in Minneapolis in the summer of 2020, sparked a series of spontaneous demonstrations in numerous cities and towns, with participants recalling earlier moments of the same sort in which the police also claimed they had used reasonable force.

Events resound with pluri-potentiality, calling up sheets of past that may point toward a different future.

It is also true that each act of perception can be construed as an event, organized out of relations between layered memories and sensory reception during the half-second delay between reception and organization of a percept. That is a phenomenon to explore, too. But I focus here on more notable intrusions that open the way to tighten, revise, or reconfigure habitual arrays of affectively imbued judgments already in place.

The issue now becomes how to respond to a new event. Do you modify old concepts and strategies to bring as much nobility and presumptive generosity to them as feasible? Do you, at the other end of that pole, respond with existential resentment and look for people to punish? Or do you try to forget an event?

Contingencies, coagulations, timing, creativity, events, affect, and thought are thus interinvolved. Each is a cluster concept, co-involved with the others, with different elements gaining prominence at different moments. To pursue theory without hubris is to acknowledge the role of events of multifarious sorts in planetary processes, daily life, academic theories, social movements, and regime politics. So, again, an event to me involves a contingency, or intersection between two or more processes, that affects the fate of specific constituencies, human or nonhuman. It could be an earthquake, an imperial invasion, a massive volcano, a new democratic movement, a new love, a rapid surge of fascism, a coup, the global spread of a new disease, a revolution, an encounter with a new thinker, and so on and on. Events keep coming, in large and small doses, with past events folding into new memories and happenings. New events bristle with residues from past events. But perhaps the key is that an event finds you before you find it.

Covid-19 is a recent event of global consequences with small beginnings. It (probably) arose out of chancy conjunctions between viruses, bats, an animal intermediary, and humans in an open meat market in Wuhan. It was then propelled rapidly across the globe via the ship, auto, truck, and air travel that mark a fast-paced world.

A crucial question becomes how to become worthy of the events we encounter. That question periodically repeats itself in new variations.

• • •

I did, then, embrace fairly early the thesis that fossil capitalist emissions propel the Anthropocene, but I was slower to grasp the significant role planetary volatilities play in climate change, how they were periodically in play well before the advent of capitalism and now recoil back upon it and noncapitalized regions differentially. The conjunctions between planetary volatilities, cultural spirituality, and capital processes increasingly became critical to me.

I now pursued the question of planetary events, accelerating the pace after placing a 2007 book by Fred Pearce, *With Speed and Violence*, in a seminar.[38] Pearce interviews cutting-edge climate scientists, oceanographers, glaciologists, paleontologists, climatologists, and geologists about the transdisciplinary work they do as the manifold event of climate change accelerates. And I began to read several earth scientists closely, with Stephen

Gould, Richard Alley, James Hansen, Naomi Oreskes, Michael Mann, Wally Broeker, Jan Zalasiewicz, Marcia Bjornerud, Michael Benton, Bill McBride, and Arnold Taylor high on the list. Many of these scientists played up the utter severity of an unfolding climate crisis well ahead of the consensus in their own fields. They were often said to be outliers then; today they are recognized to have been prescient.

These forays, it became clear, required significant augmentation from humanists and postcolonial theorists addressing imbrications between imperial capital, volatile planetary processes, and the highly unequal regional and racial and class modes of suffering they engender. Theorists and activists such as Donna Haraway, Peter Van Dooren, Rob Nixon, Bruno Latour, Anna Tsing, Bhrigu Singh, Naveeda Khan, Anand Pandian, Wangari Maathai, Brian Fagan, Mike Shapiro, James Der Derian, Deborah Danowski, Eduardo de Castro, Naomi Klein, Anatoli Ignatov, Jairus Grove, Dipesh Chakrabarty, and Catherine Keller now began to draw closer attention. Was it possible, too, to augment these two streams of thought through new engagements with Nietzsche, James, Deleuze, and Whitehead on how diverse planetary temporalities infuse and impinge upon one another as they move at different speeds and modes of complexity? I was primed to think so. Some authors on that second list, such as Latour, Danowski, de Castro, Singh, Haraway, Grove, and Keller, thought so, too.

• • •

A World of Becoming 2011), The Fragility of Things (2013), and Facing the Planetary (2017) present the results of these engagements.

During this period of ferment I also taught seminars with Nicholas Jabko, Jane Bennett, Bentley Allan, and P. J. Brendese—each seminar engaging an aspect of these issues. Nicholas is a comparativist studying political economy. He and I explored how to bring complexity theory to political economy, focusing on creative actions by economic actors and theorists. Jane was pursuing another dimension of "new materialism." Influx and Efflux: Writing Up with Walt Whitman, was in production as this study proceeded.[39] That book, as earlier noted, focuses on multiple kinds of atmospheric ingressions into the human sensorium and the visceral register of cultural life. It also explores how the ingressions are variously synthesized to help to constitute human subjectivity. Bentley works on how rapid climate change requires significant changes in IR theory, with his book Scientific Cosmology and International Orders appearing in 2018.[40] P. J. explores racial and indigenous dimensions of these same issues, with a fine book now from Oxford University Press called *Segregated Time*.[41]

Some friends and colleagues, when I engaged them in urgent conversation about the Anthropocene as a mass of galloping, intersecting temporalities that now infect every issue addressed in the humanities and human sciences, warned me not to become a crisis monger. They responded, no doubt, to the shrill tone that often rose when I spoke about the issues as well as to real worries about how crisis-mongering on the Right can overwhelm the Left.

I concur that the Right thrives on disaster porn. But its crises are manufactured in part to cover up a real global crisis with active sources in capitalist states and its most dramatic contemporary effects hitting nonwhite polar, subtropical, and tropical regions. The question: How to disseminate a looming crisis without exacerbating self-protective drives to avoidance already there? Deferralism, denialism, casualism, skepticism, and nihilism are a few faces climate avoidance assumes. A major danger in the old luxurious capitalist states today, you might say, is *normality porn*.

Facing the Planetary: Entangled Humanism and the Politics of Swarming (2017) contests both secular presumptions of planetary gradualism and complementary theological faiths in a providential world. The volatility of the earth presented in the theophany of the book of Job is introduced to contest both visions. It may even suggest that human beings are not the most important beings to the divinity as the Nameless One surveys the multiple forces and life forms it has ushered into being. The study then turns to four disparate, secular thinkers in Euro-American thought tethered—in varying degrees and ways—to planetary gradualism and sociocentrism. The diverse theorists selected are Jean Jacques Rousseau, Friedrich Hayek, Isaiah Berlin, and Karl Marx. Sociocentrism is the drive to explain key cultural and social processes by reference to other social processes alone, with partisans debating which of the latter are most fundamental. It, in turn, often rests upon the cosmic assumption of planetary gradualism—the idea that profound changes in climate, ocean currents, ocean levels and acidification, drought patterns, glacier flows, monsoon patterns, hurricane intensities, and species change always occur in long slow time, or at least did so for billions of years until the advent of capitalism and the Anthropocene. The assumption of gradualism was sealed in stone by Charles Lyell, the leading nineteenth-century geologist, and Charles Darwin, the great evolutionary theorist, both of whom wedged notions of racial hierarchy into those theories.

To come to terms with the revolution in the earth sciences launched in the 1980s, however, is to see that planetary gradualism and sociocentrism must also be transcended in the humanities writ large. Nietzsche, Deleuze, and Whitehead are placed into conversation with recent trends in the earth sciences to prod that process along. Whitehead's account of how "scars of the past" can resonate with new events to help prod new, creative interventions into being receives a long discussion.

Reviews of the five great extinction events in the past are followed by summaries of more recent planetary events, some preceding the rise of extensive agriculture and all preceding capitalism. These include the closing of the ocean conveyor 12,700 years ago, the rapid stuttering into being of the Holocene, the Medieval Warming Period, and the Little Ice Age, each with distinct sources and widely diverse civilizational effects. These considerations press us to challenge both secular images of progressive mastery of nature and providential images, doing so with a story of bumpy, intersecting temporalities of multiple sorts. Time itself, the text suggests, may be composed by multiple temporalities moving at different speeds, as their bumpy intersections turn it in different directions. The task is to rework future extrapolations of the possible and the desirable as these turns arrive. The refusal to rethink two extant models of time may be one source of climate denialism and fascist danger today.

Planetary gradualism, then, is dead, but its afterlife survives in a variety of institutional projections and belief systems.

Today capitalist carbon emissions trigger numerous self-organizing planetary *amplifiers*, so that a warming event greatly exceeds the force of the triggers. We are well on the road to a cross-species crisis, with divergent ramifications in different regions. Institutional projections of the future institutionally embedded in neoliberal investments and decisions are thus profoundly at odds with the future the world actually faces; many workers, consumers, and white evangelicals entangled in those institutions also cling to old dreams to get through mortgage payments, weekly sermons, daily work, and the night.

The text thus commends the "improbable necessity" of a cross-regional politics of swarming: *improbable* because so many institutional pressures push against it, *necessary* because only such large, concerted, cross-regional actions can speak to the scope and urgency of the challenge. The *politics of swarming* involves moving *through* eco-role experiments in homes, schools, localities, the media, corporations, churches, universities, and cross-regional meetings, *into* renewed public protests and insurgencies in electoral politics, *to* cross-regional general strikes to press old capitalist states, particularly in Europe and America, to take militant corrective actions. Such cross-regional strikes would press capitalist states from inside and outside at the same time: A militant assemblage moving across several sites of action in different regions simultaneously. An improbable necessity.

The idea is to challenge both humanism and some variants of posthumanism with an *entangled humanism* that comes to terms with racial and regional modes of oppression and human entanglements with viruses, bacteria, plants, and larger planetary processes with variable degrees of autonomy. Entangled humanism, however, is not presented as a new universal that adherents of diverse theologies and humanisms must accept. It is offered as a contestable philosophy to be placed into productive conversations with other such orientations, to the extent they embrace the reasonable contestability of their creeds in the eyes of others, without too much existential resentment.

A key question explored is how to overcome the passive nihilism through which several constituencies today believe in climate warming and yet fail to act upon it. The surfeit of huge SUVs on American streets offers merely one sign of that condition. Sure, short-term self-interest is often involved. But the issue cuts more deeply, too, into widely held images of nature and time. Various theologians are intimately familiar with such a condition as it finds expression in the vagaries of religious faith. Nietzsche addresses the quandary, too.

To Nietzsche, passive nihilism arises when a constituency begins to acknowledge at a refined level of belief a difficult or disappointing phenomenon (it might be, say, the death of God, defects of human exceptionalism, capitalist dependence on colonial, race, and class exploitation, or the gallop of the Anthropocene). But *remains of old views still persist in embodied and cultural residues. You can *dramatize* those remains as if they whisper, "Yes, this is happening, but the world ought not to be that way." Nietzsche asks, "From whence comes that 'ought not to be'?" It comes, he suggests, from cloudy *remains* of old onto-theological and secular faiths roaming around in bodies and institutions even after the refined beliefs have been altered. The result encourages immobilization among some. It might also encourage others to slide toward a more aggressive nihilism, vociferously attacking those who issue an unacceptable message they themselves sense to be true.

So a crucial problem becomes how to combat passive nihilism during the age of the Anthropocene. Role experimentations—as one dimension of the politics of swarming—thus make a second entry, providing a place to start. The proliferation of new role adjustments in response to the Anthropocene does not merely produce minor, positive effects in the world; repetition of them in the company of others also helps to *recode the visceral register of cultural assumptions and dispositional priorities.* That, anyway, is how my early friends Dewey, Kaufman, Meisel, and Mannheim join forces with Nietzsche, Whitehead, Tsing, Bennett, Chakrabarty, and pragmatic neuroscientists to address passive nihilism amid the Anthropocene.

Chapter 6 pursues a series of intersections between ecological movements in old capitalist states, decolonial movements, and new work in the earth sciences. The idea is that during an era of eco-imperialism it is essential to fold findings from each of these orientations into the others, working to induce communication between them about the character of agency, time, and causality as you proceed.

• • •

The study has received some affirmative responses to date, including one symposium in *Contemporary Political Theory* (2019) and a lively conference on it at the Free University of Brussels in the fall of 2019. There have also been, though the conjunction is of course coincidental, a growing chorus of calls in several regions for general climate strikes. I am not yet far enough removed from the text to gain much critical perspective. I do know that the themes opened in Chapter 6 need further exploration. We inhabit a planet in which viruses, trees, rivers, desertification processes, snakes, volcanic ash, climate change, ethnic migrations, monsoon interruptions, nuclear waste, intense storms, white invaders, bacterial flows, and ocean acidification transcend territorial borders, often moving faster than heretofore. Classic demands for state sovereignty too readily foster repression today as old regimes strive to secure themselves violently against the very passages, flows, and currents they help to propagate. Drives to secure sovereign white nation-states escalate amidst such conditions, while successful movements to face the planetary must cross those boundaries.

You have not discussed the recent academic scene for the Krieger School at Hopkins. A new president of the school arrived in 2009. How receptive has he been to the sort of work pursued by people in critical theory and the humanities? How, if at all, does this academic administration speak to issues you and others in the school have been posing?

Those who teach in the humanities and theoretical disciplines in the Krieger School at Hopkins have been blessed with several privileges. Teaching loads are reasonable; salaries are good; many undergrads are increasingly interested in intellectual life; grad students are exceptional and highly motivated; and humanistically oriented faculty in several disciplines pursue connections across departments. Humanists at Hopkins have taken pride in the fact that the faculty has had a fair degree of autonomy with respect to appointments and tenure and has played a role in shaping the intellectual contours of the School.

Things went well in these respects when Dan Weiss, an art historian, and Adam Falk, a quantum physicist, were respectively deans of the Krieger School. They respected the intellectual enterprise and supported a fair degree of faculty autonomy. For example, I, as chair of political science for several years during the late 1990s, sought to make each sub-field within the department intersect closely with the others. The deans were attracted to that agenda, as were a majority of the faculty.

Several of these features, however, changed rapidly upon the arrival of President Ronald Daniels in 2009. The quick departure of Adam Falk to happier hunting grounds offered an early sign of what was in store. A 2005 book by Daniels on the rationality of voucher programs in several domains of public life could have provided another sign, had we read the book at the time. In that book citizens as consumers of private/public "voucher programs" assume primacy over citizens as active participants in public life. Little sense is conveyed, either, of the crisis tendencies periodically fomented by a neoliberal economy or the racial and class consequences of the spiritual alliance between white evangelicals and white neoliberals that had been in motion in the States for decades. It is a technocratic study. In general, Daniels opposes racism without addressing the social constellations and neoliberal premises that intensify it.

It became clear to faculty members committed to critical thought and participation in university governance what was in store when the new president commissioned, at the onset of his tenure, what we called *The Cole Report*, a report written by administrators from other schools who share the president's worldview.

The Cole Report is a document of CEO governance tethered to wealthy donors and a neoliberal economy. It seeks to bring diverse schools at Hopkins under central control and pretends that valuable innovation comes almost solely from the top. That latter assumption is ridiculous in its ahistoricism. But the authors are blind to that, in part because they narrowly frame what counts as useful. Neoliberal CEOs don't engage those who challenge their assumptions. They rather command them. They often, too, reek of a sense of special entitlement to autocratic power. After all, they are CEOs and they know best, no matter how many economic crises they and their types have helped to foment . . .

The agenda is to bring faculty in the humanities and social sciences, in particular, under the president's thumb. The president quickly appointed a new repressive dean to the Krieger School, whom the humanities faculty resisted for four years until a forum of chairs and the Faculty Assembly finally unseated her. Four of us had initially been commissioned to report details to the provost about her authoritarian conduct, but to no avail. I spoke at the key assembly meeting, along with several others, and called the question on the key motion. The motion against her won by a huge majority.

As we left the room that afternoon, I said to Siba Grovogui, a friend and highly reflective decolonial theorist, that I wished we had passed a motion of no confidence. It was so de facto, he said. Indeed, it was. It also became a sign to the central administration that the traditional standing of the Faculty Assembly and the Academic Council—the latter an elected faculty body in charge of tenure and appointments—must be curtailed more effectively. Word soon seeped out that the Daniels regime labeled the Faculty Assembly a group of "malcontents" and "anarchists"; perhaps he did not know that this is how autocrats around the world always characterize those who seek a real voice in self-governance. Several departments were placed under more direct assault, too. Daniels has spent the last several years accomplishing these goals.

Daniels brings a Hayek vision of the firm to university governance. Hayek, the consummate neoliberal, gave tremendous leeway to entrepreneurs because he held them to be founts of creativity regulated automatically by an impersonal market. He adamantly opposed, for instance, similar autonomy for labor unions, even if they had effective membership accountability through elections, which of course was not always the case. And he was extremely wary of popular social movements. Labor unions and social movements both upset the impersonal beauty of the market.

Daniels demands to be a CEO himself rather than a leader who welcomes robust participation by the faculty in university life. Since valuable innovation only comes from the top, in his view, he introduced well-funded "signature" programs that stole initiative from the faculty with respect to appointments, programs, tenure, curriculum, and intellectual agendas. Daniels is extraordinarily successful at raising funds and deploying them to increase his control over the curriculum and faculty in the humanities.

Trustees, most of whom share the neoliberal world vision of Daniels, love his inordinate success as a fundraiser. But many faculty, like me, find him to embody an *authoritarian naivete* that is widespread among neoliberals— authoritarian in its mode of institutional governance and naïve about the effects upon universities and the society at large of a neoliberal economy that both redistributes wealth, job security, and income upward and spawns periodic meltdowns.

The historic Humanities Center; the Women, Gender and Sexuality Program; Anthropology; and political theory have all suffered under this autocratic regime. Coincidentally, each contains faculty members who have stood up to the president at assembly meetings and elsewhere.

Much of this came to a head in 2019 when the Grand Innovator first rigged a university-wide committee to implement more centralized control over tenure decisions and, second, imposed an armed private police force on the Homewood campus. No faculty member from the humanities or social sciences at the Krieger School was appointed to the first committee. With respect to the armed private police force, 160 faculty members in the Krieger School signed a public letter explaining why it was a bad idea on the Home-wood campus—where liberal arts programs are located—because of the accidents that were apt to follow and the deleterious effects it would have on relations with neighboring communities. Seventy-six percent of students on the Homewood campus opposed this top-down innovation, too.

Students launched a sit-in at the central administration building when it became clear that administrative "consultation" on the police issue was a charade. Faculty, students, and surrounding community members joined several protests, with two of the marches closing with speeches in front of the president's house. He did not show the courage of a democratic leader to address the demonstrators. A few of us taught a grad class or two at the sit-in site after being petitioned by students to do so and asking our classes what they thought about such a shift in venue. I at first hesitated to do so because I prefer not to mix classroom activity and political action. But given the stakes and how Daniels thumbed his nose at Homewood students and faculty, it seemed wise to override this hesitation. We advised untenured faculty members to avoid participation in these events.

I sponsored one motion in the Faculty Assembly, calling upon the president to rescind the private police force decision. It passed by a large majority. Other stringent motions were passed, too. All were simply ignored by the administration. Again it percolated down to us that the assembly initiatives were said by many administrators to be passed by "malcontents" and "anarchists" among the faculty—exactly the choice of words autocrats in various regimes deploy whenever greater participation in governance is demanded. It was by then abundantly clear that the Assembly as a vehicle of faculty governance is incompatible with a CEO image of top-down rule. "Hopkins is One," the public relations poster announces everywhere on campus; the Grand Innovator is *the* One, it means.

When the long student sit-in became a lock-out in late spring of 2019, President Daniels called the Baltimore police to end it. A huge meeting of the Assembly was then convened, with the president invited to answer questions.

But, to me and most others in the hall that day, it was now crystal clear how traditional modes of self-governance among the liberal arts faculty are, to this regime, barriers to deflect, defame, and avoid, not respected institutions of deliberation and governance. Administrative gossip about how disorganized and unruly that last meeting was helped to feed that image to administrators and to a section of the faculty. Top-down structures are smooth, innovative, and rational, or so it appears, until they introduce disastrous innovations. All this was anticipated by *The Cole Report* solicited by a new president at the start of his tenure.

•••

Daniels would work to outflank faculty dissent with a vast team of publicity agents hired to swamp press announcements made by the faculty. The assembly would pass a motion and publicize it in the local paper; the president's publicity team would state that the vote represented a small minority of the entire university faculty (even when the vote was not taken by a university assembly but the much smaller liberal arts school).

Then one day the lid blew off. On May 19, 2020, François Furstenberg, a Hopkins professor of history, published a piece in the *Chronicle of Higher Education* entitled, "When University Leaders Fail." Using the response to the Covid-19 pandemic as its launching pad, after the president had unilaterally frozen retirement contributions from the administration, the piece claimed that President Daniels is a neoliberal who captures self-governance from the faculty, sets research and educational priorities governed by narrow values, takes unwise risks with the endowment, hires expensive administrative teams to enact and defend top-down policies, and fails to install the resilience needed to help steer a university through hard times. Here are a few things Furstenberg said to a national academic audience:

> Even as the AAUP and other organizations protest, the president has consolidated power in the hands of corporate executives, "who have

little understanding of the academic mission, increasingly make decisions behind closed doors, and execute them from above";

Besides announcing hiring freezes, etc., during the pandemic, "most extraordinarily of all it [the Hopkins president] suspended contributions to its employees' retirement";

The president announced the retirement freeze for academic and nonacademic employees without consulting self-organized employee unions and faculty;

His leadership team now "looks more like the C-Suite at a public university with two senior vice presidents, 12 vice presidents, an acting vice provost, a secretary and three senior advisers";

Besides the huge salary and benefits for the president, all told "the compensation of the 28 key employees in 2018 amounted to $29 million," ignoring the "deferred compensation" for them;

Before the pandemic, "the university began recklessly expensive building projects, including the purchase of a $372.5 million building in Washington D.C.";

Hopkins did not prepare for a crisis of this sort, "but a university is not a corporation that must maximize its profitability . . . , it is, or should be, an institution with far longer time horizons.[42]

Furstenberg's indictment is potent. In closing, he says, "Reform should begin at the top. At a time when major politicians are proposing that corporate boards include workers, it is astonishing how few university boards of trustees have seats for faculty, staff and students."[43] He could have added working-class and minority parents to that list, while calling for an academic revolution that returns more authority about curriculum and research priorities to the faculty.

This story continues. A vibrant faculty-community insurrection was finally able to get the president to back down on the private police force after questions about his management of the Covid pandemic and university expenditures became so prominent. The liberal arts school has finally created a faculty Senate to propose new policies and respond more actively to administrative actions. We leave the story here for now, however.

• • •

I concur with Furstenberg and appreciate how the autocratic policies of the Hopkins president have now received a wider public airing. It is also clear, however, that the events at Hopkins track trends very much in play today at most universities in the States and elsewhere. Hopkins had been a holdout against a few of them, but this very fact is repeatedly invoked against the faculty by the current president. We should follow "best practices" elsewhere, he says selectively, while binding new innovations to his control of donor funds and signature programs.

Neoliberal university presidents maintain accountability to rich donors and trustees, most of whom are themselves infused with a neoliberal ethos. Administrative staffs grow at a frightening pace, replete with moles assigned to take notes at faculty meetings; huge public relations teams manage relations with students, the public, faculty, and the media; more and more adjunct or contingent faculty members are hired with low pay and job insecurity; the university loses interest in critical liberal arts and participatory citizenship in a democracy; centralized administrative hegemony grows over academic matters previously governed by the faculty; and well-seeded routines of administrative gossip convey disdain for independent faculty members in ways that are not too distant from things Republican Party leaders say about the professoriate as a whole. A school president may explode at this or that faculty assembly, but the faculty is always expected to be "civil." Or servile.

Faculty members at numerous schools resist these trends. But it will take larger political movements to fortify the place of critical thought, creative faculty, and active students in the academy. The issue is not merely pertinent to the academy, either. For several decades, progressive social movements have been seeded by or extended in the academy. Think of Black civil rights, gay movements, women's rights, transgender movements, voting drives, ecological movements, living-wage movements, Black Lives Matter, anti-fossil fuel movements, and anti-war struggles. (Daniels, it must be noted, sidelined one student/faculty committee that advised curtailing fossil fuel use.) Participants in these counter movements seldom wear squeaky-clean suits, or convey an aura of deference to a CEO, or demand extreme entitlement for themselves. The male suit and tie themselves, recall, are adaptations from a military uniform.

Neoliberal images and demands seep into administrative presumptions of self-entitlement to support technocratic, authoritarian practices of program innovation, curriculum construction, and university governance. Horizontal processes of governance, discussion, and protest are too messy, uncertain, and uncontrollable for their taste—or regal sense of entitlement. I am confident that no administrator at Hopkins supports the neofascist right Trump has ignited and that still often parades under the label of populism. But that dangerous formation is itself in part a response to the barrenness of the neoliberalism preceding it and the periodic crises it spawns. Neoliberals in the university combine innocence about larger social processes with dogmatic claims about their own prerogatives. I wonder whether they realize how the hubris they carry in their briefcases helps to pave the way for the very state takeovers and anti-university drives they oppose.

The nub of the matter is perhaps this: Neoliberalism—with the authoritarian hubris of its elites, its demand for massive state subsidies of corporations and the military, its exploitation and discipline of university nonacademic employees, its focus on private philanthropy (controlled by the rich philanthropists) over public programs, and its outlandish faith in market rationality—periodically spawns regime crisis. An evangelical/neoliberal resonance machine in America exacerbates those tendencies, seeding neofascist responses to the very dislocations and crises it generates. How can research universities become beacons against such ugly social trends today, given their own dependence on wealthy donors, extensive involvement in military research, propensities to autocratic rule, demand for CEO salaries and special prerogatives, and engrained hostility to the messiness of democratic governance? Earlier propensities of many scholars in the academy writ large toward narrow professionalism are now returning with top-down vengeance to haunt both the university and its manifold relations to democracy.

5
The New Fascist Revolt

In the Prologue you told us that the recent death of your younger sister was a spur to the composition of this study. It inspired you to think more carefully about the complex layering of memory, its place in thinking, and the multiple ways events jostle memory and thinking. Perhaps you could discuss now what lessons you draw from her and how the two of you communed about life and politics?

Judy Beal died in the winter of 2019. Her experiences and insights are relevant to the topic now under exploration. I will let her speak in her own voice soon from the brief memoir she bestowed late in life upon her son and daughters about her early years.

By the time Judy reached middle age she had passed through youth as a gymnast, attended nursing school, raised three sweet kids with her husband, Bob, risen from being a nurse for several years to becoming financial officer of a medical facility, created temporary refuges for young teens in the area when their family scenes cracked, participated actively in local Democratic Party politics, helped to raise a lovely granddaughter, and served as an ebullient role model for everyone who knew her—very much including her older brother. Judy increasingly reminded me of our mother as the years passed.

In middle age her health took a series of bad turns. She became diabetic. Her kidney then failed. Her son, Darren, donated a kidney to her. The transplant surgery did not go well; then, after an endless period of uncertainty, the new kidney began to function. Several years later, that transplant died. She went through five years of dialysis, with her husband, Bob, learning the delicate task of managing a dialysis machine at home several hours at a time, four days a week. They even secured a portable unit to use on vacations. Miraculously, after five years on dialysis, a second, anonymous transplant became available. It took, for a while. A few years later amputation of a toe was required, followed by amputation of the lower left leg, and eventually an amputation higher on the same leg. Now the dynamic woman was confined to a wheelchair.

Those years were marked by several near-death events, with the woman saved each time by her drive to life, a close-knit family, and local nurses and doctors devoted to the well-known former nurse. I met several of the latter during times I rushed to Flint when survival was in doubt. When we were ushered into the recovery room after the last amputation, I reported to Judy that this time the surgeon was optimistic about recovery. "Is that true, Tiffany?" the highly medicated woman asked. "Yes," her daughter said, "this surgery worked, mom." Tiffany was the one Judy interrogated whenever she needed the straight scoop. Bob, Janelle, Darren, and I were less trustworthy.

Three years later, Judy died after yet another amputation was required for the other leg and could not be performed because of the bodily trauma it would generate. The options had congealed into a bind. Now the question, for her, was not whether there is life after death but how to live now with the loved ones who will remain after her death. On her last night, under hospice care at home, she asked that the young grandchildren be allowed to run up and down the hallway so she could hear sounds of their vitality.

I review these last grim years for at least two reasons. First, Judy maintained magnificent composure and care for others during the last decade of her life. She remained a model to her husband, children, grandchildren, brother, in-laws, and innumerable friends, teaching us how to manage ourselves and care for others when health takes a series of bad turns. Or at least how we might *try* to emulate the model she presented. She wanted urgently to live; she was a fount of wisdom and care for others; and she died with as much grace as one can muster when the bodily drive to live encounters other failing bodily systems.

My desire to compose these reports crystallized several months after her death, though friends had previously suggested such a project. The death of the last loved one with whom you shared childhood events proliferates memories. Some arrive at night during dreams, others when an old smell, sound, or image returns to spur a flood of affect-soaked memories, others yet when you awaken suddenly at night and find yourself in the middle of a reverie. Death of a *younger* loved one conveys acute versions of those experiences. "An hour Is not merely an hour. It Is a vase full of scents and sounds and projects and climates, and what we call reality Is a certain connection between these immediate sensations and the memories which envelop us simultaneously with them—a connection that Is suppressed within a simple cinematographic vision."[1] Woe onto him or her who records memories merely as "snapshots." Their thinking, joys, and empathies may thereby suffer.

Memory can either congeal or become fantastical when torn loose from moorings others have provided it. Not merely do recollections lose the anchors of commonality and continuities of friendly contestation, the tacit awareness by intimate others of your gestures, dispositions, humor, gait, speech patterns, and facial quirks is lost, too. You may stop in your tracks when you encounter a stranger whose facial expression or gesture calls forth something about your sister you hadn't noted when she was alive. A gesture experienced at two different times: once amid bare consciousness of it, later when it sharpens memories of another time.

When such living pivots melt down it is wise, perhaps, to write them up, to encourage them to play positive roles in life rather than to sink into sealed vessels or slink into other darker places awaiting them. Mine the positive kernels immured in grief. There would be no grief without these kernels. A previous event is called up now in a new situation. Two events, separated by an interval of time, are now tethered together through resonance. Time regained. That is one reason to invoke Judy's life.

• • •

A second reason is that during her late convalescence Judy and I talked regularly about the political convulsions in Michigan and America during the long Clinton/Trump campaign of 2016. She found local white working men known to her as long-term Democrats to be sorely tempted by Trump, with most finally jumping to him. She found how difficult it was to call anyone back once that leap was taken. One verification of the tendency, and difficulty, occurred when she tried to organize—in the midst of illness—a Democratic election night party of the sort she and Bob had regularly hosted at their house on the eve of a presidential election. Sorry, she was told by loving friends—many of whom poured out to honor her during the packed and joyous memorial service a year and a half later—we now support Trump and cannot come this year. In most instances—but not all—husbands and wives turned together toward the salmon-faced man bellowing belligerent, violent rhetoric. Many were inclined to encourage him to blow things up.

• • •

I close this vignette on my younger sister with a few quotations from her memories of our early family days. The text from which the quotes are extracted was composed by Judy in 2007. Her daughters had pestered her to write it; they located it among her belongings after Chapter 2 of this book was sent to them.

Judy and I were ten years apart. The terse formulations, to me, reveal a nurse's matter-of-fact attitude toward life infused with existential gratitude for its abundance.

The first recorded memory, at the age of three: "My brother rode his bicycle every day up and down the steep hills on the streets and he was 'so clever in my eyes' that he had playing cards hooked on the spokes of the bike to sound like a motorcycle. . . . One day he finally let me get on the back of the bike. Since I was a barefooted little brat, it was quite an injury when my heel got caught in the spokes as he was speeding downhill. I remember crying and seeing blood, but mostly I remember how badly my brother felt and how much compassion he had for me." {There was a lot of shame and guilt in that compassion. . . .}

"Finally when I was three years old we began preparations to build a house at 3427 Ellis Park Drive, which was on a dead end road in Burton. I was sure we were rich now to get out of the city! Watching my dad and Bill work on the house was exciting. They finally let me be their 'nail girl.' {The house was actually a newly constructed shell when we moved in; we added pine floors, wallboard, woodwork, plumbing, septic tank, and drainage field, etc., as we inhabited it.}

"Our vacations were earned. We often went to Traverse City to tent in a park while my dad was working. . . . Then after a week my dad would arrive and bring food to cook Irish Stew." {We did that once. . . .}

"When I was about six, two men from Hills Ambulance Company came to our house to tell us kids that our parents had been in a horrible accident. They took Bill and Sue to the hospital with them. That accident changed our lives forever. Before my mom came home, I was bounced around to various relatives I barely knew for a few months. . . ."

"He (our dad) came home, limping and had brain damage with loss of memory, but was kind as a kitten. We became friends since he could not work, and I was told it was my job to help him know what was going on." {When he could drive again, she was allowed to go to the store with him.}

"My mother always made sure I had an extra dime (for phone calls) with me, which she taped on the back of a little mirror in my purse. . . ."

"Becoming a gymnast occupied my life from age 9 to 15 or 16. Bill's girlfriend, Inez Caon, took me to Mott College to join gymnastics at a higher level. . . . My mom sat watching me five days a week in the gym for about two hours a day."

"My brother Bill was twenty and I was ten when he was in college. I often interrupted his studying to start wrestling with him. As soon as I realized I could not win the scuffle I would start screaming for mom and tell her Billy would not leave me alone. Always she answered, 'Come on, Bill, leave your little sister alone,' and I was victorious again!"

When she was eighteen, and our mother died suddenly: "I was going to college to be a nurse but was so depressed by my mother's death that I dropped out and took a job at McClaren hospital as a clerk in the emergency room. . . . I was also pretty proud that I taught my dad how to become more independent. He was a doll and did everything that I said. I left a note in his pocket most days so he could remember where I was and what he should do."

•••

Marcel contends, after rehearsing a lifetime of lost loves and deaths of others woven into his life, that an accumulation of minor and major losses helps to prepare you to accept your own death. I agree at least that such an accumulation filters into the soul, affecting how you relate to others and respond to the prospect of your death. But there is no certainty what turns the events will set into motion. You play your last basketball game in middle age, setting aside skills crafted over the years about strategy, passing instinctively, keeping the shooting elbow in on your jump shot, and so on, facing a minor grief of setting those carefully crafted accumulations to the side. You lose a charismatic father and become a tutor of sorts to the new man he becomes. You lose a girlfriend to another and must adapt oh so quickly to single life. You teach your last class after devoting decades to nurturing the multifarious skills and care involved in teaching. You resist wars concocted out of imperial falsehoods. Your parents die. Your sister struggles with the end of life amid loved ones who desperately want her to stay. Such events are outstripped by facing a holocaust or sensing the possible end of the civilization that nurtured you as you increasingly came to see the injustices and denials upon which it was built, events such as a war, racist attacks by the police, the shock of the Anthropocene, a fall into homelessness, a pandemic lock-down, the return of aspirational fascism, or the organization of an insurrection.

The most one can say, perhaps, is that minor, major, and catastrophic events pose challenges as you work through the griefs, joys, and surprises they engender. You might mine positive existential energies from a few . . . , or one may overwhelm you so that a drive to existential revenge takes over . . . , or you may withdraw into contemplation . . . , or sink into resignation. Such events are manifold; they bristle with multiple possibilities as they slide and bump into dispositions and reflective judgments already there. Can you transfigure the anticipatory grief accompanying acceleration of the Anthropocene, for instance, into positive political energy? What about the vicissitudes of aging? Can awareness of the suffering imposed on the world by the recurrent politics of existential revenge—what Nietzsche calls *ressentiment*—foster more intensive cultivation of positive existential responses? Can you help to transmit such a temper to students and other constituencies you engage? What about the models of intellect and activism you admire? Is it possible to emulate them more fully? Such issues are not entirely settled until death do us part.

One dilemma is that as the tests accumulate in number, type, and intensity the reserve available to respond positively to them declines. That trajectory, too, needs to be folded into self-understanding and intellectual arts of the self. That is another reason that Judy provides a sterling exemplar to those who knew her. I think that these issues are important ethically and politically because, circulating inside the more proximate causes of the rampant denialisms in America with respect to the 2020 election results, racism, climate change, and the pandemic is another denialism; it takes the form of an operational refusal to come to terms affirmatively with how death itself sets a condition of life. This is a collective spiritual issue Nietzsche may have grasped above all others, though leading theologians also struggle with it. The issue infects spiritual cohorts as well as individuals, as members of the cohort respond to one another through bodily patterns of expression. Attention to the issue must be folded into readings of class, race, gender, and creedal dimensions of exploitation and insecurity marking the current age. To use the term "spirituality" in the way I do is not to invoke an ontology of idealism: it is to transfigure old, reductive materialisms until they can house the theme of spiritual cohorts partly defined by the distinctive drives they share, the cluster of hopes and resentments they house, the aspirations they pursue, and the visceral modes of communication they adopt.

• • •

Our early family experiences in Flint informed conversations Judy and I had in person and on the phone during the long 2016 electoral campaign, convincing both of us that Trump had a much better chance to win that election than polls suggested, the media asserted, and most political scientists opined. Some of my colleagues, when I voiced these worries, wondered whether I understood how election polls work. I did know that people sometimes lie to upper-middle-class pollsters when they sense that their grievances come across to them as minor or unworthy. I could also spot candidates who do not know how to speak to the hopes and grievances of white working-class people. In other respects, I had myself fallen rather out of touch with the shifting character of those latter experiences.

Judy and I worried about a Trump victory; we were upset when Hillary Clinton failed to campaign much in Michigan, Wisconsin, or Ohio. We increasingly thought she did not know how to do so, even though Bill Clinton and Barack Obama had campaigned effectively in those states. We knew that many white people who bought the Trump bill of goods would suffer after his election and that many of those he raged against would suffer much more. Until late in the day neither of us knew that Russia had organized massive invasions into the election: publicizing stolen democratic party emails, lobbying anonymously for African Americans to stay home, and priming white workers to define immigrants and other minorities as enemies. We soon caught on, even as we understood that a history of American interventions into other states was itself problematic. We did not form legal judgments about the Russian intervention and the Trump collusion. Rather, we forged evidence-rich political judgments of the sort citizens must make in appraising a candidate for election, a political appointment, a judicial appointment, or administrator of a university. People who channel too much political interpretation into legal processes take too narrow a view of democratic citizenship. Think of all those legal commentators on MSNBC who told us just to wait until the Mueller Report was completed.

•••

You have published two short books recently, Aspirational Fascism *(2017) and* Climate Machines, Fascist Drives, and Truth *(2019). It is possible to guess how they grow out of confluences between your early life and recent events. Can you tell us a bit about how they indeed unfolded? Had you yourself lost contact, in the sanctity of a private university, with class experiences pertinent to that election? Also, since some early critics charged you with unwarranted optimism in your earlier work, don't the recent studies show how your orientation has undergone a sea change in that respect? I mean, you seem to say now that the United States faces the danger of a new kind of fascism. And you seem to think that too many constituencies have waited too long to respond to the acceleration of climate change. Do you see, finally, how you have entered the age of pessimism? How, in your view, are we to respond during such a bleak era?*

I will get to your questions in good time. During six or seven summers after Judy's illnesses became severe the large family clan—nineteen or twenty of us—would gather together in a large house for a week on this or that crystalline lake in the northwestern part of the lower peninsula in Michigan, not far from that state park near Traverse City and the music camp at which I had once worked and that my two children later attended as campers. Judy loved those excursions; so did the rest of us. Occasionally we would stop at the Cherry Hut nearby, a place "world famous" for its cherry pie. It says so on the door.

One night, as the others ordered pie to finish off a meal, I asked the waitress if it was feasible to prepare a small cheese plate for me—my anti-diabetic diet ruled out pie. The nice teenager returned a few minutes later with two saltine crackers and two pieces of Kraft processed cheese. As I stared down at the plate, the table broke into uproarious laughter. A pseudo-polished Easterner, who now loved *epoisse*, was now encountering a half-forgotten fragment of the past staring up at him. Teasing ensued, especially from Jane, Judy, David, and Debbie. All the young children found the wisecracks of this foursome to be inordinately funny. Pretensions were pierced. Photos of the cheese and saltine plate were snapped—a self-styled sophisticate captured in broad daylight teetering precariously between two worlds: *Kraft* and *Epoisse*. I enjoyed the saltines. . . .

• • •

Fast forward to an event in the summer of 2016 when Jane, Judy, and I dropped into that same café to take a break from the sun, water, kayaks, pontoon, and kids. Judy loved those evening pontoon boat rides, with sunsets augmented by wine and *Epoisse* courtesy of her East Coast brother. I quote a fragment from the opening two pages of *Aspirational Fascism* (2017):

It was the middle of July, 2016. Hillary Clinton was riding high, and the media had not yet entirely overcome the drive to reduce the campaign of Donald Trump to a humorous series of mix-ups, histori-cal mistakes, tweet misspellings, and name callings. My sister, my partner, and I stopped at a café in the northwestern part of the lower peninsula of Michigan; we had been vacationing there with a large family entourage on one of those gorgeous lakes where the white sand runs thick, the water is clear, and the sunsets are stunning. . . . Politics was not on our minds that day as my two companions and I settled down to enjoy the pie the cheery Hut had made famous in the region. . . . Five working-class vacationers walked into the café, sitting a table away from us. The alpha-male wore a severe look, a baseball cap and an aggressive T-shirt; he spoke in short, definitive phrases. I grew up as a working-class boy in an urban, southern part of that state speckled with the type. Some of us made fun of that definitive de-meanor behind their backs from time to time, though we also had a sense of the pain and authoritarian discipline that contributed to their way of being. We had dads, uncles, barbers, coaches, and neigh-bors. . . . For fifteen minutes the alpha-male explained in no nonsense terms why it was absolutely necessary to defeat Hillary Clinton and elect Donald Trump. . . . There was no disagreeing with this guy; three of his partners showed no interest to do so. One woman tried to dissent mildly from time to time. "I hear what you are saying," she would say, "and I have no truck with Hillary, but doesn't Trump scare you a little sometimes?" "No," the man would blurt. "He is *exactly* what we need today!" . . . Besides, peeking just below that alpha-male bravado were vulnerabilities that doubled the hesitancy his compan-ions showed in dissenting from him. An aggressive, domineering, vulnerable man.[2]

The diatribe was still in full swing as we left the Cherry Hut. We were both shaken and amused—the first because the battery of sharp word punches still reverberated in our guts, the second because the verbal punches were free of evidence. My two companions teased me for not responding to the guy. I replied that Judy was in a wheelchair and I was too much of a coward to stir up a fight. The three of us departed that café even more concerned than before that Trump had a very decent chance to win the election. The intensity at that table had been palpable. As I said in a blog post a week or so later, favorable demographics do not guarantee victory if the other side stirs up enough belligerent intensity and produces high voter turnout as key parts of your own base become discouraged.

Aspirational Fascism: The Struggle for Multifaceted Democracy under Trumpism (2017), grew out of a seminar announced in August of 2016 for the spring term: the decision to announce that course before the election

grew out of dark premonitions Judy Beal and I had shared for several months.

The book, written in white heat over a five-month period, starts by comparing the rhetorical style Hitler elaborated in *Mein Kampf*[3] and practiced as the Führer to the style enacted by Donald Trump. The two social movements—in Germany and the United States—differ profoundly. But the rhetorical styles of these two figures display remarkable affinities. What makes a large section of the white populace so susceptible to it today? The text acknowledges that many high rollers and Republican operatives are devoted to the movement out of short-term self-interest and lack of concern for the collective future. But it focuses on an evangelical wing of the white working and middle class that buys into it intensely.

As the insecurity of this class has grown with deindustrialization and the decline of labor unions, it is caught in a bind between the noble pluralizing drives of the democratic left on one side and neoliberal magnifications of wealth, income inequality, authoritarianism at work, job insecurity, and wage stagnation on the other. It is trapped in a pincer movement. This bind tempts many white workers to pay even more heed than heretofore to a virulent movement that blames migrants of color, liberals, African Americans, and other minorities for the troubles it faces. White triumphalism is its coat of arms. Trump inhabits a rhetorical niche within that bind to capture an enlarged segment of this class, particularly white evangelicals but extending out beyond them. He also reaches out to whites in other classes who are drawn to the spirituality of *ressentiment* he spouts, or pulled by class greed, or called by both.

One problem is that the Democratic Party had neglected for decades to link its slow support of pluralizing drives to major efforts to reduce economic inequality in general, to reshape the costly infrastructure of consumption, and to protect job security. Other constituencies—Amerindians and urban African Americans most notable among them—have suffered much longer and more profoundly than the constituency solicited by Trump. But the bind of the white working class made it ripe for the taking. Moreover, well-heeled academics and journalists who ignore or explain away white working-class grievances look callous to them, especially when it becomes clear how seriously the former take their own grievances by comparison. We face troubles, but our jobs are often better than wages.

One question becomes, *How* do neofascist strategies work under such conditions of constituency stress and cultural resentment? Drawing upon the work of a maverick German sociologist, Klaus Theweleit (*Male Fantasies*),[4] the text argues that media neglect and specific bodily stresses in work and family life prime this constituency to absorb Trumpian tactics. Theweleit's summary of how an early modern ballet *insinuates* a message of class hierarchy, royal power, and male authority into the bodily dispositions and proclivities of viewers is illuminating. Sure, representation is important to life. "But more is involved too. The tight choreography of male and female bodies *enacts* an intensive, rhythmic organization of muscles, movements, brain activities, eye contacts and hormonal secretions that fold specific relations of authority, exoticization, and subordination into bodily habits, instincts, and routines of desire."[5] Viewers of such a performance do not merely watch it. "Simulations of these bodily movements are folded, if prior susceptibility to them is operative, into the bodily practices and modes of relational attunement of viewers during the performance."[6] If you are a tennis player or dancer, attend occasionally to your own mini-bodily *simulations* as you watch a tennis match or dance performance. Our bodies are absorbent machines, replete with synthesizing powers drawn from internalized dispositions congealed from past influxes, rhetorical practices, and bodily rhythms. It is the resonances between congealed dispositions, rhetorical practices, and disruptive events that do the work.

Trump's rhetorical practice—with its harsh repetition of words, gestures, facial grimaces, intense accusations, Big Lies, aggressive pointing, and exaggerated intonations—insinuates itself into the hormonal secretions, gaits, rhythms of conduct, facial habits of expression, vocal patterns, and memory-laden perceptions of those already primed to absorb it. It becomes contagious. Enthusiastic audiences don't always *believe* everything he says; many rather become attached to the *pegs* upon which he hangs their anxieties, grievances, prejudices, and hostilities. Belief, after all, is a layered, many-splendored thing. That is why Trump, the text anticipates, will run a continuous campaign after the election.

The study argues against, first, neoliberalism in its soft and hard versions, second, the sufficiency of liberal notions of rights not well attuned to economic inequality and pluralization, and third, any socialist model that invokes a unified collectivity to foster rapid growth and dominate nature. The first, in its alliance with white evangelicals, fomented conditions for the emergence of Trumpism. Indeed, American liberalism itself has become too infected with neoliberal dispositions—as the Hillary Clinton campaign displayed so well.

Egalitarian pluralism is presented as the best antidote to Trumpism and hope for the future, *if* it includes drives to curtail job insecurity, to improve social programs for workers, and to rework the compensatory hypermasculinity that Trumpism courts and exacerbates. This movement must acquire a broad cultural bandwidth: it must become installed *both* on the visceral register of cultural relations—the register liberal publicists and academics often ignore or misinterpret—*and* on the more reflective registers of cultural life. Both. The ideal of a multifaceted, pluralist, egalitarian, ecological polity needs refinement, for sure. But it has now become an improbable necessity to pursue.

The multilayered processes through which alpha-masculine drive complexes are forged by football teams, fraternities, authoritarian workplaces, action films, male gossip, police forces, and military codes also need attention. The counter-need to forge positive modes of affective communication—a positive ethos of engagement between diverse constituencies—has also become urgent. Why? Because "there is never a vacuum on the visceral register of cultural life." And that register plays an important role in the tenor of inter-constituency relations. It is thus not *if* or *when* the visceral dimension comes into play but by *what means*, to *which ends*, and with *what intensities*. Deliberative models of democracy remain relevant, but they are radically insufficient. A wideband, pluralist democracy must find expression not only in electoral politics but also in the spiritual ethos of family life, schooling, the organization of consumption, local leadership, corporations, work life, films, blogs, social movements, policing, military life, and electoral campaigns. The contemporary danger of fascism underlines such lessons. Indeed, fascist movements deploy institutions of democracy—election campaigns, media, police forces, bureaucracies, executive actions—against the ethos of democracy.

So, the book closes by presenting a positive ideal of pluralist, egalitarian democracy, one that works at multiple sites and on two cultural registers, as it strives to overcome extractive capitalism. It is not the most likely combination, of course. It is not even certain how all those elements can fit together. It is merely the formation essential to the rehabilitation of democracy during an age when democracy is placed at risk.

I reiterate the question. Haven't you now become a pessimist, dropping the mood and tone governing your earlier work? If so, that requires justification, too. Also, Freud already grasped what you call affective contagion. It seems essential to consult him on these questions. Moreover, to sort these issues out you must respond directly to those who think current movements in several countries are better understood as populist than fascist movements? Surely (2020) Trumpism is irreducible to Nazism, even in "aspiration."

Let's turn to the second issue first. In *Group Psychology and the Ego*, Freud links authoritarian modes of mass contagion to two things: first, to "memory traces" of alpha male monopoly of sexual relations in prehistoric hordes, when young males excluded from sexual pleasure finally killed the domineering father and then internalized intense guilt for having done so.[7] The emergence of alpha males in positions of authority in modern life spark fragments of these memories; they can spur desires to obey the ruler by imposing suffering on those below you in the social structure.

Freud's anthropology is important because he thinks carefully about how influences slide into the unconscious. But I am wary of its invocation of a primal horde, even if the theme is held to *fabulate* tendencies that would otherwise be obscured without the fabulation. I take a drive to be a purposive impulsion bodily implanted through previous cultural experiences. Drives are real forces in life, then, but their character and intensities are closely bound to cohort embodiment of specific cultural histories in societies divided by class, race, religion, and so on. So different cohorts in the same society often internalize rather different drive complexes, each equipped with specific modes of intercommunication through styles of walking, facial contours, sense of humor, modes of intonation, and so on. Contending spiritual constituencies, if you will, invade cultural life.

It can now be seen how a political constituency could be mostly anchored in a specific class or creed but also draw many outside those social positions into it because the parties communicate spiritual affinities across those differences in subject position. Any viable interpretation of fascism or democracy must, I think, come to terms with such connections across class, gender, and race, identifying cohorts who have come to share spiritual affinities—that is, to share existential affinities of orientation to the world. The turn by a minority of Black males to Trump in the 2020 election helps to teach that lesson.

Also, the very embodied and layered character of cultural drives/spiritual cohorts means that it does not suffice to ground ethical life in higher deliberative processes alone, as Freud himself was tempted to do to ward off the dangers of fascist contagion. Since affective communication, to him, primarily flows from autocrats to masses, he wants to minimize that mode of communication. I agree with Nidesh Lawtoo in *(New) Fascism*, however.[8] The affective, visceral register of culture must be activated and enlivened democratically if democracy is to thrive.

Democracy, then, must find expression at multiple sites and on at least two registers of cultural experience. There is much to learn from Freud about the unconscious, but I emphasize less how unconscious, purposive strivings are grounded partly in primordial traces from a primal horde and more how they emerge from resonances between past encounters, current anxieties, and new situations. Neither a language-soaked, intersubjective image of culture nor a notion of generic drives, then, *suffices* to the dynamic, visceral dimension of democratic culture. If Freud was moved to overcome what I call the effects of the visceral register by pursuing refined ethical precepts, I contend that fascism and democracy—though in very different ways—both draw sustenance from the visceral and refined registers of cultural life in tandem. That's why the vitality of pluralist democracy, if it is to be, must find expression in a wideband ethos of family life, schools, work life, corporate practices, localities, policing, the military, churches, and rhetorical practices, as well as in electoral politics and governmental institutions. A wideband democratic culture is fragile in part because it must find expression on both the reflective and visceral dimensions of culture and be manifest on both the macro- and micro-dimensions of politics. Democracy is fragile today partly because its course is increasingly at odds with new turns in capitalism and partly because its nurturance involves work on different registers at the same time. The emergence of aspirational fascism out of democratic practices teaches us a lot about the requirements of democracy itself.

•••

That being said, it might appear, as you charge, that the two recent studies exude a new aura of pessimism. I do not read the difference exactly that way, however. I construe both optimism and pessimism to be spectatorial in orientation, when what is needed are action-oriented perspectives infused with care and positivity under new, rough conditions. Further, my hunch is that several theorists who now write under the star of pessimism, despair, the negative, or nihilism continue to react to their existential disappointment that the larger nonhuman world is not as predisposed as they had previously assumed to either capitalist or socialist projects of world mastery. So, democratic socialism, too, needs to be reworked under new conditions of being. Disappointment following such existential shocks can readily morph into pessimism as you come to resent viscerally the shaky place of humanity in the cosmos. This is the way of the world, you may assert explicitly, while a cloudy Double from the past whispers back, "But it ought not to be that way." The second voice—the Double—expresses visceral remainders of an ontology you now reject on the more refined registers of belief but have not reworked all the way down. Immobilization and pessimism reflect an impasse between these two registers. It is the Double that must be worked upon.

So while it is true that old capitalist states are locked into self-defeating and destructive agendas for the future and that it is hard to discern new energies sufficient to put things on the right track, the task of the intellectual still includes identifying improbable necessities and seeking ways to enact them. The point, then, is this: White, affluent people over fifty in old capitalist states have no right to despair. It is our task to reorganize old Doubles and to respond as intelligently as possible to threats posed by fascism, imperialism, racism, and the Anthropocene. Pessimism, too, can be a mode of self-indulgence.

Part of the problem resides in a widespread existential insistence that the nonhuman world *must be* highly predisposed to human mastery, a disposition embedded in the institutional priorities of capitalism. And the organic image traditionally wheeled out to challenge this disposition also encounters weekly body blows from wildfires, floods, droughts, and hurricanes intensified by the Anthropocene. The quest now is to affirm ties to a world that fits neither the myth of human mastery nor that of organic belonging, as you struggle intelligently and militantly to reconstitute extractive capitalist institutions organized meticulously around the forlorn project of mastery. You now acknowledge a nature more "wild, arbitrary, fantastic, disorderly and surprising" than it has appeared in most modern categories and debates.[9] You become ready, for instance, to reform both the infrastructure and ethos of consumption in old capitalist states, doing so to replace automobiles as primary modes of transportation as you also rethink housing design, modes of energy use, dominant diets, and a million other things.

• • •

Earlier books of mine, from at least *The Ethos of Pluralization* on, projected possible fascist responses to established democracies unless the social projects of diversification, class equalization, and a positive ethos of engagement were pursued together. That claim was soon joined to the contention that unless radical steps were launched to respond to the Anthropocene in cross-regional ways, the danger of fascism would grow. The positive responses needed soon became defined as "improbable necessities," *improbable*, again, because massive work on multiple fronts is required to enact them, and *necessary* because the danger grows with each delay in doing so. Aspirational fascism, indeed, thrives on such delays. Neoliberal capitalism is the major source of these dangers, along with the dangerous political spiritualities it foments. We will not, however, arrive home free even today if it is overcome. Old collectivist ideals of productivism must be reworked, too. That is why I support an interim agenda now: a cross-regional politics of swarming and the interim policy agendas pursued by it.

• • •

Realism in its dominant mode in the American academy, at least, proceeds by appraising existing approaches to a problem and adopting one with a high degree of probable acceptance. C. Wright Mills, writing about the dangers of nuclear war in the 1960s, labeled such proponents "crackpot realists." Their unrealism resides in a refusal to forge responses proportionate to the severity of the danger.

A "visionary realist," on the other hand, as Bonnie Honig defines the phrase, appraises salient *dangers* of the day and then devises *possibilities* that could speak to them if undertaken.[10] For many old realists have not caught on to how volatile planetary forces exacerbate the effects of capitalist exploitation. Visionary realists fold the urgency of time into their appraisals and proposals. We work to make the needed responses more probable. The old idealist/realist debates need to be redefined under contemporary conditions of being.

You speak of those who aspire to fascism and the danger of fascism. That has sometimes seemed like an overstatement to many—an exaggeration that borders on the hysterical. Many have come to terms with recent turns in several democratic states to the right by addressing the danger of populism. Does not such a lens of analysis suffice? It may even be dangerous to overstate contemporary dangers.

Yes, shortly after *Aspirational Fascism* appeared, a spate of essays and books came out addressing Trumpism and associated movements elsewhere under the title of "populism." Two examples of that genre are Steven Levitsky and Daniel Ziblatt, *How Democracies Die*, and Federico Finkelstein, *From Fascism to Populism in History*.[11] There are valuable points in each text. But I diverge from both on key counts, including their demands to replace the language of fascism with that of populism. Note that in a profound earlier text, *The Great Transformation*, Karl Polanyi identified thirteen or fourteen fascist movements that arose in Europe and the Americas during the Great Depression.[12] He explored shifts in the global order—especially the worldwide Great Depression—that propelled such movements. And he refused to allow the horrendous particularities of the Nazi regime to monopolize the term "fascism." I also note how few authors today invoking the label "populism" really address either the global severity of the Anthropocene or how these new revolts belligerently deny it. My thinking, indeed, is much closer to that of Nidesh Lawtoo in *(New) Fascism*. He emphasizes the role that affective communication plays in fascist movements, in which political mobilization works on the visceral and more refined registers of cultural life simultaneously and how the specter of the Anthropocene can work on both registers.

My views on this question were initially elaborated a year after *Aspirational Fascism* appeared in a symposium on How Democracies Die in *Perspectives on Politics* (December 2018) and a post in *The Contemporary Condition* entitled "Populism or Fascism?"[13] The contentions to follow extend those themes.

First, the term "populism" tends to paint Left- and Right-wing movements with the same brush, leaving only moderate liberal movements in the center as viable. But long-term liberal neglect of egalitarian proposals that animate left populism helped to prime democratic regimes for racist, fascist revolts. It is also true that movements in the 1930s called themselves fascist while the new ones usually do not. But the new movements do not call themselves racist or misogynist, either. Nor do their leaders call themselves ruthless narcissists. The new stealth movements at first avoid public identification with the very histories they reignite under new conditions. Movements the first time around did not have to avoid the later associations. It is further pertinent to note that Nazism was the most extreme expression of fascism in the 1930s, but in fact numerous social movements in several countries paraded under the label of fascism without falling into the unique pit of Nazism.

Second, fascist movements in several countries during the 1930s did eliminate competitive elections when possible. That is, to many commentators today, a master fact that separates populist movements now from old fascist movements. Such a master line of division, however, no longer holds. The Trump juggernaut, for instance, mobilizes powerful drives to suppress voting of vulnerable minorities such as Muslims, African Americans, the poor, and Amerindians; it conspires with Russia to engineer domestic elections; it accepts massive infusions of dark money from the donor class; it aligns itself at the hip with powerful right-wing media; it spreads fake news and Big Lies systematically while accusing its opponents of doing so; and it seeks to bring courts, intelligence agencies, and the Republican party fully under its control. The *aspiration* of the Trump movement, and others like it, is to retain scraps of electoral legitimacy while stripping elections of broad representation. These are movements, then, that would eliminate elections if they could get away with it. Aspirational fascism, in the early going, is stealth fascism.

Third, proponents of a populist reading tend to discount how capture in the early 1980s of the Republican Party by an evangelical/neoliberal machine in America exacerbated white triumphalism, planted seeds of economic crisis, attacked public schooling, closed many white, black, and brown workers out of the gains of economic growth, promulgated fictional theories of the economy, and helped to inspire white spiritual migrations toward Trumpism. These accounts indeed underplay the role spiritual and existential shifts can play in politics, because spiritual movements do not mesh well with the secular terms of analysis they often adopt. The issues of today are electoral, governmental, economic, and spiritual at the same time; they are not merely electoral and governmental, as critics of populism tend to think.

Fourth, if you yourself deprecate the *bifocal* character of democracy—as critics of left populism do—you are apt to pretend that a return to elite protection of old guardrails will suffice to save democracy. But that route promotes a return to the very conditions that helped to foment fascist revolts in the first place. *Bifocal* democracy, however, invokes both representational politics *and* periodic social movements to place selective pressure on old guardrails to promote diversity and reduce inequality. Democracy is thus essentially bifocal. There would not have been historic advances by labor, African Americans, gays, lesbians, transgender people, ecology, and non-Christian religious minorities if the second rail of democratic culture did not periodically disrupt the first. Today you must either attach egalitarianism to minority social movements or crouch in a defensive posture to protect old guardrails. Black Lives Matter, feminist movements, the Occupy movement, transgender movements, climate strikes, public unionization, and urban police reform campaigns exemplify recent social movements that express the bifocal character of democracy. Unifocal democracy in a neoliberal culture, again, sows the seeds of fascist revolt.

Fifth, Trump's violent drive to ignite a coup after the election of 2020 blew populist readings of Trumpism out of the water. It involved racist drives to overturn by any means possible the clear election results in cities such as Philadelphia, Detroit, Milwaukee, and Atlanta. On November 10, a few days after the election, I joined others in my Facebook cohort, such as Jeffrey Isaac, Jeff Tullis, Thomas Dumm, Jairus Grove, and Melissa Williams, in contending that Trump was preparing a coup attempt. But I did not know what form it would take. With support from police, media, and Republican

Party allies, Trump had braced followers for such an event for years, spouting big lies repeatedly and demeaning the media regularly, now tweeting endlessly the lie that he had in fact won the election by a large margin and was only thwarted by massive miscounts in several states—miscounts, however, that apparently only applied to him at the top of the ballot, not to down-ballot Republican victories.

On January 6, the day the Biden victory was being certified by both houses of Congress, I was celebrating my pandemic birthday with a few shivering friends around a small firepit in our backyard. Phone calls from other friends soon interrupted that sweet event. An insurrection was underway. Trump had called armed storm troopers to town—led by the Proud Boys, the Oath Keepers, QAnon, and the Three Percenters—to march on the Capitol building. It was clear to anyone watching and heeding online chatter before the event that they intended violence. They invaded the Capitol building, threatening legislators, disrupting the proceedings, injuring and killing several, and threatening the vice president and Speaker with death. The goal was to stop the election certification and, very probably, to create enough violence and havoc to allow Trump to announce martial law. It was an attempted coup.

The undermanned Capitol police put up a valiant defense, and many were injured, though some officers perhaps sympathetic to the white fascist insurrection seem to have treated the invaders with kid gloves never given to Black Lives Matter demonstrators and seldom given to peaceful anti-war protests. And then there was Trump's unconscionable delay in allowing police reinforcements, reinforcements that finally had to be ordered by others.

The insurrection was defeated. But after Congress returned several hours later to complete the certification, around 150 Republican legislators voted to oppose certification—with no evidence presented on behalf of their "no" votes. The event was followed by insistent Republican/media repetitions of the Big Lie that the election had been stolen, using that lie to justify new state legislation to further suppress the minority and poor voters.

This event was fascistic through and through, fomented for months by a fascist president, Republican extremists, armed militia, and social media allies. Trump announced on the mall that day that he would march with the vigilantes to the Capitol, but in fact he went to the White House to enjoy the proceedings on TV. What's more, he forced a delay in allowing National Guard aid from Maryland to reach legislators crouching beneath their desks or in a bunker under the Capitol building.

Later, fascist publicists propagated yet another Big Lie, claiming that left-wing activists had infiltrated the Trump rallies and that they had ignited the violence. The startling fact that a large majority of Republican senators voted against conviction of Trump in the second impeachment trial for fomenting the insurrection does not merely mean they were afraid of the Trump machine, as too many commentators continued to say. They are part of that machine; their refusal shows that they are ready to go this far again if the opportunity arises. Even further.

Karl Polanyi has demonstrated how the worldwide effects of the Great Depression make purely internal accounts of 1930s fascism insufficient to that era: similar movements arose in several regimes during the same period, though many were defeated. Today, the Anthropocene constitutes a new worldwide danger with racialized consequences for different regions and subordinate constituencies within the same region. White workers in old capitalist regimes are told by aspirational fascists that only by returning to the good old days of white supremacy, fossil extraction, auto and steel production, Christian hegemony, and rapid economic growth can they regain their standing. Meantime, refugees fleeing effects of accelerating climate change and bloody wars are treated as threats to that restoration. Fascist national movements and climate denialism are thus increasingly woven together in old capitalist states. Those who merely focus on the loss of old domestic guardrails tend to skip over the global and planetary dimensions of the late-modern condition.

The populist story, to me, thus dies on all counts. Doing so, it underplays how much work must be done to sustain and augment democracy under new conditions of danger. The recent coup attempt, to the Trump movement, is merely the first attempt, to be followed by others.

• • •

I agree, certainly, that it is now extremely difficult to win back a large portion of evangelical whites within the working and lower middle classes as you strive to reduce inequality, protect pluralism, and address the Anthropocene. Hardened white racists, misogynists, and the right edge of Christianity will doubtless remain entrenched; but others in similar social locations are potentially susceptible to recruitment if the invitations are real and sustained. There is even evidence that the number of whites who identify themselves as evangelicals is now in decline.

As fascism itself shows, the cultural distribution of spiritual cohorts does not mesh entirely with differences of class, gender, race, ethnicity, religious creed, sexuality, or age. Secularists thus ignore the spiritual dimension of political life at their own peril. They fail to perceive how affinities of spirituality can cut across differences in creed, gender, race, and class, thus making real differences in politics—as, in a negative way, when the fateful alliance between white evangelicals and white neoliberals was fomented in America decades ago. Or as in a positive way, when an affirmative ethos of egalitarian pluralism is negotiated across differences of race, class, gender, and faith.

•••

I am not entirely convinced. But this debate, as you stake out a stance on it, overlooks another innovation implemented during the Brexit campaign, the Trump campaign, Bolsanaro's campaign in Brazil, Putin's regime, and elsewhere. That is the systematic use of psychographic data scraped from millions of Facebook subscribers to target slivers of undecided voters, analyzing data about their fears, anxieties, and hostilities, igniting their passions, and striving to steer those passions in particular directions. Scraped data from phone usage, credit card purchases, Facebook usage, etc., etc., can be effective in right-wing campaigns. Does it not need to be included in the accounts both you and critics of populism articulate? Why have you not done so?
Right. Foucault pulled social theory down this trail. But I have yet to engage new developments in it enough. It is extremely pertinent. Given the visceral register of culture and the dynamics of affective contagion, such a weaponization of data becomes critical to the success of authoritarian spirals. When Cambridge Analytica posted false, anonymous ads about a violent Black Lives Matter meeting to a group of prejudiced whites in southern Michigan during a close, tense election in 2016, it motivated the target group to become more racist and intensify its support for Trump. Similarly, the Russian invasion of Facebook in America was designed to discourage African Americans from voting in swing states. Such instances merely scratch the surface of this phenomenon.

Big Data scraping works best when the target constituency shares a set of fears, anxieties, preferences, and vulnerabilities, is unaware of the data collection, and becomes targeted by anonymous ads that circle back on them. The ads and fascist rhetoric work together. So, authoritarian campaigns, Big Lies delivered to large crowds, and Big Data weaponization form a spiral. If the behavioralists of the 1950s and '60s sought to collect unshared information to predict voting behavior, Big Data weaponization is the latest stage in the evolution of a dangerous game. Its objective is to render a target population as calculable and manipulable as possible.

It is revealing how intensely owners of large platforms such as Facebook resist releasing the data they hold on targeted individuals and constituencies or regulating their platforms in the interests of transparency and factual truthfulness. This shows again how, when new events place market autonomy in peril, CEOs and technocrats often cast their allegiance to aspirational fascism. We now know that Mark Zuckerberg and the Donald Trump family had an unpublicized dinner together as the challenges to Facebook were gathering.

Such manipulation works best, again, when the targets are unaware that it is being done and by whom. But my grasp of these processes remains at an early stage. It demands close attention from critical intellectuals equipped with a variety of skill sets, particularly those attuned to scraping algorithms and those who understand how affective contagion works.

• • •

A related issue is also critical: the need to reconfigure familiar, classical *challenges* to capitalism. We inhabit a time when neoliberal capitalism imposes tremendous suffering on many inside and outside old capitalist states. But classical versions of social democracy, socialism, and communism need some reworking today, too. Their early variants too often pursued material abundance by promising rapid growth and mastery over the earth.

It is not necessary to start from scratch. As authors such as J. K. Gibson-Graham, J. Cameron, and S. Healy have shown in *Taking Back the Economy*,[14] numerous extant constituencies now practice cooperative modes of manufacture, etc., within capitalism that provide living examples upon which to build. The task is to amplify each and to support social production, pluralism, post-fossil energy, and egalitarianism together. Indeed, one task is to learn better how to take joy in life when old middle-class assumptions about the relation between the established infrastructure of consumption and the good life are no longer workable. A demanding task, indeed.

The significance of the issue can be underlined by saying that while neoliberal capitalism generates periodic crises and exploits racial, religious, gender, and class constituencies, the most widely publicized alternatives to it no longer capture the imaginations of many troubled participants, either. This bind, indeed, can render fascist movements tempting during periods of duress. Those who resist fascism, while grasping how conventional liberal and socialist responses need revamping, thus have a lot of work to do. The task is to rethink democratic socialism during the acceleration of the

Anthropocene, multiple pressures to minoritize the world, and established infrastructures of consumption ill-suited to the reduction of inequality and elimination of fossil extraction. It is to redefine the future appropriate to bifocal democracy.

•••

You may now begin to see how the historic conjunction between capitalism and electoral democracy itself forms a large part of the problem. Why not reject the current terms of democracy in order to visualize a noncapitalist future?
It is true that democracy itself has again lost credibility within some segments of the Left. I do not share that response, even though I think the times call upon us to rework the idea of democracy. To some, democracy is merely a varnish plastered on top of capitalism, glossing over its exploitations and crisis tendencies. I note that Theodore Adorno, who once held a view close to that, took it back in *Minima Moralia* after the collapse of Weimar democracy and the triumph of Hitler.[15] He now saw how capitalism without democracy can so readily become fascism. The latter happens because, when the populace is denied the free speech, evidence-based media, a reliable court system, and active social movements previously in play—with all their limits—it now takes massive repression to keep it under wraps. Trump, for instance, would be fully prepared to initiate such draconian controls, if he could get away with it.

Actually existing democracy, to me, is thus more like a skin covering capitalism than a varnish plastered over it. Neoliberal capitalism poses severe limits, particularly to urban minorities systematically closed out of its benefits and white, black, and brown workers facing wage stagnation. Struggles must thus be intensified to overcome the racism, misogyny, imperialism, and religious bigotry that permeate democratic capitalism. But if the democratic skin were torn off, the whole would become a bloody mess, and hope would be lost.

What is needed today, then, is reconstruction of democracy to rise above the evils of fossil capitalism, to nationalize key sectors of the economy, to encourage worker and consumer cooperatives, to promote local control of electric power generation by renewable means, to nurture multifaceted, egalitarian pluralism, and to take urgent actions at multiple sites to respond to the Anthropocene. Any viable theory of democracy today must address together the danger of fascism, galloping climate change, the need for an independent media, the call of diversity, and the demands of egalitarianism. A rough assignment indeed. An improbable necessity.

• • •

I recently explored one dimension of these dilemmas: the dicey relation between the dreadful duo of climate denialism and casualism on the one hand and accentuation of fascist drives in old capitalist-democratic states on the other.

Climate Machines, Fascist Drives, and Truth is a short book.[16] It explores how the climate denialism and casualism of the cultural right helped to pave the way for fascist movements of bellicose denialism and cultural fantasies of return to a mythic time in the 1950s when industrialism, extractive capital, and white supremacy triumphed together. "Donald Trump came to power not only by attacking precarious minorities, pushing white triumphalism, slamming the media, courting white evangelicals, demeaning democratic allies of America, pushing misogyny, conspiring with Putin, talking endlessly about a territorial wall, and promising battered workers a return to an old manufacturing regime. He also ridiculed warnings about climate change. . . . One way to court a deindustrialized white working lower- and middle class—especially those in 'flyover zones' between the two coasts—is to promise that you will bring back the old industrial world by returning to the coal, oil, car, steel, truck, labor, race, highway, and gasoline regime that was in place during a golden age."[17] Trump showed how a now dispersed, less urban, deindustrialized white working class could become even more susceptible to fascist, racist, and climate denialism together.

Capitalism in that study is construed to be an "axiomatic" consisting of private profit, primacy of the commodity form, wage labor, racial imperialism, and an infrastructure of consumption that presses poor and low-income earners to make ends meet. The axiomatic is replete, then, with powerful tendencies; it also contains margins of choice as new events, many of which it helps to foment, periodically rock it.

New synergies are urgently needed today between recent work in the earth sciences and cultural theory to publicize how capitalist practices of CO_2 emissions, deforestation, and agricultural methane burps *trigger* a series of planetary *amplifiers* that render the results much more severe than the triggers alone. Fifteen such amplifiers are noted in the study, with adverse consequences often concentrated in different places from their origins. This planetary machine thus generates sharp asymmetries in regional modes of suffering, with tropical and polar regions receiving the largest blows and capitalist regimes in temperate zones propagating the most severe triggers. The planetary climate machine itself consists of heterogeneous forces bound together: capitalist exploitation, Co_2 emissions, numerous planetary amplifiers, a host of refugee drives, and fascist temptations in old capitalist states work back and forth upon each other. Potential monsoon interruptions in India and China, to take one instance, are the composite result of growing emissions of fossil capitalism, intensification of El Niños in the Pacific, and weakening of seasonal winds moving from west to east. Such monsoon interruptions have occurred before. Fifteen amplifiers are reviewed in the text, ranging from how melting ice increases the albedo rate and thus sets a melting spiral into motion to how ice-melts in Greenland provide settings for algae growths that further accelerate the melt. A climate tiger is swinging us around by our tails.

Critical theorists today must also counter false neopositivist charges that they opt for a "post-truth" world, doing so by reworking classical correspondence images of truth. The text explores how a pragmatist *regime* of truth and the *lure* of truth can work back and forth upon each other in ways that both explode the neopositivist story and transcend correspondence models. Neopositivists who blithely accuse critical theorists of dropping the pursuit of truth are, indeed, often those who themselves failed, until late in the day, to gauge true relays between sociocentrism, accelerating climate machines, and fascist assaults upon racialized minorities, refugees, and the media. One way to solicit such efforts is to show how a series of cultural theorists in the "minor tradition" of European thought—such as Sophocles, Mary Shelley, Gilles Deleuze, Alfred North Whitehead, and Michel Foucault—help to challenge assumptions of the "major tradition" while placing Euro-American theorists in better positions to commune with recent decolonial theory and new turns in the earth sciences.

This book thus draws together themes from *Facing the Planetary* and *Aspirational Fascism*.

So, I guess you do struggle to ward off pessimism during a dark time. You think that the unpreparedness of so many secular and theological constituencies within luxurious societies of productivity to address a volatile world not highly disposed to humanity is part of the problem. You strive to ward off a dark future while soliciting more people to affirm that planetary processes are not that highly predisposed to us. You think that secular models of mastery and theological models of organic belonging complement one another more than their proponents acknowledge. Existential and institutional issues thus become interfolded on such a reading. And the prospect of enough political leaders, media pundits, academics, and citizens coming to terms with this

*combination in time are not that high. Let us, then, laugh together, on
principle . . .*

•••

I also think that the very organization of the academy today poses part of the
problem. Let's use the occasion of Covid-19, then, to think further about
how and why disciplinary boundaries have been sliced and diced as they are
in the academy. Let's think again about the intellectual bases of old firewalls
between the natural sciences, the social sciences, and the humanities. The
issues invoked touch conflicting ideas about the character of time itself.

If you, rather crudely, trace one vector from Descartes through Newton
to Einstein, you arrive at a dogma in Einstein that advises practitioners of
physics—"the queen of the sciences"—either to ignore the humanities,
social sciences, and softer natural sciences *or* to subjugate them to its
categories.

Descartes bestowed agency upon humans and God alone, with humans
themselves bifurcated between soulful agency and mindless bodies or
mechanisms, though these separations became softened a bit through his
discussions with a critic, Princess Elizabeth. Nonhuman animals were said
to be thoughtless brutes. He also defined time as a series of instants held
together only by the providence of an omnipotent God. He thus conceded
the onto-fragility of things, since confidence in his providential God
depended upon an ontological proof that was shaky. Without God's constant
attention and benevolence, the duration of the world itself would collapse.
In the *Meditations*, Descartes thus says, "For the whole duration of my life
can be divided into an infinite number of parts, no one of which is
dependent upon the others, and so it does not follow from the fact that I
have existed a while that I should exist now, unless at this moment some
cause produces and creates me."[18] That *eminent* cause, again, is God.
Descartes's idea of eminent causality is grounded in the assumption that
only a higher, more complex entity can cause a lower one, a theme that
supports the existence of an omniscient God, rules out emergent causality,
and denies species evolution. One piece of Descartes persists in Einstein's
later image of time.

In his 1922 debate with Henri Bergson, Einstein insisted that the Bergsonian story of delicate intersections between past and future in the creative
protraction of the present—or "duration"—misreads the very reality of time
as such grounded in the constant rate of the speed of light, assumed to be
the fastest speed in the universe. Light itself is composed of instants,

"particles," or, as he later called them, "photons." Not only does relativity show how the clock time of two travelers moving at extremely different speeds will vary, it also shows, in Einstein's words, how to "the believing physicist this division into past, present, and future has merely the standing of an obstinate illusion."[19] The result is a species of "eternalism," in which (according to one version) a multiverse collects every result somewhere *now* in space. Human experiences of the passing of time are thus illusions. So much the worse, too, for philosophies of agency in which judgments, choices, and creative adventures unfold through irreversible time. Irreversible time does not necessarily mean progressive time, but it does assert that no specific juncture is ever repeated in its entirety.

The rhetorical brilliance of Einstein found expression in his assertion that Bergson explored only "psychological time," while the scientist himself grasped "real time." I cannot rehearse the details of that debate further here; my capacity to do so is indeed limited. But, as Jimena Canales traces in *The Physicist and the Philosopher*, the debate has persisted across several permutations for a century.[20]

The key points, however, are, first, that Bergson in fact accepted Einstein's math and tests, but not his philosophy of time. Second, Bergson did not in fact restrict his claims to *human* experiences of time and agency, let alone to a unique human illusion of time. Even the title of one of Bergson's key books, *Creative Evolution*, shows this, as does this quotation from it picked almost at random: "The feeling we have of our evolution and of the evolution of all things in pure duration is there. . . . Mechanism and finalism agree in taking account only of the bright nucleus, shining in the center. They forget, that is, that this nucleus has been formed out of the rest by condensation."[21] Bergson extended experiences of temporality well beyond humans and discerned how closely notions of time and agency are bound together. In the admirable words of Donna Haraway, he appreciated the diverse, intersecting temporalities of innumerable "critters."[22]

Einstein's metaphors nonetheless stuck the most: one rigorous theory grounded in the objective constancy of the speed of light combating a human self-illusion grounded only in fuzzy self-reports. Each party to that debate, however, actually drew upon a specific aspect of human experience and then extrapolated from it: Einstein upon faith that the world itself conforms to a mathematical structure humans bring to it and Bergson upon the faith that extrapolations from human experiences of duration help to illuminate other agencies and forces in the world. Positivists such as Hans Reichenbach, Rudolf Carnap, and Bertrand Russell carried variants of the Einstein story into the human sciences; process theorists such as James,

Whitehead, Mead, Latour, Deleuze, Haraway, and Canales herself have championed variants of the Bergsonian image.

Immediately pertinent to the 2020 pandemic, then, is how complexity theorists in biology and ecology began to construe the diverse agencies and experiences of duration of, say, bees, crows, elephants, dogs, crocodiles, sunflowers, whales, bacteria, and viruses in ways that buttress the Bergson theory taken broadly, *contending that experiences of agency as striving and time as duration both include and exceed diverse human cultures.* These latter experiences are thus construed by complexity theorists in several nonhuman sciences to be neither illusionary nor unique to humans. Such formulations thus download challenges to Einstein into biology and ethology—that is, into several nonhuman sciences. They shake and rattle the intellectual foundations of a science/humanities bifurcation in the academy.

Let's turn to a formulation by Stuart Kauffman, a complexity theorist in biology, about the agency of bacteria, in which past experience and current striving into the future enter into their behavior. A bacterium, he says, possesses *some* characteristics of agency as purposive striving. It *pursues* sugar as an end while climbing a sugar gradient; it *adjusts* its behavior to attain the end during micro-moments of duration; and it *feels* satisfaction if it achieves its end. Thus, says, Kauffman, "Teleological language becomes important at some point in the tree of life. Let us stretch and say that it is appropriate to apply it to the bacterium. We may do so without attributing consciousness to the bacterium. My purpose . . . is to try to trace the origin of action, value, and meaning as close as I can to the meaning of life."[23]

Drawing upon Kauffman, it now becomes feasible for Euro-American thinkers to appreciate complex human entanglements with multiple nonhuman agencies set on different scales of temporality *and* to emphasize—with Whitehead and recent neuroscience studies of gut-brain relations—how complex micro-agencies within human beings contribute to our own modes of thought, mood, judgment, and agency also set in larger cultural contexts. Every action is marked by duration, however brief. Bonnie Bassler supplements Kauffman's account by exploring "quorum calls" of bacteria in the gut through which collective bacterial actions are undertaken.[24] Others have identified the collective agency of crocodiles, an understanding missed by early European adventurers at their peril.

It is also pertinent to resist the familiar ploy to relegate those who multiply sites of agency within and beyond humans to be mere theorists of individualism who forgo the study of larger structures. The human/nonhuman relations themselves, for instance, form assemblages, set in relatively open systems, each intersecting with several others. Indeed, the tired "individualist/collectivist/structuralist debate" in the human sciences is too often set in a larger frame of human exceptionalism and sociocentrism. The task now becomes to explore heterogeneous entanglements within and between individuals, cultural systems, and nonhuman assemblages set in intersecting temporalities operating at different speeds and capacities.

What about viruses and pandemics, though? Virology is a young science by comparison to physics, which itself gained new solidity in the sixteenth and seventeenth centuries. The first virus was detected apparently in 1892, the first coronavirus in 1898, the first human virus in 1900, and the measles virus in 1911. The electron microscope, which can observe viruses directly, was invented only by 1933. The first zoonotic virus—viruses like Covid-19 that spill over from one animal to another—was discovered in 1955. Ebola, HIV, SARs, and other coronaviruses spilling over from other animals into humans were identified later yet. Various viral vaccines trailed into the world after that, mostly after the 1950s.[25] Viral transmissions have also been identified, as we have seen, to be key agents in horizontal gene transfer, a second source of co-evolution that transfigures Darwin's old oak tree into a tangled bush or even a rhizome.

Covid-19 is a coronavirus that (probably) leaped from bats to an intermediary (perhaps a snake, pig, or pangolin) and then made a second crossing into humans. It is very impressive. It proliferates among humans after a crossing, most often through droplets inhaled from others. Covid-19 is apparently less lethal and more transmissible than several other coronaviruses. (Coronaviruses are viruses with jagged crowns that become attached to human cells and proliferate rapidly.)

Detection, virion movement, crossings, attachment, rapid evolution, stubborn persistence, resistance to antibodies. Are viruses alive, then? Do they participate in nano-strivings? The dominant view has been that, since they are immobile before attaching to host cells—they are not cells themselves—they do not fit the definition of life. They hover in a zone of indiscernibility between life and non-life. But that judgment (and definition) is now contested by some virologists. Here is what Patrick Forterre, a virologist, says in "To Be or Not to Be Alive":

Viruses use the same nucleic acids and cellular organisms for the reproduction and expression of genetic information. This indicates that viruses and cells fit into the same historical process we call life; . . . the viral genome remains inactive within a viral particle *until* it encounters a susceptible cell that can be infected [my emphasis];

. . . most biologists profoundly underestimate viral "creativity," the opportunity for emergence and selection of novel traits encoded by viral genomes. This is probably because *viruses*, confounded with their *virions*, are assimilated to passive, inert objects [my emphasis];
   . . . this implies that viruses actually originated before cells;
   . . . viruses are thus living entities because they are both genetic and metabolic entities.[26]

The Forterre thesis, though supported by some other virologists, is highly controversial, as such a proposal for a paradigm shift in a science must be. As a rank amateur on this terrain myself, let me take a viral leap nonetheless and speculate that Forterre is on the right track. Why? Well, the first reason is that a central consideration—among others—to treat viruses as nonliving has been that they cannot survive in the absence of a host. True. But other modes of life need hosts, too. Take trees in a forest connected by fungal networks. Humans also need wombs, food, gut bacteria, oxygen, parenting, and the earth to flourish, even though a couple of those items can now be provided artificially. These modes of dependence must be emphasized today—since the advances of fossil capitalism place several at risk. A second reason is that the Forterre proposal takes another step toward resolving a persistent impasse (and hierarchy) between the natural sciences and humanities that continues to confound the academy.

Here is the impasse: *Neither mode of inquiry in its dominant mode can render key aspects of the world intelligible as it stands, but each needs sustenance from the other to do its own work.* Einsteinian scientists, for instance, ask whether an "anthropic exception" exempts them from a world otherwise constituted as timeless. The impasse, again, is that each needs the other to render intelligible processes pertinent to it, but each, at least in its majoritarian guise, advances themes that make it difficult to do so in intellectually tenable ways.

Attention to the impasse calls into question the Einsteinian insistence to ground time itself *only* on the observed constancy of the speed of light. It may also encourage humanists to come to terms more closely with how human cultures are profoundly entangled with a heterogeneous set of nonhuman cultures, cultures as diverse as viruses, bacteria, algae, plants, fungi, bats, birds, forests, pangolins, whales, leopards, livestock, and pets. Cultures that provoke essential intersections between heterogeneous agents, such as the orchid and the wasp, bacteria and human moods, forests and fungi, viruses and antibodies, vultures and rats.

If you now link the Forterre account of viral life to studies of multi-species perspectivalism in several non-Western cultures, and both of these to accounts by biologists such as Lynn Margulis, Stuart Kauffman, and Terrence Deacon on how life itself may have emerged from chancy conjunctions between diverse, nonliving, complex molecules, you sow a seedbed that helps diverse academic disciplines to speak intelligibly to one another across old ontological boundaries.

Now, Euro-dualism and reductionism lose their standing as the only alternatives to entertain in a world composed of multiple, entangled, temporal systems. A story of multiple trajectories, periodically crossing into one another, now encourages closer contact in Western academies between anthropologists, non-Western cosmologies, bacteriologists, virologists, global theorists, climatologists, and ecologists as they study complex intersections of multiple sorts.

Biology, ethology, anthropology, and ecology, on this account, now become something closer to linchpin sciences, shuffling Einsteinian unilateral images of time to an outer edge to face challenges from quantum theory, biological sciences of nonhuman life, process philosophy, indigenous peoples, and decolonial movements. These modes of inquiry begin to suture assumptions about the "bifurcation of nature" (as Whitehead called it) within the academy itself, opening a door to yet new adventures.

The new linchpins do not promise a unified science, now placing administration of the old academic hierarchy under one tent. Rather, they provide clues to follow when those in the humanities and natural sciences need to draw resources from each other to explore a critical problem. Virologists, for instance, find that to trace a specific viral spillover into human cultures they need to do lab work, conceptual work, and field work simultaneously. They become amateur anthropologists in that latter task, as social scientists may become amateur virologists or climatologists at other times to follow the complexities of a problem. We all become more problem-oriented practitioners—appreciative of how new events of different sorts periodically interrupt regularities to which we have been habituated—prepared to push against the boundaries of our fields on occasion rather than huddling inside tattered disciplinary cocoons.

The discovery, for instance, of how one bat coronavirus, before Covid-19, spilled into humans after evolving sufficiently to make the leap, required investigators to study virus samples in the lab and then to map in the field how large tree bats deposit excrement on a delicate fruit, the sap of which is drunk as a delicacy by locals. In different variations this example is already repeated over and over in eco-viral studies, as David Quammen reviews so artfully in *Spillover*.[27]

Another critical possibility may be augmented, too. Those in Euro-American settings who explore entanglements between diverse modes of human and nonhuman life may therefore become better equipped than heretofore to engage rich traditions of cross-species perspectivalism advanced in several non-Western regions as well as in indigenous peoples now partitioned by "reservations" in "settler" societies. We may therefore become better prepared to rise above a nature/culture bifurcation of our own making. More reciprocal modes of intellectual dialogue now become more feasible across regions, not because of a change in this dimension alone, of course, but by linking it to studies that oppose imperial captures by capitalism and the nature/culture divisions tethered to those captures.

Opportunities may now become augmented to learn from less productivist-oriented cultures how to promote resilience during an age of rapid climate change and periodic pandemics, doing so to help challenge the hegemony of private profit, stratification, racism, economic growth, and mastery over nature. Such dialogues have been underway for a while beneath the gaze of those who defend imperialism, linear time, and the bifurcation of nature.

Another issue may now become open to closer inquiry, too: The vulnerabilities and susceptibilities to ingression that make human beings susceptible to viral contagions and bacterial infusions are also those that make us beings susceptible to affective modes of communication that work on the visceral register of cultural life. Such infusions help to spawn the proclivities, premonitions, and prejudgments that constitute the visceral register of diverse cohorts in cultural life. Theorists who bypass the processes of viral crossings and contagions are thus apt to be those who downplay or ignore how the contest between fascism and democracy is waged in part on the visceral register of cultural life.

As this report has wound along, we have encountered reflections on memory in which new events incite distinctive recollections, tap dispositions without recollection, and jostle loose remainders bouncing into the present from the past. Diverse modes of memory ignited by an event are mobilized into a non-contemporaneous sheet of past. Heterogeneous elements on the sheet intercommunicate and often propel new affect-laden ideas—you know not exactly how—into consciousness for rejection, resistance, acceptance, or modification. Given your early experiences as a working-class white boy—including a move from the country to the city, the importance of the labor movement to your family, the role of sports in youth, youthful encounters with white evangelicalism, family brushes with McCarthyism, the coma and partial recovery of your father, that secretary at school who ordered you to attend a meeting, the decision to pursue an academic career, the inspirational imprint of mentors such as Kaufman and Meisel, diverse episodes of joy and good fortune, challenges posed by neo-positivism, periodic punctuations of academic life with politics, and a shift from atheism to nontheism; given later experiments in theory, the shock of the Anthropocene, the threat of fascism, the rapid circulation of a viral pandemic, and the projection of improbable necessities into the future—what can you say now about how relays between events, thinking, and politics proceed? Do some events, say, determine future thought? Do they determine thought-imbued moods and temper, too? If so, how can you assure us now that you are not merely articulating a new set of determinations rather than offering reflections pertinent to today? If the formulation of determinism is too simple, what kind of imbrications between such diverse elements do you project? How do you support that projection?

I do not, certainly, believe that later actions, judgments, and texts are blindly *determined* by previous encounters. Such an assumption reflects a flat ontology, difficult to defend when articulated in close awareness of assumptions built into one's own actions. It denies the element of autonomy in thinking and the modest place for creativity in the uneven and intersecting temporalities of life. Indeed, it is difficult to get through a day without projecting the relative autonomy of thought and the importance of creative interventions to life.

I do imagine, however, that resonances back and forth between early experiences, later vicissitudes and joys, large political happenings, tactics of self-cultivation, surprising planetary events, periodic shifts in the earth sciences, and experimental adventures of thought can and do become entwined in loose tangles. The tangles—each with loose threads trailing out of it—can be jostled, touched, or pulled but not fully known. If pulses of real creativity do mark the world, the quest to chart a full set of determinations becomes a fool's errand. Even a god or demon with full "information" could not chart all the twists and turns of thought in advance.

Rather, at key moments you may strive to break an old habit or two by tapping into old residues as you sink into a reverie. Resonances between old remains and the new situation may help to foment new thoughts, even though the remains that help to contribute to them escape clean representation. The remains are too cloudy and incipient for that. But that does make them without efficacy. Out of such ventures a new concept more appropriate to the moment may sometimes be forged; it can then be carried forward to replace some established parameters of thought. You may now offer a revised theory, trying to move the established terms of debate to some degree. But events keep coming, and the new result, even if it becomes more persuasive, does not suffice for long.

And yes, a new generation of entangled humanists, who have learned things from the Anthropocene and viral crossings, may well be besieged again by a militant academic cadre that seeks to force the objects of inquiry into narrow molds to make them susceptible "in principle" to full explanation. That shopworn game has been pushed again and again, and it has been challenged intellectually over and over. The old professional agenda could again be endowed with signature status by university administrators who love the grant prospects available to such projects. Such cohorts apparently cannot sustain self-confidence in their own self-image *unless* such an agenda prevails in their departments and universities. The unquestioned primacy they demand discloses the fragility of the self-image they project.

Let them pursue such agendas, I say, without imposing them on others in compulsory ways—by administrative fiat, presidential signature initiatives, arbitrary tenure decisions, etc., etc. We are wiser than they: more attuned to the fragility of things; better equipped to probe dangers and pulses of novelty that periodically course through the world. Indeed, another name for the demand to impose a single disciplinary standard on everyone is authoritarianism; it is not so different from a royal command to impose belief in the same god on all subjects of a kingdom. Its essence is denial of the intimate relations between thinking and plurality.

We demand, then, not so much that the missionaries of explanatory hubris forgo adding new twists to an old agenda that has failed so often before. Rather, we insist that they acknowledge the extent to which it remains profoundly contestable, and reasonably so, in the eyes of so many. That they embrace intellectual plurality, while bringing better evidence and argument to bear on their favorite schemes.

The conjunction between singular demands for authority, dogmatism, and explanatory hubris poses key dangers to intellectual life in the academy today, whether it emanates from a neoliberal president of a university, trustees, a dean, a chair, departmental colleagues plastering new varnish on rusty ideals, or several of them aligned together, all flickering under the dim light of an old dream that has now become a nightmare. The humanities, philosophy, history, and the human sciences are highly susceptible to such cultural drives. But the purveyors of hubris always underplay both the recurrence of surprising events in life and the periodic need for creative experimentation in thought.

Quests to draw periodic draughts of insight from dicey intersections between new events, old habits of thought, and loose remains remain indispensable to intellectual life. You occasionally stretch into a domain beyond your current reach, admitting your amateur status as the problem you pursue demands explorations in new fields of inquiry. You periodically pause in fecund moments of suspension, allowing diverse elements to rumble back and forth, to see what happens to thinking next. Valves of thought sometimes become dilated during these periods, and a new, partly formed thought, concept, or stirring may spring up for further reflection. These are among the ways, or so I propose, that new sensitivities and creative thinking are cultivated together. Perhaps, too, ways through which "the courage of truth"—as Foucault called it late in life—can be cultivated and enacted by intellectuals in the academy.

Epilogue
Echoes and Spiritualities

I

I have seen *Hair* three times. Each time the musical has elevated my spirits in the company of others, bolstering drives to spiritual affirmation and strengthening political commitments to resist wars and redress injustices.

The first time was in Los Angeles in 1969. I was a participant in a four-week symposium on philosophy and politics at UC-Irvine. Arnold Kaufman, who died a couple of years later when a Phantom jet crashed into the commercial plane he was taking to an anti-war rally, was one of the organizers. We renewed our acquaintance amid the continuing horror of the Vietnam War. My new, young friends and I would attend symposia all day and then often streak to the shore in a rental car to body surf before returning to the dorm to catch dinner at the last minute.

Hair was making its West Coast debut in Los Angeles, and Dale Keller, who was now a popular sports toastmaster in Phoenix after starring as flanker back at the University of Arizona, drove out to take in the musical with us. He quickly mesmerized the young academic crew, satirizing our intellectualism in the robust style of Jonathan Winters. Each time we responded to him it would just incite a new wave.

We were all blown away by *Hair*. The performance lifted our spirits and defiance as the Vietnam War continued to grind along. Doubtless it fed energies needed to fuel the protests waged on our campuses, localities, and national gatherings.

The second time was in London, as George W. Bush presided over a disastrous war in Iraq. Once again, the performance elevated the spirits and determination of the crowd in the hall as the audience joined performers in belting out "Aquarius," "I Got My Aaass," and "Let the Sun Shine In" at the close of the play. The first event resonated with the second. At least, I felt compelled to tell Jane all about the first time and the protests it helped to inspire as we left the London Hall together.

The third time was in Catonsville, Maryland, in the summer of 2019, a small town outside Baltimore where the Catonsville Nine—led by the Berrigan brothers—had committed civil disobedience against the Vietnam War in 1969, destroying draft files with homemade napalm. A lovely waiter at the coffee shop we frequent told Jane and me she would be in a play there that weekend. "What is the name?" Jane asked. "*Hair.*" "We will be there," the two of us said in unison. We were joined by a friend, the feminist philosopher Emily Parker.

From one point of view the performers were a ragtag group, consisting of amateurs holding down arduous day jobs. Tattoos were abundant, or so it seemed to an older member of the audience. The performance was set in open air, on a farm on the outskirts of town, with a ramshackle stage backed by a dense stand of bamboo trees and fronted by a hill upon which the audience sat on blankets. All three zones were deployed in the performance, with the bamboo stand serving as a forest from which the dead vet emerges. The theater collective had dropped the acid Berger character, to good effect, distributing his best songs to other members. The performance was incredible, lifting spirits and activating energies again, this time in the middle of the racist, imperial, misogynist regime of Donald Trump—a regime resisted with humor and passion by performers and audience on the hill.

Three events, the spirit of the first two called up again as the third was performed, all three set on a single sheet of time mixing music, dancing, war, resistance, joy, and loss together. Memory is a series of echo chambers within which thinking vibrates.

II

Events of different sorts, sizes, clarity, and consequences slide, bump, and blast into the world. They accumulate in this or that way within the social structures of the soul and other institutions. A new event, rattling or delighting those who encounter it, gathers selective elements from the past, a sheet composed of events experienced at disparate times, replete with affinities and divergencies as well as variable degrees of susceptibility to recollection. Each event was first encountered in its moment; each carries preliminary weight now as it resonates with others. A sheet of the past, in this sense, is nonchronological; it assembles, as Gilles Deleuze would say, disparate moments in the face of an encounter with a new event. You sometimes become transfixed as sheet and event resonate strangely together on the fringes of conscious awareness; perhaps that transfixion encourages a new idea or plan to slip into consciousness for further processing. The creative element in thinking can be activated by a sheet of past; trauma can be, too, freezing you; more often yet, a sheet may consolidate old grooves in which thought and presumptions of action are set. A sheet can arrive loaded with trials, jolts, traumas, and joys that resonate together in a new situation.

Some of us seek to rework modestly dominant Western images of thought and time. Our readings of the relations between events, thinking, and memory support those efforts. Attention to indigenous traditions of what Viveiros de Castro calls multi-species "perspectivism" can help, too, as some recent students such as Stephanie Erev, Anatoli Ignatov, Adam Culver, Chad Shomura, and Jairus Grove have pressed upon me. So, too, can studies of fine, rhizomatic fungal networks operative in forest underlands. Such intra-forest networks of sustenance amid organic communication shatter old market-like models of competition between trees for space, soil, light, and air: "The mycorhizal fungi whose hyphae grow into hot spots—all of them frothing and tangling and fusing, making a network that's connecting holly to holly but also to beech, and to a seedling of something else over there, layering and layering and layering— until, well, it blows your computational brain."[1] It does so in part because computer models of the brain do not capture its own complexity.

Indeed, indigenous perspectivism coalesces with some recent practices of neuroscience and mycorhizal studies to scramble computational images of body/brain/culture organization. A body/brain/culture network is rhizomatic and layered, with fungal processes in our guts making differences to behavior on their own as they also percolate into conscious forests of thought. New consolidations occur, but they too are not final.

It is critical to remember how a fact both is real and bristles with more than it is. Every fact simmers with diverse potentials. Performances of *Hair* morph, a car rusts, a cluster of bacteria evolves, a constituency becomes inspired, a virus jumps across species, a civilization ossifies, an ocean conveyor slows, a sweet woman dies, a glacier melts at an accelerated rate, a body decays, a seasonal monsoon pattern stutters, a mood dissipates, a lava flow hardens into a granite field, two dispositions intersect, a new desire crystallizes, a thought gestates, an orgasm arrives of its own accord. Yes, individuals and social structures too bristle with more than either is, setting up preliminary strains that could be ignited by a new event. Everything is unfinished. It intersects with numerous others set on temporalities of diverse speeds and complexity.

III

James Baldwin, suffering from the darts and grinds of both white supremacy and heterosexism, nonetheless concluded with one of his heroes, Nietzsche, that to the extent it is possible to do so people in differently subject positions might consider cultivating little moments of joy as they strive to affirm the unruly character of the universe as such—that is, to affirm the very cosmos that enables us to be. Acknowledge and oppose militantly systemic exploitation and accidental suffering; but in doing so do not overlook or demean moments of joy, intellectual and otherwise. Such joys can stir energies beyond those required to get through the day, surpluses from which to consolidate positive compositions with others. Indeed, he surmised, the carefully guarded refusal to cultivate surpluses stretching beyond their enclosed identities constitutes one of the sources of white racism, among others. Here is what he says: "Most people guard and keep; they suppose that it is they themselves that they are guarding and keeping, whereas what they are actually guarding and keeping is their system of reality. . . . One can give nothing whatever without giving oneself—that is to say, risking oneself." Again, "I speak of change not on the surface but in the depths—change in the sense of renewal."[2]

Change in the depths, of both cultures and selves. I concur with Baldwin and Nietzsche. Those in the most dreadful circumstances cannot always marshal positive surpluses—though many surprise others by doing so. Many others, including most of those who teach, write, participate in the arts, work in the media, run for office, run cash registers at stores, preach in churches, promote social movements, and partake in diverse professions are capable of doing so, however. Here the ethico-political stakes rise. I speak for a moment to them, to us, to me.

One virus circulating through systemic racism, misogyny, imperial demands, investment portfolios, and climate denialism today is an implacable demand to blast institutional projections of capitalism into the future even as barriers to the attainment of that future pile up. The demand is centered in some classes, to be sure, but it is sprinkled across several. Larger planetary processes, defenders of such a spirituality insist, *must* be mastered in ways compatible with the future projected by extractive capitalism; if evidence piles up that they cannot be, it now becomes existentially imperative to hold vulnerable scapegoats responsible for conveying a fraudulent message. The recent flood of right-wing blog and Twitter assertions that Dr. Anthony Fauci—the U.S. expert on viral transmission—is an agent of the "deep state" reflect merely one manifestation of such spiritual drives. It manifests an extreme version of the cultural drive to "guard and keep," often piled on top of self-interest but sometimes, too, cutting against it. The drive to guard can persevere, even as counter-evidence accumulates against it; it finds expression as cruel readiness to sacrifice subordinate, marginal, and abjected constituencies to protect an existential creed from demise. It can readily become entrenched in the institutions of capital, the white working class, neofascist media, the military, small businesses, and urban police forces, rendering them more virulent and encouraging them to band together in ways that accentuate that virulence.

Ressentiment, says Nietzsche, expresses, among other things, underground, implacable resentment of the cosmos when you yourselves suspect it does not mesh with the religious, political, or economic possibilities you have officially invested in it. Constituencies loaded with *ressentiment* eagerly identify others—particularly those whose ways or faiths jeopardize their own self-confidence merely by being—to punish for the gap between the way the world must be to them and event-laden evidence accumulating against that insistence. You do not have to be an atheist to find insight in the Nietzschean reading of *ressentiment*, as it waxes and wanes during good and bad times. Indeed, atheists who replace God with secular insistence that the world itself must be amenable to consummate analysis and economic mastery readily fall prey to *ressentiment*, too. They cannot be happy until everyone is an atheist of their analytic type; they do not allow appreciation of deep pluralism to well up within and around them. In addition, many theists of diverse sorts transcend the spirituality of existential resentment, as we saw earlier, especially when they affirm the reasonable contestability of their own creed in the eyes of others and work to rise above resenting that persistent feature of human existence.

There is an alternative route to pursue. Individuals and constituencies can articulate their existential creeds and spirituality to the extent possible—knowing that creed and spirituality are connected but not equivalent—and then strive to negotiate positive spiritual assemblages across differences of creed and social position. For no single nation, creed, race, gender, class, region, or sexuality suffices to rise to the urgent challenges of today. Today, pluralist assemblages, forged across multiple differences of social position and creed, are essential to fend off fascist danger and to promote positive responses to the Anthropocene. No single constituency can carry this off.

You try not to "guard and hold" an image of the world that requires the propagation of scapegoats to sustain itself. You may even rework your own creed from within in the face of new events; and you work to forge spiritual connections to others who pursue overlapping objectives from diverse creedal starting points. By creed, of course, I include theology, philosophy, economic theory, aesthetic theory, and political theory, for they all contain creedal characteristics. Nietzsche called the propagation of such relations "the spiritual-ization of enmity"; I call it forging a cultural ethos of agonistic respect across diverse constituencies. As you do so—here the "you" is both singular and plural—you acknowledge that when national unitarians or fascists oppose a pluralist ethos implacably, a militant pluralist assemblage must be organized to take them on. We do not forge a centralized party or counter-nation to do so because we do not wish to become a variant of the thing we oppose in the act of opposing it.

Writers can strive to allow such a noble agenda to find expression in their prose. Such a presumptive ethos can also become infused into blended fami-lies, creedal congregations, political parties, egalitarian social movements, gen-der relations, race relations, and regional associations between youthful minorities struggling against the destructive world older generations in luxu-rious regimes have bestowed upon them. The quality of the spirituality infus-ing such practices and institutions, of course, is not everything. But it is always an important thing.

IV

Some academics shy away from such ontological, cosmological, and spiritual articulations—though the destructive power on the ontological right of the evangelical-neoliberal machine in America over the last forty years may well make them think twice about that. They do so, perhaps, partly because they sense that their own is highly contestable, partly because they may fear that such explorations siphon energy from critical explorations of race, gender, sexual-ity, equality, and empire, and partly because they cling to the story that the spiritual component is dispensable from social practices. But spiritually in-fused onto-assumptions—of this or that sort—are ineliminable from thought, critique, theology, everyday life, economic thought, social movements, and sci-ence. To quarantine this register is to practice a denialism that may well backfire in precisely the zones upon which you concentrate. It is to court dogmatism.

Others prize invitations to forge spiritual relations of agonistic respect be-tween constituencies from different social positions confessing alternative creeds. They may affirm, for instance, that no white academic over fifty has the right to peddle despair. We are obligated by care for the world to explore positive possibilities and alliances, especially during grim times. We know we must furiously resist fascism; we are convinced that to do so also involves court-ing deep, egalitarian pluralism.

Indeed, several constituencies seek to fold such relational spiritualities into the social movements they prize, as participants in the magnificent Woman's

March did after the Trump election in 2016, as Black Lives Matter has done in the wake of innumerable police killings of African Americans, as devotees of theologies of the earth increasingly do, as teenagers around the world do when they confront the ugly effects of rapid climate change, and as those vibrant performers of *Hair* in Catonsville did recently. They seek to extend alliances as they sharpen critiques of late-modern cruelties. Many pursue improbable necessities today. The stakes of the age intensify the urgency of the pursuits.

As earlier chapters have shown, I do not deny the importance of social structures, *if* they are conceived as interfolded institutions that enable some practices, disable others, and abound with loose ends and energies that exceed them. That is how the issues of sensibility, ethos, and spirituality remain important to "immanent naturalists," "new materialists," and "theologies of the earth" today, as we seek to broaden our spiritual connections to others and bear in mind that this very project requires resisting and opposing narrow nationalist movements enacting bellicose spiritualities.

V

We inhabit a world in which social structures reverberate with excess energies, as they periodically encounter events that jostle, rattle, enliven, or swamp them. In such a world it may be important for more intellectuals to forge spiritualities that affirm the rockiness of the world, as they seek both to grasp it better and to act experimentally with others upon it.

One hope governing these reports by an old academic is that a few young adventurers, grappling with the uncertain vocation of critical thought in a demanding age, might draw this or that current of sustenance from them, doing so by absorbing a few tips here or there and working elsewhere upon the reports in light of new experiences. The text itself merely charts the bumpy course of one refugee from the working class as he negotiates the rigors of the academy, new political events, and the powerful intersections between social life and planetary processes. The academy provides some room for intellectuals to do noble work in the company of others. But its disciplinary structures, administrative priorities, and alliances with old capitalist priorities also make it increasingly difficult to carry them out.

Such a condition intensifies the tasks of intellectuals in and around the academy while making it imperative to think and rethink how to pursue them. At least we have a sense of the task. The task of engaged intellectuals is to become worthy of events that impinge upon us as we work to broaden the scope of the us.

Acknowledgments

In an adventure of this sort, a list of acknowledgments could readily spread into a chapter of its own. So many contributions have been internalized into the twosomes and threesomes of myself, sometimes as inspirations, sometimes as indispensable rivals. Some of those to whom I am grateful have passed from this world. I now bear witness to them. The death of another slips and slides into memory, rendering it more fragile and vibrant at the same time.

I start with my parents. Pluma and William T. carved out decent lives for their children and themselves, balancing the tasks of finding adult pleasures, nurturing their children, participating in progressive union and party politics, and earning enough money to feed and house a large family, doing all this amidst a couple of wars, McCarthyism, an auto accident, labor strikes, health issues, and economic recessions. I sensed I was a lucky child, as I witnessed a few working-class men in my neighborhood abusing their wives and children. But, of course, deeper appreciation of my parents arrived later.

Dale Keller, indeed, faced such patriarchal onslaughts, and my mother took him in for a period after his dad had thrown him out of the house for a minor infraction. Our two lives have been entangled from the time we were foolish boys in the eighth grade, through sports adventures in high school that influenced the way each of us entered adult life, to later lives when we both worked to shed some engrained masculine habits and communed across geographical distances about life, politics, and philosophy. Dale often joined our family during the later years when the Larger Beal-Connolly clans would gather in northern Michigan for a joyous week. He now copes valiantly with Parkinson's, providing a stunning model of how to cope with existential hardship.

Key teachers, particularly those at the Flint University of Michigan, followed soon by Arnold Kaufman and James Meisel in graduate school at UM, have left indelible imprints on my thinking and sense of the world. Their deaths amplify their influences. Then there are theorists such as Peter Bachrach and David Kettler, whose work energized me early on and who helped me get started during the early days as a teacher and writer. They inhabit chambers where later colleagues and associates now reside, too: Michael Best, P. J. Brendese, Judith Butler, James Der Derian, Thomas Dumm, Jean Elshtain, Richard Flathman, Glen Gordon, Siba Grovogui, Kathy Ferguson, Nicolas Jabko, Steve Johnston, Bonnie Honig, Steven Lukes, Nidesh Lawtoo, George Kateb, Catherine Keller, Michael Sandel, Mike Shapiro, Mort Schoolman, Charles Taylor, Cornel West, Stephen White, and Sheldon Wolin. Through a series of fortuities, I can single out John Buell, Tom Dumm, Jairus Grove, Anatoli Ignatov, Mike Shapiro, James der Derian, Catherine Keller, Nidesh Lawtoo, Davide Panagia, Bonnie Honig, Stephanie Erev, Steve Johnston, Jane Bennett, and Mort Schoolman as intellectuals with whom I regularly commune today, to my great profit. Those connections have outlasted the contingencies through which they began. Charles Taylor and George Kateb play definitive roles as indispensable rivals spurring me on. Thanks, too, to Dean Alfange and Mike Best for checking my memory about key moments during the years in the Pioneer Valley; to Jane Bennett, Shane Butler, Naveeda Khan, P. J. Brendese, and Nidesh Lawtoo for doing the same with respect to Hopkins; and to Deborah, David, Tiffany, Janelle, and Bob Beal for reviewing the halcyon days with Judy Beal. Judy was a thinker and caretaker, folding each activity seamlessly into the other. Mike Best's influence on me also ranges well beyond the early days at UMass.

That 1984 NEH faculty summer seminar on "Genealogy and Interpretation" proved to be one of those turning points for me. It was delightful to find, at an APSA review of that seminar thirty-five years after its occurrence, that it had played a similar role for Kathy Ferguson, Tom Dumm, Stephen White, Bill Corlett, and Alex Hooke.

Several people read parts of early drafts or the whole manuscript. Besides Mike Best, Bonnie Honig, Mort Schoolman, Michael Sandel, Stephen White, and Dean Alfange, already noted, Emily Parker read and commented on some chapters, as did Deborah Youngblood, Nicolas Jabko, Steve Johnston, Shane Butler, Tiffany Beal, and Janelle Stewart, all also helping to check my thinking and memory about key moments. Tvrtko Vrdoljak, a brilliant theory student at Hopkins now writing a dissertation on the components of a "new naturalism," not only prepared the Bibliography and Index for this book, but also discussed early drafts with me as the manuscript slowly shook out into its current shape. I recall how we debated the role of the Interlocutor, and, more generally, to what extent writing strategies need to be simply enacted or announced as strategies. Others such as Adam Culver and Stephanie Erev, recent Hopkins grad students now teaching at Portland State, also read parts of an earlier draft. A special shout-out, too, to Jessica Croteau, Henry Scott, Matt Scotti, and Mary Simonsen, who discussed late drafts of some of these chapters with me in 2021 in a thoroughly audacious graduate seminar on "How to Be(Come) an Intellectual." We studied Karl Mannheim, Daniel Bell, C. Wright Mills, Charles Taylor, Jimena Canales, Donna Haraway, Michel Foucault, Judith Butler, Louis Althusser, Stefano Harney, Fred Moten, Mike Davis, and Gilles Deleuze as contending, overlapping exemplars of how to become intellectuals in universities that today both support the assignment in some ways and block it in others. If the task of the intellectual is to follow a major event where it takes you, if it is also to craft oneself to incorporate care for the world and pursue positive possibilities into your teaching and writing even in bleak situations, that task remains today more important than ever. I also thank Tom Lay, a thoughtful, supportive editor at Fordham University Press, for insightful help in giving this book its final shape.

I would also like to thank *Theory & Event* for permission to publish a revised portion of "Life, Time, and Pandemic Events" [(October 2020): 7–21], in Chapter 5 of this study.

This text is dedicated to the memory of Judy Beal, to the vitality of David Connolly and Deborah Youngblood, and to the vibrant intellect and distinctive adventurousness of Jane Bennett. Anyone who knows me knows that, from at least 1985, Jane has joined those three in the warmest chambers of my soul. She and I create new seminars together whenever possible; we read first drafts of each other's texts; and she helps me to sharpen and enliven themes as I strive to craft them into a text. This book is no exception to that rule.

Notes

1. Professionals and Intellectuals

1. Mike Davis, *The JFK Assassination Evidence Handbook* (New York: Independently Published, 2018).

2. W. E. B. Du Bois, *The Souls of Black Folk* (1903) (New York: Millennium, 2014).

3. "They're Certain the Election Was Stolen . . . ," *New York Times*, December 15, 2020.

4. Karl Mannheim, *Ideology and Utopia: An Introduction to the Sociology of Knowledge*, trans. Louis Wirth and Edward Shils (1929) (New York: Routledge & Kegan Paul, 1936).

5. Thomas S. Kuhn, *The Structure of Scientific Revolutions* (Chicago: University of Chicago Press, 1962).

6. Charles Lyell, *Principles of Geology* (1830–33) (New York: Penguin Classics, 1997); Charles Darwin, *On the Origin of Species* (1859) (New York: Gramercy, 1979).

7. Stephen Gould, *Wonderful Life: The Burgess Shale and the Nature of History* (New York: W. W. Norton, 1989).

8. William E. Connolly, *Political Science and Ideology* (New York: Atheron, 1967).

9. Connolly, *Political Science and Ideology*, 107.

10. Connolly, *Political Science and Ideology*, 155.

11. Marcel Proust, *In Search of Lost Time*, vol. 6, *Time Regained*, trans. Andreas Mayor and Terence Kilmartin, rev. D. J. Enright (1913) (New York: Modern Library, 1993), 247–48.

12. Peter Bachrach, *The Theory of Elitist Democracy: A Critique* (Boston: Little, Brown, 1967).

13. Sheldon Wolin, "Political Theory as a Vocation," *American Political Science Review* 63, no. 4 (1969): 1062–82.

14. C. Wright Mills, *The Sociological Imagination* (New York: Oxford University Press, 1959).

15. J. M. Burns and J. W. Peltason, *Government by the People*, 1st ed. (Englewood Cliffs, N.J.: Prentice Hall, 1957).

16. G. W. F. Hegel, *Phenomenology of Spirit* (1807), trans. A. V. Miller (New York: Oxford University Press, 1977).

17. René Descartes, *Discourse on Method and Meditations*, trans. Laurence J. Lafleur (1637; 1641) (New York: Macmillan and Library of Liberal Arts, 1952).

18. Gilles Deleuze, *Difference and Repetition*, trans. Paul Patton (1968; repr. New York: Columbia University Press, 1995), 139, 144.

2. A Fifty-Yard Dash

1. Cara N. Daggett, *The Birth of Energy: Fossil Fuels, Thermodynamics, and the Politics of Work* (Durham, N.C.: Duke University Press, 2019).

2. John Huston, director, and Arthur Miller, writer, *The Misfits* (1961).

3. W. E. B. Du Bois, *The Souls of Black Folk* (1903) (New York: Millennium, 2014), 86.

3. The Pioneer Valley

1. Deborah R. Connolly, *Homeless Mothers: Face to Face with Women and Poverty* (Minneapolis: University of Minnesota Press, 2017).

2. George Kateb, *The Inner Ocean: Individualism and Democratic Culture* (Ithaca, N.Y.: Cornell University Press, 1992).

3. Mark Rudd, "Political Passion Turned Violent," *New York Times*, March 6, 2020.

4. A. W. H. Adkins, *From the Many to the One: Study of Personality and Views of Human Nature in the Context of Ancient Greek Society, Values, and Beliefs* (Ithaca, N.Y.: Cornell University Press, 1970).

5. Glenn A. Albrecht, *Earth Emotions: New Words for a New World* (Ithaca, N.Y.: Cornell University Press, 2019).

6. William Apess, *On Our Own Ground*, ed. Barry O'Connell (Amherst: University of Massachusetts Press, 1992).

7. William E. Connolly, *The Ethos of Pluralization*, 2nd ed. (1995; Minneapolis: University of Minnesota Press, 2000).

8. Jürgen Habermas, *Legitimation Crisis*, trans. Thomas McCarthy (1973; repr. Boston: Beacon Press, 1975); James O'Connor, *The Fiscal Crisis of the State* (New York: St. Martin Press, 1973).

9. Fred Hirsch, *The Social Limits to Growth* (Cambridge, Mass.: Harvard University Press, 1977).

10. William E. Connolly and Glen Gordon, eds., *Social Structure and Political Theory* (Lexington, Ky.: D. C. Heath, 1974).

11. James Der Derian and Michael Shapiro, eds., *International/Intertextual Relations* (New York: Lexington, 1989).

12. Morton Schoolman, *A Democratic Enlightenment: The Reconciliation Image, Aesthetic Education, Possible Politics* (Durham, N.C.: Duke University Press, 2020).

13. Sheldon Wolin, *Politics and Vision: Continuity and Innovation in Western Political Thought* (Princeton, N.J.: Princeton University Press, 1960).

14. Charles Taylor, *Sources of the Self: The Making of the Modern Identity* (Cambridge, Mass.: Harvard University Press, 1989).

15. Jacques Derrida, *Of Grammatology*, trans. Gayatri Spivak (1967) (Baltimore: Johns Hopkins Press, 1974).

16. Nathan Widder, *Political Theory after Deleuze* (New York: Continuum International, 2012).

17. Friedrich Nietzsche, *On the Genealogy of Morals*, trans. Walter Kaufmann and R. J. Hollingdale (1887) (New York: Vintage, 1967), 78.

18. William E. Connolly, *Appearance and Reality in Politics* (New York: Cambridge University Press, 1981).

19. Michel Foucault, *Herculine Barbin: Being the Recently Discovered Memoirs of a Nineteenth Century French Hermaphrodite*, trans. Richard McDougal (1978) (New York: Pantheon, 1980).

20. Judith Butler, *Gender Trouble: Feminism and the Subversion of Identity* (New York: Routledge, 1990).

21. Butler, *Precarious Life: The Powers of Mourning and Violence* (New York: Verso, 2004).

22. Martin Heidegger, *Being and Time*, trans. John Macquarrie and Edward Robinson (1927) (New York: Harper and Row, 1962); Foucault, *The Order of Things: An Archeology of the Human Sciences*, trans. anonymous (1966) (New York: Random House, 1970); Foucault, *Discipline and Punish: The Birth of the Prison*, trans. Alan Sheridan (1975) (New York: Pantheon, 1978); Foucault, *The History of Sexuality*, vol. 1, *An Introduction*, trans. Robert Hurley (1976) (New York: Random House, 1978).

23. Hubert L. Dreyfus and Paul Rabinow, *Michel Foucault: Beyond Structuralism and Hermeneutics* (Chicago: University of Chicago Press, 1982).

24. Jane Bennett, *The Enchantment of Modern Life* (Princeton, N.J.: Princeton University Press, 2001); *Vibrant Matter: A Political Ecology of Things* (Durham, N.C.: Duke University Press, 2010); *Influx and Efflux: Writing Up with Walt Whitman* (Durham, N.C.: Duke University Press, 2020).

25. Steven Johnston, *American Dionysia: Violence, Tragedy, and Democratic Politics* (New York: Cambridge University Press, 2015).

26. Kathy Ferguson, *Emma Goldman: Political Thinking in the Streets* (Lanham, Md.: Rowman and Littlefield, 2011).

27. Thomas Dumm, *Michel Foucault and the Politics of Freedom* (Washington, D.C.: Sage, 1995).

28. Stephen K. White, *Sustaining Affirmation: The Strength of Weak Ontology in Political Theory* (Princeton, N.J.: Princeton University Press, 2000).

29. Bennett, *Thoreau's Nature: Ethics, Politics and the Wild* (Lanham, Md.: Rowman and Littlefield, 1994).

30. Alexander E. Hooke, *Alphonso Lingis and Existential Genealogy* (East Alresford: John Hunt, 2019).

31. Taylor, "Foucault on Freedom and Truth," *Political Theory* 12, no. 2 (1984): 152–83.

32. William E. Connolly, "Taylor, Foucault, and Otherness," *Political Theory* 13, no. 3 (1985): 365–76.

33. Connolly, "Beyond Good and Evil: The Ethical Sensibility of Michel Foucault," *Political Theory* 21, no. 3 (1993): 365–89.

4. The Hopkins School of Theory

1. Bonnie Honig, *Emergency Politics: Paradox, Law, Democracy* (Princeton, N.J.: Princeton University Press, 2011).

2. Friedrich Nietzsche, *Daybreak: Thoughts on the Prejudice of Morality* (1881) (New York: Cambridge University Press), 1982, 384.

3. William E. Connolly, The *Ethos of Pluralization* (1995; 2nd ed. Minneapolis: University of Minnesota Press, 2000), 182–83.

4. Kimberlé Crenshaw, "Demarginalizing the Intersection of Race and Sex: A Black Feminist Critique of Antidiscrimination Doctrine, Feminist Theory and Antiracist Politics," *University of Chicago Legal Forum* (1989): 139–68.

5. Cornel West, *Black Prophetic Fire: In Dialogue with and Edited by Christa Buschendorf* (Boston: Beacon Press, 2014).

6. James Baldwin, *The Fire Next Time* (Boston: Dial, 1962).

7. Adam Culver, "Race and Vision: A Tragic Reading" (Ph.D. diss., Johns Hopkins University, 2015).

8. David Campbell and Morton Schoolman, eds., *The New Pluralism: William Connolly and the Contemporary Global Condition* (Durham, N.C.: Duke University Press, 2008).

9. P. Bové, et al. "Left Conservatism: A Workshop; Following On," *boundary 2* 26, no. 3 (1999): 1–61.

10. Connolly, *Why I Am Not a Secularist* (Minneapolis: University of Minnesota Press, 1999).

11. Talal Asad, *Formations of the Secular: Christianity, Islam, Modernity* (Stanford, Calif.: Stanford University Press, 2003).

12. John Thatamanil, *The Immanent Divine: God, Creation, and the Human Predicament* (Minneapolis: Fortress, 2006).

13. Catherine Keller, *The Face of the Deep: A Theology of Becoming* (New York: Routledge, 2003).

14. Keller, *Political Theology of the Earth: Our Planetary Emergency and the Struggle for a New Public* (New York: Columbia University Press, 2018).

15. Connolly, *Neuropolitics: Thinking, Culture, Speed* (Minneapolis: University of Minnesota Press, 2002).

16. Connolly, *Neuropolitics*, 101–2.

17. Francesco Varela, *Sleeping, Dreaming, Dying: An Exploration of Consciousness with the Dalai Lama* (Somerville, Mass.: Wisdom, 1997).

18. Asad, *Genealogies of Religion: Discipline and Reason in Christianity and Islam* (Baltimore: Johns Hopkins University Press, 1993).

19. Eduardo Viveiros de Castro, *Cannibal Metaphysics*, trans. Peter Skafish (2009) (Minneapolis: Univocal, 2014).

20. Édouard Glissant, *Poetics of Relation*, trans. Betsy Wing (1970) (Ann Arbor: University of Michigan Press, 1997).

21. Nidesh Lawtoo, *The Phantom of the Ego: Modernism and the Mimetic Unconscious* (East Lansing: Michigan State University Press, 2013).

22. Jane Bennett, *Influx and Efflux: Writing Up with Walt Whitman* (Durham, N.C.: Duke University Press, 2020).

23. François Jullien, *Vital Nourishment: Departing from Happiness*, trans. Arthur Goldhammer (2005) (New York: Zone, 2007).

24. Jairus V. Grove, *Savage Ecology: War and Geopolitics at the End of the World* (Durham, N.C.: Duke University Press, 2019).

25. Connolly, "The Evangelical-Capitalist Resonance Machine," *Political Theory* 33, no. 6 (December 2005): 869–86.

26. Connolly, *Capitalism and Christianity, American Style* (Durham, N.C.: Duke University Press, 2008).

27. Connolly, *Capitalism and Christianity*, 49.

28. Lisa Duggan, *Mean Girl: Ayn Rand and the Culture of Greed* (Oakland: University of California Press, 2019).

29. Elizabeth Anker, *Orgies of Feeling: Melodrama and the Politics of Freedom* (Durham, N.C.: Duke University Press, 2014).

30. Nancy MacLean, *Democracy in Chains: The Deep History of the Radical Right's Stealth Plan for America* (New York: Penguin Random House, 2017).

31. Michel Foucault, *The Birth of Biopolitics: Lectures at the Collège de France, 1978–1979*, trans. Graham Burchell (2004) (London: Palgrave MacMillan, 2008).

32. Chantal Mouffe, *The Democratic Paradox* (New York: Verso, 2009).

33. Stephen K. White, *Sustaining Affirmation: The Strength of Weak Ontology in Political Theory* (Princeton: Princeton University Press, 2000), 3.

34. David Howarth, "Pluralizing Methods: Contingency, Ethics and Critical Explanation," in *Democracy and Pluralism: The Political Thought of William E. Connolly*, ed. Alan Finlayson (New York: Routledge, 2010).

35. Connolly, *Identity/Difference*, 24.

36. Connolly, *Identity/Difference*, 24–25.

37. Richard Rorty, *Contingency, Irony and Solidarity* (New York: Cambridge University Press, 1989).

38. Fred Pearce, *With Speed and Violence: Why Scientists Fear Tipping Points in Climate Change* (Boston: Beacon Press, 2007).

39. Bennett, *Influx and Efflux: Writing Up with Walt Whitman* (Durham, N.C.: Duke University Press, 2020).

40. Bentley B. Allen, *Scientific Cosmology and International Orders* (New York: Cambridge University Press, 2018).

41. P. J. Brendese, *Segregated Time* (Oxford University Press, 2021).

42. François Furstenberg, "When University Leaders Fail," *Chronicle of Higher Education*, May 19, 2020, 2–6.

43. Furstenberg, "When University Leaders Fail," 8.

5. The New Fascist Revolt

1. Marcel Proust, *In Search of Lost Time*, vol. 6, *Time Regained*, trans. Andreas Mayor and Terence Kilmartin, rev. D. J. Enright (1913) (New York: Modern Library, 1993), 289.

2. William E. Connolly, *Aspirational Fascism: The Struggle for Multifaceted Democracy under Trumpism* (Minneapolis: University of Minnesota Press, 2017), xiii–xiv.

3. Adolf Hitler, *Mein Kampf*, trans. Ralph Manheim (1925) (Boston: Houghton Mifflin, 2001).

4. Klaus Theweleit, *Male Fantasies*, vol. 1, *Women, Floods, Bodies, History*, trans. Stephen Conway (1977; repr. Minneapolis: University of Minnesota Press, 1987); vol. 2, *Male Bodies: Psychoanalyzing the White Terror*, trans. Erica Carter and Chris Turner (1978; repr. Minneapolis: University of Minnesota Press, 1988).

5. Connolly, *Aspirational Fascism*, 46–47.

6. Connolly, *Aspirational Fascism*, 47.

7. Sigmund Freud, *Group Psychology and the Ego*, trans. James Strachey (1922) (New York: W. W. Norton, 1959).

8. Nidesh Lawtoo, *(New) Fascism: Contagion, Community, Myth* (East Lansing: Michigan State University Press, 2019).

9. Friedrich Nietzsche, *Gay Science*, trans. Walter Kaufmann and R. J. Hollingdale (1882) (New York: Vintage, 1974), 255.

10. Bonnie Honig, "12 *Angry Men*: Care for the Agon and the Varieties of Masculine Experience." *Theory & Event* 22, no. 3 (2019): 701–16.

11. Steven Levitsky and Daniel Ziblatt, *How Democracies Die* (New York: Crown, 2018); Federico Finkelstein, *From Fascism to Populism in History* (Oakland: University of California Press, 2017).

12. Karl Polanyi, *The Great Transformation: The Political and Economic Origins of Our Time* (1944; repr. Boston: Beacon Press, 1957).

13. Connolly, "Populism or Fascism?," *Contemporary Condition*, June 17, 2018, http://contemporarycondition.blogspot.com/2018/06/populism-or-fascism.html.

14. J. K. Gibson-Graham, J. Cameron, and S. Healy, *Take Back the Economy: An Ethical Guide for Transforming Our Communities* (Minneapolis: University of Minnesota Press, 2013).

15. Theodor Adorno, *Minima Moralia: Reflections from Damaged Life*, trans. E. F. N. Jephcott (1954) (London: New Left, 1974).

16. Connolly, *Climate Machines, Fascist Drives, and Truth* (Durham, N.C.: Duke University Press, 2019).

17. Connolly, *Climate Machines*, 1.

18. René Descartes, *Discourse on Method and Meditations*, trans. Laurence J. Lafleur (1637; 1641) (New York: Macmillan and Library of Liberal Arts, 1952), 105.

19. Dean Buonomano, *Your Brain Is a Time Machine: The Neuroscience and Physics of Time* (New York: W. W. Norton, 2017), 156.

20. Jimena Canales, *The Physicist and the Philosopher: Einstein, Bergson, and the Debate That Changed Our Understanding of Time* (Princeton, N.J.: Princeton University Press, 2015).

21. Henri Bergson, *Creative Evolution*, trans. Arthur Mitchell (Mineola, Tex.: Dover, 1998), 46.

22. Donna Haraway, *Staying with the Trouble* (Durham, N.C.: Duke University Press, 2016).

23. Stuart A. Kauffman, *Reinventing the Sacred: A New View of Science, Reason, and Religion* (New York: Basic Books, 2008), 80.

24. Bonnie L. Bassler and Kai Papenfort, "Quorum-Sensing Signal-Response Systems in Gram-Negative Bacteria," *Nature Reviews Microbiology* 14 (2016): 576–88.

25. Michael B. A. Oldstone, *Viruses, Plagues, and History: Past, Present, and Future* (New York: Oxford University Press, 2010).

26. Patrick Forterre, "To Be or Not to Be Alive: How Recent Discoveries Challenge the Traditional Definitions of Viruses and Life," *Studies in History and Philosophy of Biological and Biomedical Sciences* 59 (2016): 100, 101, 103, 105.

27. David Quammen, *Spillover: Animal Infections and the Next Human Pandemic* (New York: W. W. Norton, 2012).

Epilogue: Echoes and Spiritualities

1. Robert Macfarlane, *Underland: A Deep Time Journey* (New York: W. W. Norton, 2019), 101.

2. James Baldwin, *The Fire Next Time* (Boston: Dial, 1962), 86, 92.

Bibliography

Citations to Works by William E. Connolly

Connolly, William E. *Political Science and Ideology*. New York: Atheron, 1967.
———. *The Terms of Political Discourse*. Lexington, Ky.: D. C. Heath, 1974.
———. *Appearance and Reality in Politics*. New York: Cambridge University Press, 1981.
———. "Taylor, Foucault, and Otherness." *Political Theory* 13, no. 3 (1985): 365–76.
———. *Politics and Ambiguity*. Madison: University of Wisconsin Press, 1987.
———. *Political Theory and Modernity*. Oxford: Basil Blackwell, 1988.
———. *Identity/Difference: Democratic Negotiations of Political Paradox*. Ithaca, N.Y.: Cornell University Press, 1991.
———. "Beyond Good and Evil: The Ethical Sensibility of Michel Foucault." *Political Theory* 21, no. 3 (1993): 365–89.
———. *The Augustinian Imperative: A Reflection on the Politics of Morality*. Newbury Park, Calif.: Sage, 1993.
———. *Why I Am Not a Secularist*. Minneapolis: University of Minnesota Press, 1999.
———. *The Ethos of Pluralization*. Minneapolis: University of Minnesota Press, 1995. Second edition, with new preface, 2000.
———. *Neuropolitics: Thinking, Culture, Speed*. Minneapolis: University of Minnesota Press, 2002.
———. "The Evangelical-Capitalist Resonance Machine." *Political Theory* 33, no. 6 (December 2005): 869–86.
———. "Europe: A Minor Tradition." In *Powers of the Secular Modern: Talal Asad and His Interlocutors*, edited by David Scott and Charles Hirschkind, 75–92. Stanford, Calif.: Stanford University Press, 2006.

———. *Capitalism and Christianity, American Style*. Durham, N.C.: Duke University Press, 2008.

———, ed. *A World of Becoming*. Durham, N.C.: Duke University Press, 2011.

———. *The Fragility of Things: Self-Organizing Processes, Neoliberal Fantasies, and Democratic Activism*. Durham, N.C.: Duke University Press, 2013.

———. *Aspirational Fascism: The Struggle for Multifaceted Democracy under Trumpism*. Minneapolis: University of Minnesota Press, 2017.

———. *Facing the Planetary: Entangled Humanism and the Politics of Swarming*. Durham, N.C.: Duke University Press, 2017.

———. "'How Do Democracies Die?' A Symposium on Steven Levitsky and Daniel Ziblatt's *How Democracies Die*." *Perspectives on Politics* 16, no. 4 (2018): 1095–96.

———. *Climate Machines, Fascist Drives, and Truth*. Durham, N.C.: Duke University Press, 2019.

Connolly, William E., and Michael Best. *The Politicized Economy*. Lexington, Ky.: D.C. Heath, 1976. Revised edition 1983.

Connolly, William E., and Glen Gordon, eds. *Social Structure and Political Theory*. Lexington: D.C. Heath, 1974.

Connolly Symposia and Blog Citations

Symposia

Bové, P. et al. "Left Conservatism: A Workshop; Following On." *boundary 2* 26, no. 3 (1999): 1–61.

Connolly, William E. "Populism or Fascism?" *Contemporary Condition*, June 17, 2018. http://contemporarycondition.blogspot.com/2018/06/populism-or-fascism.html.

———. "What Was Fascism?" *Contemporary Condition*, June 24, 2010. http://contemporarycondition.blogspot.com/2010/06/what-was-fascism.html.

———. "The Fragility of Things." *Contemporary Condition*, August 16, 2010. http://contemporarycondition.blogspot.com/2010/08/fragility-of-things.html.

———. "Aspirational Fascism." *Contemporary Condition*, September 27, 2011. http://contemporarycondition.blogspot.com/2011/09/aspirational-fascism.html.

———. "The Politics of the Event." *Contemporary Condition*, April 3, 2011. http://contemporarycondition.blogspot.com/2011/04/politics-of-event.html.

———. "Melancholia and Us." *Contemporary Condition*, April 26, 2011. http://contemporarycondition.blogspot.com/2012/04/melancholia-and-us.html.

———. "The Dilemma of Electoral Politics." *Contemporary Condition*, March 20, 2013. http://contemporarycondition.blogspot.com/2013/03/the-dilemma-of-electoral-politics.html.

———. "Toward an Eco-Egalitarian University." *Contemporary Condition*, July 27, 2014. http://contemporarycondition.blogspot.com/2014/07/toward-eco-egalitarian-university.html.

———. "Fake News and 'Postmodernism': The Fake Equation." *Contemporary Condition*, May 5, 2018. http://contemporarycondition.blogspot.com/2018/05/fake-news-and-postmodernism-fake.html.

———. "Dietetic Capitalism." *Contemporary Condition*, August 16, 2018. http://contemporarycondition.blogspot.com/2018/08/dietetic-capitalism.html.

Ignatov, A., et al. "Entangled Humanism as a Political Project: William Connolly's *Facing the Planetary.*" *Contemporary Political Theory* 18, no. 1 (2019): 115–34.

Moon, D. J., et al. "Reflections on The Ethos of Pluralization." *Philosophy & Social Criticism* 24, no. 1 (1998): 63–102.

All Other Citations

Adkins, A. W. H. *From the Many to the One: Study of Personality and Views of Human Nature in the Context of Ancient Greek Society, Values, and Beliefs.* Ithaca, N.Y.: Cornell University Press, 1970.

Adorno, Theodor. *Minima Moralia: Reflections from Damaged Life.* Translated by E. F. N. Jephcott. 1954. London: New Left, 1974.

Albrecht, Glenn A. *Earth Emotions: New Words for a New World.* Ithaca, N.Y.: Cornell University Press, 2019.

Allan, Bentley B. *Scientific Cosmology and International Orders.* New York: Cambridge University Press, 2018.

Anker, Elizabeth. *Orgies of Feeling: Melodrama and the Politics of Freedom.* Durham, N.C.: Duke University Press, 2014.

Apess, William. *On Our Own Ground.* Edited by Barry O'Connell. Amherst: University of Massachusetts Press, 1992.

Asad, Talal. *Genealogies of Religion: Discipline and Reason in Christianity and Islam.* Baltimore: Johns Hopkins University Press, 1993.

———. *Formations of the Secular: Christianity, Islam, Modernity.* Stanford, Calif.: Stanford University Press, 2003.

Bachrach, Peter. *The Theory of Elitist Democracy: A Critique.* Boston: Little, Brown, 1967.

Baldwin, James. *The Fire Next Time.* Boston: Dial, 1962.

Bassler, Bonnie L., and Kai Papenfort. "Quorum-Sensing Signal-Response Systems in Gram-Negative Bacteria." *Nature Reviews Microbiology* 14 (2016): 576–88.

Bennett, Jane. *Thoreau's Nature: Ethics, Politics and the Wild.* Lanham, Md.: Rowman and Littlefield, 1994.

———. *The Enchantment of Modern Life.* Princeton, N.J.: Princeton University Press, 2001.

———. *Vibrant Matter: A Political Ecology of Things.* Durham, N.C.: Duke University Press, 2010.

———. *Influx and Efflux: Writing Up with Walt Whitman.* Durham, N.C.: Duke University Press, 2020.

Bergson, Henri. *Creative Evolution*. Translated by Arthur Mitchell. Mineola, Tex.: Dover, 1998.

Buonomano, Dean. *Your Brain Is a Time Machine: The Neuroscience and Physics of Time*. New York: W. W. Norton, 2017.

Burns, J. M., and J. W. Peltason. *Government by the People*. Englewood Cliffs, N.J.: Prentice Hall, 1957.

Butler, Judith. *Gender Trouble: Feminism and the Subversion of Identity*. New York: Routledge, 1990.

———. *Precarious Life: The Powers of Mourning and Violence*. New York: Verso, 2004.

Campbell, David, and Morton Schoolman, eds. *The New Pluralism: William Connolly and the Contemporary Global Condition*. Durham, N.C.: Duke University Press, 2008.

Canales, Jimena. *The Physicist and the Philosopher: Einstein, Bergson, and the Debate That Changed Our Understanding of Time*. Princeton, N.J.: Princeton University Press, 2015.

Connolly, Deborah R. *Homeless Mothers: Face to Face with Women and Poverty*. Minneapolis: University of Minnesota Press, 2017.

Crenshaw, Kimberlé. "Demarginalizing the Intersection of Race and Sex: A Black Feminist Critique of Antidiscrimination Doctrine, Feminist Theory and Antiracist Politics." *University of Chicago Legal Forum* (1989): 139–68.

Culver, Adam. "Race and Vision: A Tragic Reading." Ph.D. diss., Johns Hopkins University, 2015.

Daniels, Ronald J., and Michael J. Trebilcock. *Rethinking the Welfare State: Government by Voucher*. New York: Routledge, 2005.

Daggett, Cara N. *The Birth of Energy: Fossil Fuels, Thermodynamics, and the Politics of Work*. Durham, N.C.: Duke University Press, 2019.

Darwin, Charles. *On the Origin of Species*. 1859. New York: Gramercy, 1979.

Davis, Mike. *The JFK Assassination Evidence Handbook*. New York: Independently Published, 2018.

de Castro, Eduardo Viveiros. *Cannibal Metaphysics*. Translated by Peter Skafish. 2009. Minneapolis: Univocal, 2014.

Deleuze, Gilles. *Difference and Repetition*. Translated by Paul Patton. New York: Columbia University Press, 1995. Originally published in 1968.

Der Derian, James, and Michael Shapiro, eds. *International/Intertextual Relations*. New York: Lexington, 1989.

Derrida, Jacques. *Of Grammatology*. Translated by Gayatri Spivak. 1967. Baltimore: Johns Hopkins Press, 1974.

Descartes, René. *Discourse on Method and Meditations*. 1637; 1641. Translated by Laurence J. Lafleur. New York: Macmillan and Library of Liberal Arts.

Dreyfus, Hubert L., and Paul Rabinow. *Michel Foucault: Beyond Structuralism and Hermeneutics*. Chicago: University of Chicago Press, 1982.

Du Bois, W. E. B. *The Souls of Black Folk*. 1903. New York: Millennium, 2014.

Duggan, Lisa. *Mean Girl: Ayn Rand and the Culture of Greed*. Oakland: University of California Press, 2019.

Dumm, Thomas. *Michel Foucault and the Politics of Freedom*. Washington, D.C.: Sage, 1995.

Ferguson, Kathy. *Emma Goldman: Political Thinking in the Streets*. Lanham, Md.: Rowman and Littlefield, 2011.

Finkelstein, Federico. *From Fascism to Populism in History*. Oakland: University of California Press, 2017.

Forterre, Patrick. "To Be or Not to Be Alive: How Recent Discoveries Challenge the Traditional Definitions of Viruses and Life." *Studies in History and Philosophy of Biological and Biomedical Sciences* 59 (2016): 100–108.

Foucault, Michel. *The Order of Things: An Archeology of the Human Sciences*. Translated by anonymous. 1966. New York: Random House, 1970.

———. *Discipline and Punish: The Birth of the Prison*. Translated by Alan Sheridan. 1975. New York: Pantheon, 1978.

———. *The History of Sexuality*. Vol. 1, *An Introduction*. Translated by Robert Hurley. 1976. New York: Random House, 1978.

———. *Herculine Barbin: Being the Recently Discovered Memoirs of a Nineteenth Century French Hermaphrodite*. Translated by Richard McDougal. 1978. New York: Pantheon, 1980.

———. *The Birth of Biopolitics: Lectures at the Collège de France, 1978–1979*. Translated by Graham Burchell. 2004. London: Palgrave MacMillan, 2008.

Freud, Sigmund. *Group Psychology and the Ego*. Translated by James Strachey. 1922. New York: W. W. Norton, 1959.

Gibson-Graham, J. K., J. Cameron, and S. Healy. *Take Back the Economy: An Ethical Guide for Transforming Our Communities*. Minneapolis: University of Minnesota Press, 2013.

Glissant, Édouard. *Poetics of Relation*. Translated by Betsy Wing. 1970. Ann Arbor: University of Michigan Press, 1997.

Gould, Stephen. *Wonderful Life: The Burgess Shale and the Nature of History*. New York: W. W. Norton, 1989.

Grove, Jairus V. *Savage Ecology: War and Geopolitics at the End of the World*. Durham, N.C.: Duke University Press, 2019.

Habermas, Jürgen. *Legitimation Crisis*. Translated by Thomas McCarthy. Boston: Beacon Press, 1975. Originally published in 1973.

Haraway, Donna. *Staying with the Trouble*. Durham, N.C.: Duke University Press, 2016.

Hegel, G. W. F. *Phenomenology of Spirit*. 1807. Translated by A. V. Miller. New York: Oxford University Press, 1977.

Heidegger, Martin. *Being and Time*. Translated by John Macquarrie and Edward Robinson. 1927. New York: Harper and Row, 1962.

———. *Basic Writings*. New York: Harper Collins, 1977.

Hirsch, Fred. *The Social Limits to Growth*. Cambridge, Mass.: Harvard University Press, 1977.

Hitler, Adolf. *Mein Kampf.* Translated by Ralph Manheim. 1925. Boston: Houghton Mifflin, 2001.

Honig, Bonnie. *Political Theory and the Displacement of Politics*. Ithaca, N.Y.: Cornell University Press, 1993.

———. *Emergency Politics: Paradox, Law, Democracy*. Princeton, N.J.: Princeton University Press, 2011.

———. "*12 Angry Men*: Care for the Agon and the Varieties of Masculine Experience." *Theory & Event* 22, no. 3 (2019): 701–16.

Hooke, Alexander E. *Alphonso Lingis and Existential Genealogy*. East Alresford: John Hunt, 2019.

Howarth, David. "Pluralizing Methods: Contingency, Ethics and Critical Explanation." In *Democracy and Pluralism: The Political Thought of William E. Connolly*. New York: Routledge, 2010.

Huston, John, director, and Arthur Miller, writer. *The Misfits*. 1961.

Ignatov, Anatoli. *Ecologies of the Good Life: Forces, Bodies and Cross-Cultural Encounters*. Ph.D. diss., Johns Hopkins University, 2014.

———. "The Earth as Gift-Giving Ancestor: Nietzsche's Perspectivism and African Animism." *Political Theory* 45, no. 1 (2017): 52–75.

Johnston, Steven. *American Dionysia: Violence, Tragedy, and Democratic Politics*. New York: Cambridge University Press, 2015.

Jullien, François. *Vital Nourishment: Departing from Happiness*. Translated by Arthur Goldhammer. 2005. New York: Zone, 2007.

Kateb, George. *The Inner Ocean: Individualism and Democratic Culture*. Ithaca, N.Y.: Cornell University Press, 1992.

Kauffman, Stuart A. *Reinventing the Sacred: A New View of Science, Reason, and Religion*. New York: Basic Books, 2008.

Keller, Catherine. *The Face of the Deep: A Theology of Becoming*. New York: Routledge, 2003.

———. *Political Theology of the Earth: Our Planetary Emergency and the Struggle for a New Public*. New York: Columbia University Press, 2018.

Kuhn, Thomas S. *The Structure of Scientific Revolutions*. Chicago: University of Chicago Press, 1962.

Lawtoo, Nidesh. *The Phantom of the Ego: Modernism and the Mimetic Unconscious*. East Lansing: Michigan State University Press, 2013.

———. *(New) Fascism: Contagion, Community, Myth*. East Lansing: Michigan State University Press, 2019.

Levitsky, Steven, and Daniel Ziblatt. *How Democracies Die*. New York: Crown, 2018.

Lyell, Charles. *Principles of Geology*. 1830–33. New York: Penguin Classics, 1997.

Macfarlane, Robert. *Underland: A Deep Time Journey*. New York: W. W. Norton, 2019.

MacLean, Nancy. *Democracy in Chains: The Deep History of the Radical Right's Stealth Plan for America*. New York: Penguin Random House, 2017.

Mannheim, Karl. *Ideology and Utopia: An Introduction to the Sociology of Knowledge.* Translated by Louis Wirth and Edward Shils. 1929. New York: Routledge & Kegan Paul, 1936.

Mills, C. Wright. *The Sociological Imagination.* New York: Oxford University Press, 1959.

Mouffe, Chantal. *The Democratic Paradox.* New York: Verso, 2009.

Nietzsche, Friedrich. *On the Genealogy of Morals.* Translated by Walter Kaufmann and R. J. Hollingdale. 1887. New York: Vintage, 1967.

———. *Will To Power.* Translated by Walter Kauffman. 1901. New York: Random House, 1967.

———. *Thus Spoke Zarathustra.* Translated by Walter Kaufmann. 1885. New York: Vintage, 1968.

———. *Twilight of the Idols.* Translated by R. J. Hollingdale. 1889. New York: Penguin, 1968.

———. *Gay Science.* Translated by Walter Kaufmann and R. J. Hollingdale. 1882. New York: Vintage, 1974.

———. *Daybreak: Thoughts on the Prejudice of Morality.* 1881. New York: Cambridge University Press, 1982.

O'Connor, James. *The Fiscal Crisis of the State.* New York: St. Martin Press, 1973.

Oldstone, Michael B. A. *Viruses, Plagues, and History: Past, Present, and Future.* New York: Oxford University Press, 2010.

Pearce, Fred. *With Speed and Violence: Why Scientists Fear Tipping Points in Climate Change.* Boston: Beacon Press, 2007.

Polanyi, Karl. *The Great Transformation: The Political and Economic Origins of Our Time.* 1944. Boston: Beacon Press, 1957.

Proust, Marcel. *In Search of Lost Time.* Vol. 6, *Time Regained.* Translated by Andreas Mayor and Terence Kilmartin. Revised by D. J. Enright. 1913. New York: Modern Library, 1993.

Quammen, David. *Spillover: Animal Infections and the Next Human Pandemic.* New York: W. W. Norton, 2012.

Rorty, Richard. *Contingency, Irony and Solidarity.* New York: Cambridge University Press, 1989.

Schoolman, Morton. *A Democratic Enlightenment: The Reconciliation Image, Aesthetic Education, Possible Politics.* Durham, N.C.: Duke University Press, 2020.

Taylor, Charles. "Foucault on Freedom and Truth." *Political Theory* 12, no. 2 (1984): 152–83.

———. "Connolly, Foucault, and Truth." *Political Theory* 13, no. 3 (1985): 377–85.

———. "Overcoming Epistemology." In *After Philosophy: End or Transformation,* edited by Thomas McCarthy et al. Cambridge, Mass.: MIT Press, 1987.

———. *Sources of the Self: The Making of the Modern Identity.* Cambridge, Mass.: Harvard University Press, 1989.

Thatamanil, John. *The Immanent Divine: God, Creation, and the Human Predicament.* Minneapolis: Fortress, 2006.

Theweleit, Klaus. *Male Fantasies.* Vol. 1, *Women, Floods, Bodies, History.* Translated by Stephen Conway. 1977. Minneapolis: University of Minnesota Press, 1987.
——. *Male Fantasies.* Vol. 2, *Male Bodies: Psychoanalyzing the White Terror.* Translated by Erica Carter and Chris Turner. 1978. Minneapolis: University of Minnesota Press, 1988.
Varela, Francesco. *Sleeping, Dreaming, Dying: An Exploration of Consciousness with the Dalai Lama.* Somerville, Mass.: Wisdom, 1997.
West, Cornel. *Black Prophetic Fire: In Dialogue with and Edited by Christa Buschendorf.* Boston: Beacon Press, 2014.
White, Stephen K. *Sustaining Affirmation: The Strength of Weak Ontology in Political Theory.* Princeton, N.J.: Princeton University Press, 2000.
Widder, Nathan. *Political Theory after Deleuze.* New York: Continuum International, 2012.
Wolin, Sheldon. *Politics and Vision: Continuity and Innovation in Western Political Thought.* Princeton, N.J.: Princeton University Press, 1960.
——. "Political Theory as a Vocation." *American Political Science Review* 63, no. 4 (1969): 1062–82.

Index

academia, 1, 3–5, 14, 15, 23, 24, 28–29, 38, 39, 87, 175, 184; and field divisions, 175–81; Flint Junior College, 59, 67, 70; and graduate school, 1, 3, 7, 9, 14, 22, 72, 76; and Harvard University, 109–10; as the Humanities Center at the Australian National University, 95; and Johns Hopkins University, 38, 97, 108, 142–50; as neoliberal, 29, 33, 34, 142–50; as Ohio University, 30–31, 33, 35–37, 39; as Oxford University, 93–95; as Princeton Institute of Advanced Study, 95; as Stanford Center for Behavioral Studies, 95; as the University of Exeter, 95; as University of Massachusetts, 39, 73, 76, 78, 84, 86, 92–93, 98, 101, 108; as University of Michigan, 9, 16, 27, 35, 44, 72; as white and male, 14
Alfange, Dean: at University of Massachusetts, Amherst, 85, 87–88
Allan, Bentley, 138
ambiguity, 26
analytic-synthetic dichotomy: limits of, 75, 78, 82–83, 124
Anker, Elisabeth: and American melodrama, 131
Anthropocene, 4–5, 17, 37, 66, 100, 126, 129, 137, 139–41, 169
Appearance and Reality in Politics, 95
armored males, and fascism, 158–61
Asad, Talal, 125; and secularism, 121
Aspirational Fascism, 156, 158–61, 164–66
The Augustinian Imperative, 114

authoritarianism, 10, 36; and capitalism, 89; as lure, 53; and university administration, 144–45, 148–49

Bachrach, Peter: and critique of elitist democratic theory, 27
Baldwin, James, 117, 119; and existential affirmation, 188
Bassler, Bonnie: and quorum calls of bacteria, 177
Beal, Judy, 4, 13, 14, 31, 32, 60, 70–71, 75, 150
behavioralism, 16–18, 20–23, 29, 81
Beiner, Ronald, 93–95; at Oxford University, 93–95
Bennett, Jane, 56, 75–76, 93, 100, 106, 120, 126, 138; and influx and efflux, 125; and tactics of the self, 103
Bergson, Henri: on time, 175–77
Berlin, Isaiah: at Oxford University, 94
Best, Michael: and *The Politicized Economy*, 87–88; at the University of Massachusetts, Amherst, 84–90
bifurcation points, 3; as forks, 3–4
big data, 16, 170
Big Lies, 160, 168, 169
Book of Job: and the volatility of nature, 2, 65, 66, 139
Bowles, Samuel: at the University of Massachusetts, Amherst, 88
Brendese, P. J., 138–39; and Hopkins School of Theory, 114

WILLIAM E. CONNOLLY is Krieger-Eisenhower Professor at Johns Hopkins, where he teaches political theory. His books include *Climate Machines, Fascist Drives, and Truth* (Duke, 2020), *Aspirational Fascism* (Minnesota, 2017), *Facing the Planetary* (Duke, 2017), *Capitalism and Christianity, American Style* (Duke, 2008), *Why I Am Not a Secularist* (Minnesota, 1999), *The Ethos of Pluralization* (Minnesota, 1995), and *The Terms of Political Discourse* (Princeton, 1983, 3rd ed., 1993). In a poll of American political theorists published in 2010, he was named the fourth most influential political theorist in America over the last twenty years, after Rawls, Habermas, and Foucault.

CPSIA information can be obtained
at www.ICGtesting.com
Printed in the USA
JSHW030819050222
22616JS00001B/19

9 781531 500238